W9-BCG-243

LANGUAGE LEARNING
AND THOUGHT

PERSPECTIVES IN
NEUROLINGUISTICS AND PSYCHOLINGUISTICS

Harry A. Whitaker, Series Editor
DEPARTMENT OF PSYCHOLOGY
THE UNIVERSITY OF ROCHESTER
ROCHESTER, NEW YORK

LANGUAGE LEARNING AND THOUGHT

Edited by

JOHN MACNAMARA

Department of Psychology
McGill University
Montreal, Quebec, Canada

ACADEMIC PRESS   New York   San Francisco   London   1977

A Subsidiary of Harcourt Brace Jovanovich, Publishers

ACADEMIC PRESS, INC.
111 Fifth Avenue, New York, New York 10003

United Kingdom Edition published by
ACADEMIC PRESS, INC. (LONDON) LTD.
24/28 Oval Road, London NW1

Library of Congress Cataloging in Publication Data

Main entry under title:

Language learning and thought.

(Perspectives in neurolinguistics and
psycholinguistics series)
Includes bibliographies.
1. Children—Language. 2. Thought and
thinking. 3. Psycholinguistics. 4. Artificial
intelligence. I. Macnamara, John Theodore.
P118.L37   410'.01   76-55980
ISBN 0-12-464750-2

Contents

List of Contributors

Numbers in parentheses indicate the pages on which the authors' contributions begin.

WILLIAM J. BAKER (85), Department of Linguistics, University of Alberta, Edmonton, Alberta, Canada

EVE V. CLARK (147), Department of Linguistics, Stanford University, Stanford, California

BRUCE L. DERWING (79, 85), Department of Linguistics, University of Alberta, Edmonton, Alberta, Canada

PAUL KIPARSKY (47), Department of Linguistics and Philosophy, Massachusetts Institute of Technology, Cambridge, Massachusetts

JOHN MACNAMARA (1, 11, 141, 261), Department of Psychology, McGill University, Montreal, Quebec, Canada

LISE MENN (47), Research Laboratory of Electronics, Massachusetts Institute of Technology, Cambridge, Massachusetts

SHANNON DAWN MOESER (227), Institute for Research in Human Abilities, Memorial University of Newfoundland, St. John's, Newfoundland, Canada

KATHERINE NELSON (117), Department of Psychology, Yale University, New Haven, Connecticut

DAVID R. OLSON (111, 177), Department of Applied Psychology, Ontario Institute for Studies in Education, Toronto, Ontario, Canada

SEYMOUR PAPERT (137, 289), Artificial Intelligence Laboratory, Massachusetts Institute of Technology, Cambridge, Massachusetts

ZENON W. PYLYSHYN (37, 169), Department of Psychology, University of Western Ontario, London, Ontario, Canada

GILLIAN SANKOFF (223), Department of Anthropology, University of Montreal, Montreal, Quebec, Canada

I. M. SCHLESINGER (215, 251), Department of Psychology, Hebrew University of Jerusalem, Jerusalem, Israel and Israel Institute of Applied Social Research, Jerusalem

DAN I. SLOBIN (185), Department of Psychology, University of California, Berkeley, Berkeley, California

Preface

Unusual circumstances apart, a person who knows a language like English is able to express his thoughts in English and understand the thoughts of others when expressed in English. It follows that to learn English, for infant or adult, includes learning how to express thoughts in English. A child whose cognitive powers grew, but who failed to develop language would be a mute; one who developed language but did not express thoughts in it would be no better than a parrot. To know what children are doing in learning language, then, includes finding out how they come to relate thought to language.

This book is a study on that subject. Each contributor was assigned one particular facet of the relationship between thought and language and asked to discuss it developmentally. The major facets which were so assigned are:

1. The contribution of nonverbal signs to the understanding of language.
2. Thought and the learning of phonology.
3. Thought and the learning of morphology.
4. Thought and the strategies of vocabulary learning.
5. Concepts and words.
6. Thought and the learning of syntax in natural language.
7. Thought and the learning of syntax in artificial language.
8. Propositional operations involved in the understanding of sentences.

Although this list does not cover all possible areas, for example, the social functions of speech (to communicate, to amuse, to draw attention, etc.), the book is more comprehensive than most others on child language.

The contributors come from a variety of disciplines and theoretical orientations. In planning the book the aim was to include at least one contribution from each of the following vantage points: developmental psychology, artificial intelligence, linguistics, anthropology, and philosophy. But more than just a contribution from each was wanted; the goal was that each contribution would be influenced by or take into account the viewpoint of the others.

Accordingly, the eight topics were drawn up and eight persons selected to write on these topics. Eight other persons were then selected to react in writing to one or more of the eight main essays. The eight essays were circulated to all 16 participants, who met for a 4-day workshop where everyone discussed the main essays and the formal comments on them. Because the written work had been circulated beforehand, the workshop was devoted largely to general discussion. Afterward, participants went home to revise their work. The main essays were first revised and sent again to those who were to write comments on them.

One of the advantages of this method is that among those who commented on papers were several who are not identified as students of child language. This was express policy. The study of child language is as much in danger of incest as any. People who have not made a particular study of a topic are happier reacting to a paper than writing one on their own.

The one exception to the procedure just outlined is the first chapter. Since all other contributions deal with a particular facet of language learning and thought, it seemed fitting that one should explore the topic as a whole. So I wrote one. It is what the French call an *esquisse*, or sketch, because the topic is large enough for a book in itself. The point of view it expresses is personal, but it is the only point of view I have. While I doubt that all would agree with it, I am confident that it does not contradict what the other contributors have written for this book.

The book is not meant for undergraduate students as an introductory text on psycholinguistics. It is intended for all serious scholars and students interested in language learning, whatever their home ground: developmental psychology, linguistics, speech pathology, second-language teaching, linguistic anthropology, philosophy of language. The book might also serve as a text in specialized classes on developmental linguistics or psycholinguistics and as supplementary reading in a variety of academic courses.

Work on this book was aided by a generous grant from The Canada Council to bring the authors together for the 4-day workshop. The preparation of the manuscript was supported by a grant from the Faculty of Graduate Studies, McGill University and by the Department of Psychology of McGill. We are grateful to these bodies for their support and sympathy.

1

On the Relation between Language Learning and Thought

JOHN MACNAMARA

McGill University

The core of the problem to which this paper addresses itself comes from accepting, as I do, the general position that language and thought are autonomous systems. The claim that they are autonomous has continually been made by Noam Chomsky, and I will attempt to summarize here what I see as the evidence in its support. The claim itself, in the form that I would like to make it, is that one *cannot* express linguistic rules in terms of semantic or conceptual structures. To accept this claim is to pose the problem of how we manage to express our thoughts in language, and how the child learns that certain sentences express certain messages or meanings.

Of necessity the paper must be short, with the result that the pace is too hurried. Brevity, then, must be my excuse for not making all the necessary qualifications, for treading on philosophical toes, and for being clearer than the matter really permits. On the other hand, it does seem appropriate that at least one essay, even a brief one, should be devoted to the general topic of language learning and thought in a book where the bulk of essays take up individual issues within the topic. To begin: some statements of basic position which, it is hoped, do not need to be established here!

I will assume without apology that language and thought are distinct, that J. B. Watson was wrong in claiming that thought is subvocal speech. I will assume, too, that language normally expresses thought. I will assume that Noam Chomsky is right in saying that knowledge of a language involves the ability (not always used) to process speech in terms of form classes and combinatorial rules which are not given in the physical speech signal. That is, the production or perception of a sentence frequently involves combinatorial rules which can be expressed only in terms of such entities as noun, noun phrase, subject of the main verb, and the like. In Chomsky's words, the linguistic analysis of normal speech by the normal listener may involve linguistic categories that are "abstract" with respect to the speech signal. These categories are then contributed by the mind to the linguistic analysis of the signal. Finally, with the bulk of workers in artificial intelligence, I will assume that thought is comprised of concepts and operations that are also abstract with respect to the form of any sensory input. In other words, my knowledge of the world is in the form of representations whose function as representations does not depend on any resemblance between themselves and the objects represented.

Since the term "abstract" comes up twice—to denote the relation between knowledge of language and the speech signal, and that between thought and the known objects—perhaps an illustration, inspired by Ernst Cassirer, is warranted. Mathematicians represent a straight line by the expression $y = bx + c$. The expression does not look like a straight line; or if it does, the resemblance is accidental. The mathematician merely means that as x varies through a continuum for constant b and constant c, the point x, y describes a straight line on a graph. This ability of A to represent B independently of the physical properties of either is part of what is denoted by the word "abstract," or by the expression "A is abstract with respect to B."

If all this be granted, the question arises: What is the relation between thought and language? Is it, too, abstract? The interest of the solution is that it bears directly on our understanding of the child's task in learning a language. If the relation is abstract, the child must develop somehow both the domain of thought and, separately, the domain of language; and in addition, he must set up a representing relation between the two. If, however, the relation between the two is not abstract or is not fully abstract, then the child's task appears, superficially at least, easier. The resemblance between language and thought would facilitate the learning of the two and would be a grounding for the relation between them.

It is highly improbable that there is any physical resemblance between thought and language. Linguists generally find that at least most everyday messages can be expressed in languages as physically different as English, Russian, and Chinese. And while there are such things as linguistic universals of syntax and vocabulary, they are not located in physical properties. It follows that thought is abstract with respect to speech.

Though most of those who work in artificial intelligence agree with the foregoing, they seek to establish a mapping from thought to language which is complete. So an important word like a noun elicits a "conceptual structure," and the grammatical relation between the noun and the rest of the sentence elicits a relation (often computed on the spot) between the noun's "conceptual structure" and some other "conceptual structure(s)" in the computer's memory. This is an oversimplification of the types of operation that computers have been programmed to perform in "interpreting" sentences. But as a rough characterization it suffices. The computer's interpretation is related to the incoming sentence by a physically causal chain of connections and computations. In all the work I have seen, the linguistic analysis has been shallow, and the linguistic corpus to be handled has been, understandably, restricted. That I think the computer analogy misleading will become clear as we proceed.

There have been two movements in linguistics that have a close affinity with the work in artificial intelligence. Case grammars attempt to establish a formal (and automatic) mapping from semantic functions, such as agent, object acted upon, and instrument, onto syntactic relationships such as subject of main sentence, and direct object. It is my opinion, expressed here much too abruptly, that this movement has failed. The reason seems to be the lack of a clear idea of how to define the semantic functions. Moreover, the number of such functions seems to be greatly in excess of that (usually a dozen or less) proposed in any case grammars I have seen. Consider the following sentences:

(1)
    a. *John struck Mary.*
    b. *John loved Mary.*
    c. *John loved nobody.*
    d. *John loved telling stories.*
    e. *John loved listening to stories.*
    f. *John loved mowing the lawn.*
    g. *John loved idleness.*

Mary is not the case of "person acted upon" in the same sense in both (1a) and (1b). In the first sentence she is the recipient of a blow, while if John is shy she may, in the second sentence, be the recipient of nothing at all. Obviously *John* is a different type of agent in the two cases. Should we then have as many semantic cases as we have types of agent? Matters are complicated by the fact that in (1c) *John* does nothing, and there is nobody acted upon in any sense. In (1d) *telling stories* can hardly count as an object in the sense that *Mary* is one. Again, must we say that the *Johns* of (1d) and (1e) are different types of agents? The list of such sentences can be lengthened. What is evident is that in each sentence *John* is the subject and the expression following *loved* is the direct object. These are linguistic notions. There seems to be no hope of providing a principled mapping from such linguistic structures to a compact set of semantically defined cases. Part of the reason that the difficulty shows up so clearly is that case grammars have not confined themselves to a restricted corpus of English.

The other linguistic movement that has an affinity with the work in artificial intelligence is called generative semantics. It went further than artificial intelligence models in claiming that semantic structures were of the same formal nature as syntactic ones. It also abolished the distinction between semantic and syntactic at all levels of analysis deeper than surface structure. The attraction of such a move is that the elements and the bulk of the combinatorial rules of thought as well as those of language need to be specified only once, not twice. The trouble with the move has been suggested in principle, but one point is worth pursuing. One generative semanticist (McCawley, 1971) suggested that the notions "noun phrase" (of linguistics) and "argument of a function" (of logic) were interchangeable. Turn back again to the sentences of (1) and consider the noun phrase which is direct object of the verb in each sentence. There is nothing to stop us from rebaptizing it "argument of the verb *loved.*" However, that is no more than a rebaptism. The equivalence class of such arguments is established not in semantics, but in linguistics; it is the equivalence class of those words which can be the direct object of *loved.* In another language the set of words expressing the same set of concepts might not all be possible direct objects. For example, in Irish the normal way to express (1b) is *Thug Seán grá do Mháire* ('John gave love to Mary') where the word for *Mary* is the indirect object, not the direct one.

This is not just a particular phenomenon. It is very general across the linguistic rules of phonology, morphology, phrase structure, and transformations. There are probably some structures of English grammar that in most uses have a simpler mapping onto semantic structures. For example, the possessive, *John's hat,* probably has a straightforward mapping onto the semantic notion of ownership; though one should not forget such aberrations as *John's going away* and even *John's age.* However, over the whole range of linguistic rules, the mapping, if such there be, is vastly complex.

What these three movements (artificial intelligence, case grammar, and generative semantics) have in common is the desire to specify a complete mapping from the forms and structures of sentences to the abstract representations of thought. Noam Chomsky, if I follow him correctly, has stood for a theory deeply at odds with all three. He has argued that language and thought are autonomous systems. At the least, this means that the elements and combinatorial rules of language can be stated without reference to semantics. This is broadly true. However, I wish to go beyond that now and go on to suggest that the rules of grammar cannot be stated in semantic terms. Now if there were a complete mapping from language to thought, clearly that claim would be false. We have every reason to be cautious in this area, but the burden of my argument up to the present has been to support the stricter interpretation. It has been to show that thought is not only abstract with respect to language, but that it is autonomous in the strict sense from language. The form classes and combinatorial rules of language cannot be specified in semantic terms, even awkwardly.

All this, however, seems to make the task of the infant language learner more difficult since it complicates the relationship between thought and language. Moreover it seems, at least at first sight, to make trouble for the theory I once proposed (Macnamara, 1972) that the child uses meaning, independently divined, to decipher the grammar of his mother tongue. It is now necessary to outline a theory of how the child brings thought and language into relationship, and to explore how thought can be the clue to language. In order to do so, I will make use of an analogy. It is inevitable that we shall be led into a general discussion of human intelligence and evidence. I make no apology for this, since it would be impossible to proceed without some general notions about the capacity that humans possess to think and to interpret speech.

When a detective is summoned to the scene of a murder, his whole attention is on locating the culprit. He examines footprints in the shrubbery, fingerprints in the room, signs of a struggle, the weapon, and possible motives for murder. He finds that the footprint matches that of Harry Trent, and even that an irregularity in the left heel of Harry's shoe exactly corresponds to something in the footprint. The detective then concludes that Harry was in the shrubbery. Notice that he is not caused so to think. He treats his observations as evidence that Harry was there. Harry's being there explains the footprint. He finds, further, that Harry wanted to marry the dead man's wife who, owing to the terms of her father's will, could not seek a divorce without forfeiting her inheritance. Taking one thing with another, he concludes that Harry committed the murder.

Though the scraps of evidence I have given are conventional enough, it is obvious that there cannot be a finite list of clearly specified items that will serve as evidence for murder. Neither can there be such a list for what will serve as evidence that somebody was in a certain place. And while Harry's walking in the shrubbery was, if the detective was right, the one and only cause of the footprint, the reasons that might justify the conclusion that he was there could be very numerous and cannot be exhaustively listed a priori. The reason we cannot do this is really very profound: We cannot explain our capacity to explain. Only if we could specify the process that draws conclusions from evidence, could we specify all the evidence that would lead to a particular conclusion.

While nearly all psychologists would agree that we cannot explain explanation at the moment, not all would agree that we cannot in principle, or that we will never be able. Indeed whether or not I agree with this as a statement of principle myself depends on how "explain" is interpreted. I agree with it if "explain" is taken to mean specified in the manner of a computer program. My reason is based on the distinction that Brentano (and, in a related sense, Husserl) drew between the intentional domain and the physical. This is not the place to elaborate on the distinction. It is based on the fact that phenomenologically understanding (or explaining) is something one experiences, for example, understanding some proof in Euclidean geometry. And this is the understanding that would have to be explained (or understood). It is not an event in the observable physical environment. It cannot be studied from the outside, as say physics can (though "outside" here is in need of explication). It seems to be correlated with events in brains, but as Fodor (1975) so convincingly argues, it can no more be reduced to a brain event than economics can be reduced to physics. All this is not to be confused with dualism. One is not accused of being a dualist if one says economics does not reduce to physics. Neither should one be accused of dualism if one claims that intentional events (understanding, wanting, believing, judging, seeing, etc.) do not reduce to brain events. But neither do they reduce to events in computers. Computers are just as external to intentionality as brains are. If I am right in all this, it follows that those who work in artificial intelligence are modeling brains, not intentional events.

All this will strike most readers who are involved in psychology as strange, yet I think it is implicit in the claim that language and thought are autonomous, a claim several psychologists accept. Against the general point, workers in artificial intelligence claim, reasonably, that whatever is stateable is computable. So if ever we succeed in stating what it is to explain, we could model explanation in a computer. My suspicion is, and here I have some support from early introspectionists, that there is a deep-rooted difficulty in expressing the essence of an intelligible relationship. In proving, say, that the angles of a triangle sum to two right angles, I make a series of statements. But among those statements there is an intelligible relation not expressed even by the order of their occurrence; the intelligible relation is simply understood. If I attempted to express this relation, I would have to employ another set of statements, whose interrelationships with each other and with the original statements would remain unexpressed. This leads to an awkward regress. I can hint at the relation between a pair of statements by adding the word *because*, but this no more expresses the intelligible relation than the word *check* specifies a particular structure on a chess board.

As a final indication that there is a partly inexpressible relation between thought and language, let us take what Bertrand Russell called propositional attitudes, and let us confine ourselves to a single example. If I utter the sentence "The word *horse* is written on the blackboard," I may either be describing a state of affairs or I may be giving an example of an English sentence. If a listener were to question me about my real propositional attitude, I could say "I am truthfully and sincerely describing a state of affairs when I say, 'the word *horse* is written on the blackboard.'" However, the question can again be asked, was this whole long expression really intended to describe a state of affairs or merely to give an example of a sentence for some other purpose. And so on ad infinitum.

In the spirit of the detective analogy it seems that an utterance (and other forms of expression) should be taken as evidence that the speaker holds some view or has some intention. A language is a conventional and systematic means of giving such evidence. But we should no more seek a complete mapping from meaning to language than we should seek such a mapping from criminal behavior to the conclusions of detectives.

This, as Merleau-Ponty (1967) points out, does not rule out the possibility of experimental cognitive psychology. It merely rules out experiments and interpretations that exclude the phenomenology of intentional events, at least as bearing on the core of cognitive psychology. Such a phenomenology is, incidentally, implicit in all work or perception and indeed on the interpretation of sentences.

It may help to summarize the argument up to this point. I have tried to establish that thought is abstract with respect to language, and that the two are autonomous systems such that the rules of language cannot be expressed in semantic terms. I have argued that the reason for this autonomy is that thought takes place in the intentional domain but the construction and utterance of sentences do not. The relation between the two is akin to that between evidence and conclusions.

These remarks treat the psychophysical parallel not as a nuisance but as a basis for fruitful insight. Of course, more needs to be said to explain that evidence is not in the intentional domain. By this I mean that there is a sense in which the detective's evidence is external to the detective; for that which is to be known is external, and the act of knowing is not. Language, too, insofar as it is semantically uninterpreted is also external to the act of interpreting. That is what we mean by saying it is autonomous from the interpretative system. Language can (hopefully) be described as a system that can be fully represented in a computer. In a sense related to that in which I use evidence, language is that by means of which I know.

If this affords some insight into the process of interpreting language, what can be added about the use of meaning to guide the deciphering of language? The detective's search for clues is guided by his schema of how murders occur. That is what guides him to look for signs that point to the identity of all who had recently entered the apartment. That is what guides him to look for clues to a motive. The schema does not specify a list of what will serve as clues.

It is possible to illustrate more pertinently from some experimental work on language learning. Katz, Baker, and Macnamara (1974) studied babies' learning of the linguistic marking in English for the distinction between common and proper nouns. In general, common nouns can take determiners, e.g., *a horse, the horse, some horses*. And in general, proper names cannot; one can say *Harry* or *Jane*, but one cannot say *a Harry* or *the Jane*. The related semantic facts are that *horse* refers to a class of objects; *Harry* refers to an individual and not a class. Things are not of course quite so clear, even for young children. Expressions like **my** *doll* and **the** *doll* refer to individuals, though the nouns are common. Similarly, expressions like *come here,* **child** and *hello,* **doggie** refer to individuals though the nouns are common and though they are not preceded by determiners such as *my* or *the*. On the other hand, expressions like *the* **horse** *eats grass* and *the* **lion** *is the king of the beasts* refer to classes.

We anticipated that children make a sharp distinction, conceptually, between, on the one hand, objects whose individuality is not salient, such as spoons, hankies, and apples, and, on the other, objects whose individuality is salient because of their class membership, such as Dada, Mama, and Freddie the dog. We anticipated that the conceptual distinction might set the child looking for linguistic means to mark it. In our experiment with $1\frac{1}{2}$-year-olds, we introduced them to new pairs of objects: a pair of dolls or a pair of blocks. We named one of each pair either with a new proper noun or with a new common noun (in fact, nonsense syllables). Later we asked the child for the named object. I cannot here repeat all the relevant details of the design. However, the children tended to hand the named object only when it was a doll that had been given a proper name. Otherwise they treated the members of the pair as interchangeable. They did not tend to single out an individual block even when it had received a proper name. We interpreted this as linguistic learning that was stimulated by the salience of the individuality of dolls, as surrogate people. If instead the learning had been stimulated by some autonomous linguistic acuteness, the children ought to have treated the block that received the proper name as they did the corresponding doll. Notice that the relevant linguistic learning was the absence of a determiner: *Zav* denoted an individual doll; *a Zav* or *the Zav* suggested a common noun. Perhaps the semantic correlates of the presence or absence of a linguistic determiner are more reliable than those of most linguistic devices. Nevertheless, the correlation is far from perfect. But the main point is: The observations do not attempt to explain what it is to refer to something by means of a word. Referring is left unanalyzed and the research asks how children learn to refer in one way rather than in another.

All of the papers in this volume take a point of view that is at least not incompatible with the foregoing. They all speak of the child forming linguistic hypotheses, in itself a very cognitive approach to language learning. In addition, most papers explore the possibility that his linguistic hypotheses are inspired by nonlinguistic knowledge. Though none of the papers take up the matter explicitly, my suspicion is that implicit in seven of the eight main papers (that on miniature artificial languages being the exception) is the theory that thought and language are related as evidence and conclusions, and that the process of interpretation cannot be specified in the form of a computer program. By this I do not mean that the authors accept such a theory, or would accept it if it were proposed to them. But none of the seven main papers is looking for a complete mapping from language to meaning; each seems content with a much looser type of relation not unlike what I am proposing here. In the eighth paper, Moeser does not allow the issue to arise, since she has constructed a visual display to map completely and exactly onto a miniature artificial language.

REFERENCES

Fodor, J. A. *The language of thought*. New York: Crowell, 1975.

Katz, N., Baker, E., & Macnamara, J. What's in a name? A study of how children learn common and proper names. *Child Development*, 1974, *45*, 469–473.

Macnamara, J. The cognitive basis of language learning in infants. *Psychological Review*, 1972, *79*, 1–13.

McCawley, J. D. Interpretative semantics meets Frankenstein. *Foundations of Language*, 1971, *7*, 285–296.

Merleau-Ponty, M. Difficulties involved in a subordination of psychology. In J. J. Kockelmans (Ed.), *Phenomenology: The philosophy of Edmund Husserl and its interpretation*. New York: Doubleday, 1967. pp. 485–502.

2

From Sign to Language

JOHN MACNAMARA

McGill University

How does a baby know that his mother is talking about an object as a whole, and not just some of its qualities or its relations with other objects? For that matter, how does he know which object is being spoken about? How does he know that a remark has been addressed to him? How does he know that an utterance was a command rather than a question or a statement, and how does he come to recognize the different syntactic structures that are normally used to signal such propositional attitudes? Macnamara (1972) argues that his main strategy must be to divine the speaker's intention as a clue to language. This position presupposes that he is initially able to use nonlinguistic objects, events, and signals, as a clue to intention far more accurately than he can use speech. Such clues are likely to be objects which are present, the movement of objects, human gestures and eye-to-eye contact. In the present series of studies we shall be concerned with the baby's interpretation of such clues and how they influence his response. We shall pit them against one another and against linguistic signals to compare their relative usefulness to the child.

The basic idea for the set of experiments was suggested by Nancy Wargry. The experiments were conducted by Erica Baker. The work was funded by a grant to John Macnamara from The Canada Council. Some interesting observations on communicative gestures in babies have come to light in Carol Lord's article in *Papers and Reports on Child Language Development*, No. 8., Stanford, 1974.

St. Augustine, in his *Confessions*, suggests that there is a set of natural non-linguistic signs (*tamquam verbis naturalibus omnium gentium*) consisting of gestures, eye movements, and tones of voice which parents can use to express intention to infants. These, he maintains, provide infants with the key to language. I do not claim that in this paper we are investigating a set of natural signs, or indeed that there are signs that can be interpreted without any learning. But I do claim that Augustine is basically right in saying that babies understand nonverbal signals before they understand verbal ones, and that they use them to learn the verbal ones. Wittgenstein, in *Philosophical Investigations*, cites Augustine and disagrees with him. His central objection is to such ethereal entities as intentions. He goes on to propose his celebrated theory of use as meaning. I will return to this position after discussing the experiments, but in general I favor Augustine as against Wittgenstein. Not that I want to make of gestures a solve-all for the child; with Roger Brown (1958, p. 209) I believe that more is to be learned from objects and their functions than from gestures.

The investigation comprises five experiments with small babies. Throughout, the basic observation is the same: the baby's response to a combination of nonverbal and verbal signs that (at least to the adult) involved an object that was in front of the child. In some conditions all nonverbal and verbal signs agree (again, to the adult), and in some there is disagreement either among the nonverbal signs or between the nonverbal and verbal ones. The overall hypothesis was that nonlinguistic signs would prove more powerful than linguistic ones; and the younger the baby or the less he understood of the language, the more powerful the nonlinguistic sign. The sorts of non-linguistic signs chosen to study were certain manual gestures and eye-to-eye contact. Syntax was also varied in what seemed a perceptually obvious manner; we sometimes employed statement forms and sometimes question.

Perhaps it would be well to give an example. We might (1) take a shoe in one hand and a spoon in the other, hold out to the child the shoe, look at him and say "Take the shoe, Harry" or "Take the spoon, Harry." The response would indicate the relative efficiency of sentence and gesture in conveying to the child what to do. (2) We might, with the same objects in hand, look at the child or at his mother, offer the shoe to the child, and say "Take the shoe, Harry" or simply "Take the shoe." Responses would indicate the relative efficacy of the child's name and eye-to-eye contact in conveying to the child that he was being addressed.

The first four experiments were with children whose average age was about 17 months; the final experiment was with children whose average age was 12 months. In varying age the aim was to vary understanding of sentences, the better to reveal the role of nonlinguistic signs. With the same objective in mind, all the experiments, with the exception of the first, were conducted wholly or partly in French. All the children were in English-speaking homes, none knew French. This controlled the extent to which the children could understand the sentences on the basis of linguistic knowledge alone. By such measures it was hoped to explore the natural setting in which the child comes to grips with sentences.

All the babies lived in the west end of Montreal island in English-speaking middle-class homes. Each was seen at home and tested individually in the presence of his mother. Testing was not begun before both the mother and baby had overcome their first shyness at the presence of the tester. No other persons were present during these sessions.

The number of experiments is large, and the variables employed form a complicated set. I will describe each experiment in detail, but in the final section I will summarize the overall research strategy and findings.

EXPERIMENT 1

Method

The babies, 10 boys and 10 girls, ranged in age from 14 to 20 months with an average of 17 months. In each home, five familiar objects whose names the mother thought were known to the child were selected. These were used in pairs during the testing and pairs were varied as much as possible.

There was a set of 20 questions to put to each child. They were written on cards, one question per card, and the pack was shuffled before each session so that each child was tested with a different random order of questions.

During testing the child sat close to his mother, and both mother and child faced the tester. A pilot study of 11 children of about the same age as the group of subjects indicated that the instructions "show me X" or "where is X" were more likely to elicit a response than "take X" or "give me X." We therefore employed only the first two sentences, and we did so interchangeably.

There were three sets of variables. (1) The tester looked at the child and waited until the child returned his look, or he looked at the mother. (2) The tester added or omitted the child's name at the end of the sentence, e.g., "show me the shoe, Henry" or simply "show me the shoe." (3) The tester held out the "correct" object (the one mentioned in the sentence) to the child or to his mother; or he held out the "incorrect" one (not mentioned in the sentence) to the child or to his mother. In each of these conditions he held the second of the two objects in his other hand. A fifth condition we called "neutral"; the tester placed the two objects on the floor (or on a table) equidistant from the child. The three sets of variables were completely crossed with one another so that in all there were twenty conditions: $2 \times 2 \times 5$.

Responses were classified under three headings. *Correct*: the child took or indicated or did something to the object mentioned in the sentence; *Incorrect*: he took or indicated the object which was not mentioned; *No reponse*: the child did nothing or nothing which seemed relevant to the instruction.

Results and Discussion

We look first at the correct responses which are set out in Table 2.1. The data were quantified by attributing a value of 1 to each correct response and a value of 0 to all other responses. These scores were submitted to analysis of variance. There is the inconvenience that the data do not vary along a continuum, and therefore the results of such an analysis must be interpreted cautiously. Look, Name, and Gesture were treated as fixed factors. Look yielded a significant main effect: $F(1, 19) = 40.54; p < .001$. So did Gesture: $F(4, 76) = 10.94; p < .001$. The triple interaction of Look, Name, and Gesture was significant: $F(4,76) = 3.49; p < .05$. The only other significant effect was the interaction of Look and Name: $F(1, 19) = 4.86; p < .01$.

TABLE 2.1

Proportion of Correct Responses Associated with Look and Gesture in Experiment 1

	Object offered to child		Object offered to mother			
	Right	Wrong	Right	Wrong	Neutral	Total
Tester looks						
at child	.95	.45	.88	.82	.98	.82
at mother	.73	.40	.65	.38	.65	.56
Total	.84	.42	.76	.60	.81	

Table 2.1 shows the effects of both Look and Gesture. Across all conditions the probability of a correct response when the tester looked at the child was .82; when he looked at the mother it was only .56. We can deduce that a child weighed eye-to-eye contact heavily as an indicator that it was he who was being addressed. Interestingly, the main effect for Name, seen in Table 2.2, fell far short of significance. Note, however, that the child's name was mentioned only after the sentence, and so it may not have been as effective

as if it had been mentioned before, to alert the child to the sentence. On the other hand, eye-to-eye contact was established before the sentence was uttered, and does indeed seem to have drawn the child's attention to the sentence. Nevertheless, the interaction of Name and Look was significant. It seems that even though his name came after the sentence, it still increased the likelihood of a correct response when the tester looked at the mother. In that condition the use of his name elicited a correct response with a probability of .63; when his name was omitted, the probability dropped to .48. Thus Name is shown to have an effect subsidiary to that of Look.

TABLE 2.2

Proportion of Correct Responses Associated with Look and Name in Experiment 1

	Name	No name	Total
Tester looks			
at child	.81	.81	.81
at mother	.63	.48	.56
Total	.73	.65	

The second main effect is associated with Gesture and can be seen in Table 2.1. It would seem that the child tended to respond correctly whenever the correct object was held out. When it was held out to himself, p was .84; when it was held out to his mother, p was .76. Correspondingly, the child tended not to respond correctly when the wrong object was held out: The lowest probability occurred then, $p = .42$; when the wrong object was held out to his mother, $p = .60$. Thus the Gesture of holding out had a marked influence on responses. When the tester looked at the child and held out the correct object to him, the probability of a correct response rose to .95. Actually all 20 children responded correctly in the condition where the tester looked at the child, held out the correct object, and mentioned the child's name. Because of the significant triple interaction, it seems legitimate to single out this particular condition. This result is particularly consoling in view of the age of the children and the rather bizarre effect (to an adult, at least) of some of the conditions. The fact that all children responded correctly in this condition suggests that they did not write off the game or the tester as beyond the bounds that a reasonable human being might be expected to take seriously.

What about the relative efficacy of eye-to-eye contact and Gesture as signals that it was the child who was addressed? The answer is to be found in two conditions: The tester looks at the child and holds out the right object to the mother ($p = .88$); the tester looks at the mother and holds out the right object to the child ($p = .73$). Both factors are powerful, but eye-to-eye contact appears slightly more so. If we examine the same two conditions when the baby's name was not mentioned, the two values of p are .85 and .75. Clearly, the name was not a significant influence in this connection.

The neutral condition is especially instructive because in it is revealed the effect of language alone without the influence of Gesture. The overall probability of a correct response in the neutral condition was .81; when the tester looked at the child it was .98, and when he looked at the mother it was .65. Actually in the neutral condition all children responded correctly when the tester looked at the child and mentioned his name. Again, these results show that the tester was successful in obtaining the child's attention and in selecting objects that were familiar to him but not of such overwhelming interest that he tended to grab them no matter what the instruction or condition.

The results for the neutral condition also raise some questions. Was the child in other conditions responding to the Gesture or to the sentence? The results can all be explained by the view that the child was not aided by nonlinguistic signals, but that he was upset by them. That is, his responses did not improve when the tester looked at him or offered him the correct object beyond the level he achieved when the objects were just placed before him. However, his response was poorer when the tester looked at his mother or held out the wrong object, particularly to him. This interpretation is confirmed by the incorrect responses. Their number was negligible except in those conditions where the wrong object was held out to the child. Then there was some tendency for the child to take the offered object ($p = .34$). Indeed, in the condition where the tester looked at the child, mentioned his name, and held out the wrong object, the probability that he would take it rose to .55. Once again the significant triple interaction warrants our singling out certain conditions in this fashion.

The net result is that we have established the importance of Look and Gesture only when they are misleading.

Another question is whether the children responded to the sentence as a whole or only to the name of the object. There is nothing in the evidence so far to rule out the possibility that correct responses were due to the child's attending only to the object's name and ignoring the rest of the sentence. The remainder of the experiments are designed to answer these questions.

We can break down the child's performance which was not marked correct into incorrect responses and no-responses. The latter are set out in Table 2.3 where it can be seen that there is only one major factor. When the tester looked at the mother the child did not respond in about 36% of trials; when he looked at the child, the latter did not respond in only some 6% of trials. This again confirms the importance of eye-to-eye contact. When the tester looked at the child, errors tended to be the child's taking the wrong object.

TABLE 2.3

Proportion of No-Responses in Experiment 1

	Object offered to child		Object offered to mother			
	Right	Wrong	Right	Wrong	Neutral	Total
Tester looks						
at child	.05	.03	.13	.08	.00	.06
at mother	.30	.40	.30	.43	.35	.36
Total	.18	.22	.22	.25	.18	

EXPERIMENT 2

In order to answer the questions raised by Experiment 1, we decided to control the role of language by using French. Working with children in English-speaking homes we could be sure just how much of the sentence they would understand. The use of French, we felt, enabled us to simulate in certain key respects the situation where the infant understood nothing or very little by means of language. This would throw nonlinguistic signs into bolder relief.

Method

In order to study whether the children of the first experiment had attended to the sentence as a whole or just to the name, we devised two conditions. In one the sentence was entirely in French, e.g., *montre-moi le soulier*; in the other only the name of the object was in English, e.g., *montre-moi le shoe*.

Ten children who had not taken part in the first experiment were tested in each of the linguistic conditions. In one group there were six boys and four girls; in the other there were five boys and five girls. The average age of each group was $17\frac{1}{2}$ months, and in each ages ranged from 14 to 20 months.

Objects were selected for the tests just as in Experiment 1. In each group Look was varied: The tester looked either at the child or at his mother. In each group Gesture was varied as in Experiment 1: The named object was held out either to the child or to his mother; or the unnamed object was; or the two objects were placed in the neutral position, equidistant from the child. In short, Look and Gesture were varied precisely as in the first experiment. Since Name had proved a relatively weak clue, we omitted it in this experiment. Otherwise the testing and recording of responses were just as previously.

In particular the order in which the 10 items were administered was varied randomly anew for each child.

Results and Discussion

The data for correct responses were submitted to analysis of variance, one for each "linguistic" group. In the analysis for the all-French group there was only one significant effect, that for Gesture: F (4, 36) = 22.15; $p < .001$. The analysis for the other group yielded two significant effects. Gesture yielded F (4, 36) = 8.86; $p < .01$. The interaction between Gesture and Look yielded F (4, 36) = 2.77; $p < .05$. In Table 2.4 we set out the numbers of correct responses for the all-French group. There was only one effective

TABLE 2.4

Proportion of Correct Responses Made by All-French Group in Experiment 2

	Object offered to child		Object offered to mother			
	Right	Wrong	Right	Wrong	Neutral	Total
Tester looks						
at child	.80	.00	.50	.00	.00	.26
at mother	.80	.00	.30	.00	.00	.22
Total	.80	.00	.40	.00	.00	

Gesture, that was when the tester offered the named object to the child; then the probability of a correct response was .80. When the named object was offered to the mother, the corresponding figure was .40. In all other conditions there were no correct responses. From this we learn that the Gesture of offering can carry great meaning to a child independent of language. There was a probability of .65 that the child would take the unnamed object when it was offered to him—hardly surprising since he had no indication that it was the wrong one. And interestingly, there were no correct responses in the neutral condition. This demonstrates very powerfully the influence of the Gesture of offering.

The corresponding no-response data are given in Table 2.5, where it will be noticed that Look, again, is not an important factor, but Gesture is. In particular when the tester offered an object to the mother the probability of no-response was about .68 compared with .25 when one was offered to the child. In the absence of any comprehensible language, then, Gesture rather than Look guided the response. This is borne out by the fact that for the neutral condition, there were no-responses in 90% of the trials.

TABLE 2.5

Proportion of No-Responses for All-French Group in Experiment 2

| | Object offered to child | | Object offered to mother | | | |
	Right	Wrong	Right	Wrong	Neutral	Total
Tester looks						
at child	.20	.20	.50	.80	.80	.50
at mother	.20	.40	.70	.70	1.00	.60
Total	.20	.30	.60	.75	.90	

TABLE 2.6

Proportion of Correct Responses Made by Name-in-English Group in Experiment 2

| | Object offered to child | | Object offered to mother | | | |
	Right	Wrong	Right	Wrong	Neutral	Total
Tester looks						
at child	.90	.10	.90	.90	1.00	.76
at mother	.70	.40	.60	.50	.80	.60
Total	.80	.25	.75	.70	.90	

There were many more correct responses in the second group, the "name-in-English" group—Table 2.6. In this group when the tester held out the correct object to the child, the probability of a correct response was .80. This equals the performance of the all-French group in the corresponding conditions. We may conclude, then, that by itself the gesture of offering an object conveys as much meaning to a child as does the same gesture accompanied by the name of the object. Indeed when we compare these figures with the corresponding ones for the first experiment, we see that the new set of responses are almost, but not quite, as good, even when the babies did not understand a word of what was said to them. The point is not that small children understand little of the utterances they hear—but that they are capable of getting a great deal of meaning from signs and gestures when they do not understand what is said to them.

In the data for the name-in-English group, the influence of Gesture, though still important, was greatly reduced. Most noticeable is the probability of .90 that the child would respond correctly when the unnamed (wrong) object was held out to his mother. This shows that his attention was on the name of the object. Equally impressive is the overall probability of .90 of a correct response in the neutral condition. This is as high as the corresponding figure in Experiment 1. It follows that we are justified in attributing correct responses in that experiment to the name alone, rather than to the entire sentence.

Again we see in both groups the influence of a misleading gesture, which shows how closely the child attends to the nonlinguistic signals. The overall probability of a correct response in both groups when the tester looked at the child and offered him the wrong object was .05; the overall probability that the child would take the wrong object was .52. However, the misleading effect was less in the name-in-English group when the tester looked at the mother and offered the wrong object to the child. Then the probability of a correct response is .40. When Gesture and Look were in conflict, the object's name helped. The same effect is seen even more clearly when the tester looked at the child and offered the wrong object to his mother: The probability of a correct response is .90.

The no-response data for the name-in-English group are set out in Table 2.7. The first thing to note is that no-responses occurred in only 14% of trials, compared with 55% for the all-French group. The object's name was an important factor. In addition, Look seems to have influenced no-responses in the name-in-English group. When the tester looked at the mother there were no-responses in 24% of trials, compared with 4% when he looked at the child.

TABLE 2.7

Proportion of No-Responses for Name-in-English Group in Experiment 2

	Object offered to child		Object offered to mother			
	Right	Wrong	Right	Wrong	Neutral	Total
Tester looks						
at child	.10	.00	.10	.00	0.00	.04
at mother	.20	.40	.40	.40	.20	.24
Total	.15	.20	.25	.20	.10	

We were surprised that Look did not give rise to a significant main effect in the data for correct responses. This was the only time when we tested for it with 17-month-olds that it did not. In the all-French group the explanation is not difficult to find. They simply did not respond correctly at all in those conditions where Look had had a significant effect in the first experiment. The no-response data showed that they tended not to respond more when an object was offered to their mother, and simply to take the wrong object when it was offered to them. There was no room for a Look factor. In the correct responses for the name-in-English group there was a marked difference associated with Look between two conditions: The tester looking at the child offered the wrong object to the child; the tester offered it to his mother. The effect seems to have been so powerful, but in contrary directions, that it obliterated what in the first experiment had been a main effect. The explanation seems to be that eye-to-eye contact with the child seems to have alerted him to respond. When the wrong object was offered to him, he took it in 90% of the trials; when it was offered to his mother, he took the other, correct one in 90% of the trials. The conflict between Look and Gesture seems to have thrown him back on the object's name. The fact that Look was indeed playing a part is, as we have seen, borne out further by the no-response data. In these there was a slight tendency for no-responses to increase when the tester looked at the mother. Or to put it another way, eye-to-eye contact with the child stimulated a response.

EXPERIMENT 3

Up to the present we have employed only a single instruction: We asked the child to indicate the named object. In learning his mother tongue the child has to distinguish between many sentence types and between different speech acts. How, for example, does the small child know whether a particular utterance is a command or a question. One hypothesis was that the clue would lie in some corresponding variation in the accompanying nonlinguistic gestures. We also hypothesized, on Lieberman's (1967) suggestion, that intonation pattern would constitute a powerful clue. We thought that the child would tend to treat an utterance as a question if its final words were spoken on a rising tone, as a statement or a command if its final words were spoken with a falling tone. These considerations gave us our third experiment.

Method

We varied Intonation Pattern: question and command. We varied Gesture, either pointing at the named object or offering it to the child. We varied Look as before. We used French sentences to simulate the stage when the child was learning to understand basic sentence types. With Gesture we covaried sentence structure. The gesture of offering an object was accompanied by the sentence *prend le X*; that of pointing, by the sentence *est-ce que c'est un X?* On half the occasions, X was named in English, on the other half in French. This design meant that there were 16 test items determined as follows: two intonation patterns, two gestures (covarying with two sentences), name of object in English or in French, and eye-to-eye contact with the child or with his mother. All possible combinations of these variables number 16. Note that there were no misleading gestures.

Ten children who had not been previously tested acted as subjects, five boys and five girls. Their average age was 17 months, with a range from 14 to 20 months. Objects were chosen for the tests as in the previous experiments. The order of items was randomized afresh for each child. The administration and scoring were just as in the first two experiments.

Results and Discussion

Analysis of variance of the correct responses yielded only three significant results. Look was significant with $F (1, 9) = 14.22, p < .01$. So was Gesture: $F (1, 9) = 11.00, p .01$. Finally the interaction of Look and Gesture yielded $F (1, 9) = 8.44, p < .05$. The means for these variables are set out in Table 2.8.

TABLE 2.8

Proportion of Correct Responses by Look and Gesture in Experiment 3

	Offer	Point	Total
Tester looks			
at child	.90	.35	.63
at mother	.28	.28	.28
Total	.59	.31	

The Gesture effect is quite marked in this experiment, but we must bear in mind that it does not mean what it meant in previous experiments. It refers merely to the acts of offering an object or pointing to it. Children varied their response when the tester varied the gesture. They did so mainly by taking the object when it was offered, and doing nothing when it was pointed to. Recall that sentence type covaried with gesture: Question went with pointing, and command with offering. We cannot be sure, then, whether the children paid attention to Gesture or to Language, or to both. This will be taken up in the next experiment.

Look gives rise to an equally marked effect, responses being better when the tester looked at the child. Most interesting, however, is the interaction of Look and Gesture (Table 2.8). Look had little effect when the tester pointed, probably because children tended not to respond for that condition. However, when the tester offered the object to the child while looking at him, the probability of a correct response rose to .90.

The absence of a Language effect is surprising, particularly in view of the last experiment. When an object was named in French the overall probability of a correct response was .46; when it was named in English it was .44. In this experiment, then, both eye-to-eye contact and gesture carried more meaning for the child than an object's name. Moreover, the high probability of a correct response ($p = .90$) when the tester looked at the child and offered him the right object occurred even when the entire sentence was in French. This finding agrees with those of the first two experiments: Children are capable of getting as much meaning from certain nonlinguistic signs as adults might from the sentences with which we accompanied the signs.

But why did the object's name make so little difference in other conditions? The most reasonable answer is that in this experiment there were no misleading gestures (such as holding out the wrong object). In Experiment 2, Name had its largest effect for that condition where the tester offered the wrong object to the child's mother. It seems that in that case the misleading gesture was not so overpowering as when the tester offered the wrong object to the child. It seems that when the wrong object was offered to the mother, he was able to use the name to overcome the suggestion of the misleading gesture. That is, the effect of Name, previously, may have been to counteract the influence of misleading gestures. In Experiment 3 there were no misleading gestures and no effect of Name. We will have another opportunity to examine this interpretation in the next experiment.

The absence of a significant effect associated with Intonation Pattern is surprising and possibly informative. We had failed to find such an effect in a pilot study, but considered the matter important enough to merit closer examination. Lieberman (1967) observed that in 12 of the 14 languages on which he had information, questions could be put by employing a rising intonation pattern without altering the syntax of the declarative sentence. We had imagined that rising intonation pattern might constitute a "natural sign" for the child. The present experiment, at any rate, gives no support to that view. It should be noted, however, that the rising intonation pattern is ambiguous in language addressed to a small child. The rising tone at the end of the sentence is often an indication of command or request rather than question. However the no-response data, Table 2.9, indicate that rising tone had no effect. If the children had interpreted it as a command, they should have responded more frequently when they heard it. But there is no evidence of such a tendency.

Indeed, the no-response data match the correct response data rather closely. The number of no-responses fell off sharply when the tester looked at the child and offered the object. There is no effect of Language apparent in these data either.

TABLE 2.9

Proportion of No-Responses by Gesture, Intonation Pattern, and Look in Experiment 3

Gesture:	Offer		Point		
Intonation:	Statement	Question	Statement	Question	Total
Look:					
at child	.05	.15	.45	.45	.27
at mother	.70	.75	.65	.55	.66
Total	.38	.45	.55	.50	

EXPERIMENT 4

Method

The plan on this occasion was to separate the effects that were confounded in Experiment 3, when Gesture (point and offer) was covaried with Sentence Type (command and question). We wish to pit these two variables against one another in order to reveal the child's strategy. Would he notice and pay more attention to variation in the linguistic signal than in the gesture? This gives us our first two variables: Sentence Type and Gesture.

We also varied the object pointed to or offered as in Experiments 1 and 2. In half the trials the tester pointed to or offered the wrong object (unnamed) and in half the right one (named). The final variable was Language. In half the trials the object's name was given in English and in the other half in French. In all trials the rest of the sentence was in French. The two sentence structures were: *prend le X* and *est-ce que c'est un X?*

With four variables, each with two values, we have 16 possible combinations, and so we have 16 trials for each child. The children, five boys and five girls, had an average age of $18\frac{1}{2}$ months, and ranged in ages from 15 to 20 months. They had not taken part in any of the previous experiments.

Objects were selected for the testing as previously, and the testing was carried out in the same manner. The order of items was randomly varied afresh for each child.

Results and Discussion

The correct responses were quantified as previously and submitted to a four (fixed) factor analysis of variance. Only three effects proved significant. Gesture (offering/pointing) yielded an $F(1, 9) = 9.00$, $p < .05$. Object pointed to or offered (right/wrong) yielded $F(1, 9) = 19.22$, $p < .01$. The relevant means are set out in Table 2.10.

TABLE 2.10

**Proportion of Correct Responses by
Gesture and Object in Experiment 4**

	Offer	Point	Total
Right object	.86	.45	.66
Wrong object	.025	.075	.05
Total	.45	.26	

Perhaps the first thing to note is the absence of a significant Language effect. In order to understand this we must look at some other effects. When a child was offered the correct object, the overall probability of a correct response was .88; when he was offered the wrong object it was .025. There was a similar, but weaker, effect in those conditions in which the tester pointed. How does this relate to the earlier findings and to our explanation of a corresponding absence of a Language effect in Experiment 3? Actually, as Table 2.10 shows, it relates quite well. In Experiments 1 and 2 the probability of a correct response was lowest when the tester offered the wrong object to the child. When he offered the wrong object to the mother, the child was able to use the object's name and overcome to some extent the suggestion of the misleading gesture. In Experiment 4 we did not include a condition in which the wrong object was offered to the mother. Hence, the absence of a Language effect (which is really that of telling or not telling the child the object's name). However, it does suggest that telling the child the object's name was effective mainly in that condition when the wrong object was offered to the mother. Moreover, the present finding is quite in keeping with the finding of the earlier experiments to the extent that telling the name adds nothing to the effect of offering the correct object.

The main finding of Experiment 4 is that Gesture is associated with a significant mean square, whereas Sentence Type is not. This implies that the children did not notice or did not pay as much attention to the linguistic change as they did to the change in gesture. This forms an important item of evidence suggesting that, in the process of learning their mother tongue, children rely heavily on nonlinguistic signs as a key to a speaker's intention. However, more about this in the general conclusion.

In Experiment 3 we saw that the change in Gesture from offering to pointing had a marked effect which we see again here. This time, however, we see that the effect of object is even more marked. When the tester's signal drew attention to the right object, the probability of a correct response was .66, when it drew attention to the wrong one, it was .05. It seems then that the two gestures drew attention to a particular object, and in this they may well have been equal. In addition, the gesture of offering suggested to the child that he should take the object to which his attention was being drawn.

The data for no-responses, Table 2.11, add very little to what we have just seen: Gesture was the main factor, and Syntax had no effect. As we would expect however, Object was not a significant factor in no-responses, though it was in correct responses. It seems that Object affected which object the child took, but not whether he responded or not. There was no evidence of a Language effect in the no-response data.

TABLE 2.11

Proportion of No-Responses by Gesture, Object, and Syntactic Structure in Experiment 4

Gesture:	Offer		Point		
Object:	Right	Wrong	Right	Wrong	Total
Syntax:					
Command	.10	.15	.50	.45	.30
Question	.15	.15	.50	.50	.33
Total	.13	.15	.50	.48	

EXPERIMENT 5

Hitherto we have examined children who were about 17 months old on average, and we controlled their understanding of the experimental sentences by using French. In the final experiment we adopted an additional strategy, that of using children who were on average 5 months younger. It was our ambition to repeat in one experiment with younger children as much as we could of the foregoing experimentation. Naturally, we had to make a selection among factors, and we arrived at a design somewhat more complicated than the earlier ones.

Method

Our first variable was Look—at the child or at his mother. Our second was Gesture—offer the object, point to it, or neutral (the objects placed equidistant from the infant without an accompanying gesture). The third variable, Object, is nested under the first two gestures only—we offered or pointed to the right object (named) or the wrong one (unnamed). The fourth variable, Person, is nested under the gesture of offering only—we offered the right or wrong object to the child or to his mother. This rather complicated pattern is illustrated in Figure 2.1. Only one sentence type was used, and it was French except for the name of the object, e.g., *prend le shoe.*

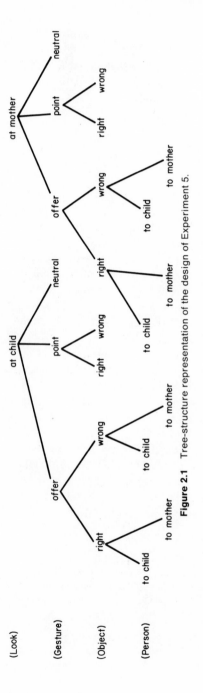

Figure 2.1 Tree-structure representation of the design of Experiment 5.

(Look)

(Gesture)

(Object)

(Person)

The children, none of whom had previously been tested, had an average age of 12 months. Their ages ranged from 11 months to 14. Five were boys, and five girls. The testing was carried out with objects selected in the manner described in the earlier experiments. The series of 14 test items was administered in different random orders.

Results and Discussion

Three separate analyses of variance were carried out for three different combinations of the correct response data. There was one overall analysis: Look × Gesture. For this, observations nested under the gesture of offering were averaged for each child, and it was these averages that were entered as the child's scores for that gesture. Scores nested under the gesture of pointing were averaged in a similar manner, and the averages were used as individual scores. This analysis yielded only one significant effect; for Gesture F $(2, 18) = 11.04, p < .01$. The relevant probabilities of a correct response were: offer, $p = .48$; point, $p = .18$; neutral, $p = .15$. Clearly the significant effect arises from the difference between the mean for offer and those for the other two gestures.

The second analysis was by Look, Gesture, and Object. However only two gestures were included: offering and pointing. The neutral one was omitted. The reason is that one could not draw attention to a particular object in the neutral condition. The analysis yielded three significant effects. For Gesture, $F(1, 9) = 16.00, p < .01$. For Object, $F(1, 9) = 18.41, p < .01$. For the interaction of Object and Gesture, $F(1, 9) = 5.44, p < .05$. The appropriate means are set out in Table 2.12 where it will be seen that responses when the object was offered were better than when it was pointed to; they were better when attention was drawn to the right object than to the wrong one; and when the right object was offered to the child, the probability of a correct response (.78) was very much higher than in any of the other conditions.

TABLE 2.12

Proportion of Correct Responses by
Gesture and Object for Second Anova in
Experiment 5

	Offer	Point	Total
Right object	.78	.25	.51
Wrong object	.18	.10	.14
Total	.48	.18	

The third analysis was by Look, Person, and Object. The data associated with pointing and with the neutral condition were not included. The analysis yielded only one significant result; for Object, F (1, 9) = 21.25, p < .01. However, the variance ratio associated with the interaction between Object and Person falls just short of significance at the 5% level: F (1, 9) = 5.0, p > .05. For significance at that level an F-value of 5.12 is required. In view of the fact that Person has been associated with significant effects in the other experiments, we have decided to treat the effect here as significant. The appropriate means are to be found in Table 2.13. Offering the right object produced better results than offering the wrong one. As before, results were best when the right object was offered to the child (p = .90) and worst when the wrong one was (p = .15). When the objects were offered to the mother, the child's level of correct responses was intermediary between the two.

TABLE 2.13

Proportion of Correct Responses by Person and Object for Third Anova in Experiment 5

	Offer to child	Offer to mother	Total
Right object	.90	.65	.78
Wrong object	.15	.20	.18
Total	.53	.43	

To sum up, significant effects were found in the now familiar directions in association with Gesture and Object, and, in one marginally significant interaction, with Person. The interesting absence of significance is associated with Look and the main effect involving Person.

The most important conclusion from all this is that the results for 12-month-old babies largely replicate those obtained with older ones. All the significant results replicate exactly the findings of the experiments with older babies; differences lie in the absence of significant results. Among the latter, the principal one is the very poor level of performance for the neutral condition (p = .15). In the first experiment this condition was associated with a p = 1.0 when the tester looked at the child and said his name. In Experiment 2 the neutral condition was associated with a very high level of correct responses in the name-in-English group (p = .90). This is exactly the neutral condition in the present experiment; the name was in English and the rest of the sentence was in French. However, none of the all-French group in Experiment 2 responded correctly in the neutral condition. The children of the present experiment come very close to them. Perhaps the explanation is that they did not understand the names of the objects. If this is the case, and it seems to be, we have indeed reached a level where the child is only beginning to understand language. On the other hand his ability to cope with gestures and signs—and to be misled by them—seems to be almost as pronounced as that of older children. For example, when the right object was offered to the child, the probability of a correct response was .90, and when the wrong one was offered, the probability dropped to .15. This is indistinguishable from the corresponding findings with older children. What the older children developed in the intervening 5 months seems to have been an increasing understanding of language, not an increase in ability to interpret the nonlinguistic signs we used.

Why then the lack of significant effect for Look? There were consistently higher scores in all conditions when the tester looked at the child, but not significantly so. We have repeatedly suggested that Look was not as important a factor in catching a child's attention as the actions of pointing or holding out an object. The present results confirm that view. Younger children paid more attention to Gesture than to Look. In particular, the gesture of offering seemed not only to have fixed the child's attention on an object but to have suggested that he do something with it. Eye-to-eye contact may well have served only to fix the child's attention on the tester. Perhaps the younger children were less able than the older ones to attend to both the tester and to the object he was manipulating. They may well, then, have concentrated on the objects and on the gestures instead.

TABLE 2.14

Proportion of No-Responses by Gesture, Object, Person, and Look in Experiment 5

Gesture:	Offer				Point			
Object:	Right		Wrong					
Person:	Child	Mother	Child	Mother	Right	Wrong	Neutral	Total
Look:								
at child	.10	.30	.20	.40	.70	.40	.80	.41
at mother	.10	.40	.20	.50	.60	.80	.70	.48
Total	.10	.35	.20	.45	.65	.60		

One or two interesting points emerge from the no-response data which we have laid out in Table 2.14. The most important factor is Gesture: The child tended to respond less when the object was pointed to. Person, too, is a factor: The child responded less frequently when an object was offered to his mother. The no-response data support our interpretation of the Person factor in the correct responses. Most interestingly, for the neutral condition when the tester looked at the child, there were no-responses in 80% of trials; when he looked at the mother there were no-responses in 70% of trials. Compare this with the corresponding cell of the first experiment when the two figures were 0% and 70%, respectively. The difference must be that the younger child did not know the objects' names. Note, however, the suggestion that eye-to-eye contact did not convey to the child any intimation of a command. At most it is an attention-getting device, but does not specify to what the child must attend, or what he must do.

GENERAL DISCUSSION

Let us for the moment lay aside methodological problems and ask ourselves what have we done and what have we discovered. We examined the ability of babies to respond to instructions under various conditions. We varied the linguistic instruction controlling the amount that the child could possibly have understood. We varied the child's age. Both of these variations were intended to reach or recreate and explore settings in which a child had to rely on nonlinguistic signals in order to interpret the linguistic instructions. We chose only a few linguistic variations: statement versus question and an entire sentence the child might possibly have understood versus the object's name alone versus nothing at all that he could possibly understand. We employed statement intonation patterns and question ones. We also varied whether or not the child's name was mentioned. We worked with two age groups: 12- and 17-month-olds. We varied only a few gestures: pointing, offering, and neutral (no gestures). We varied the object to which attention was drawn, the right one or the wrong one, and we varied the person to whom an object was offered, the child or his mother. Finally we varied the person looked at, the child or his mother.

The overall findings are clear enough. If the child can understand the linguistic instruction, he responds to it and depends largely on it, but he can be misled by a look or a gesture. Indeed when words and gestures conflict, he tends to rely on gestures. This gives the impression that of the two, gestures are the more basic and more powerful signaling system. Where the child can understand little or nothing of the linguistic sign, either because he is younger or because he has not heard the language before, he relies more heavily on the nonlinguistic signs. It is not that his performance is different in those conditions where nonlinguistic and linguistic signals agreed; he is merely more at the mercy of misleading nonlinguistic signals. And when even these fail, as in the neutral condition, he simply does not respond.

There has not, to our knowledge, been much research into the communicative role of nonverbal signs in connection with language in infants, but the mental health profession has been interested in the topic among adult patients—see Shapiro (1966, 1968), Shapiro, Foster, and Powell (1968), and Ekman, Sorenson, and Friesen (1969). There seems to be considerable agreement among them that when nonverbal cues and verbal ones conflict, the nonverbal are the more reliable. If this is correct, and it seems to make good sense, then there may be a universal of communication across all ages; the nonverbal signaling system is the basic one, partly because the verbal one rests upon it to some considerable extent. Indeed, to judge from the behavior of the children in the two age groups we studied, the progress seems to be from an understanding of objects and some nonlinguistic symbols one at a time, to a coordination of such signals, to an understanding of the object's linguistic names, and thence to an understanding of syntax. Recall that when syntax and gesture were varied independently in French, the child's response showed that he had attended to the variation in gesture but not in syntax. Our present studies do not explore how such a progression is made. We have concentrated instead on mapping it out.

We return now to the questions with which we began. How does the child know that he, and not somebody else, is being addressed? Presumably there are many clues, such as his being the only other person in the room, or the use of that special speech style that mothers reserve for babies (Snow, 1976). In our studies we looked at some possible cues, and of these the child's name was only marginally effective. It seems to have sometimes conveyed to him that he was being addressed when the tester was looking at his mother, otherwise, no. It was mentioned only after the sentence; perhaps if it had been mentioned before the sentence, it would have drawn his attention to the sentence before the sentence had faded from short-term memory.

Eye-to-eye contact was a much more powerful factor in telling the child that he was being addressed. It was established before the sentence was uttered. While it had not so decisive an effect on the child's response—which was all we had to judge by—as gesture, it had some effect in all four experiments with older children. In particular, it tended to elicit a correct response when the "wrong" object was offered to the mother. At that point, eye contact with the tester appears to have suggested to the child that he was being addressed and to have alerted him to the contrast between the object offered and the object named. The data do not support the more simple interpretation that the child took the other object, the one not offered to his mother.

Curiously, eye contact did not contribute to the number of correct responses by the younger children of the fifth experiment. We do not interpret this as a failure to signal who was being addressed, but rather as an inability on the child's part to attend to eye contact and, at the same time, to the object being offered. Of course, our interpretation is based on responses, and there is very little evidence that the child took eye contact as a sign that he was being addressed and then forgot about it as he attended to gesture. In our support there is a body of literature that underlines the importance to infants of eye-to-eye contact. This literature suggests that such contact establishes communication between infant and adult, but unfortunately it says nothing, so far as we are aware, about its role in drawing attention to speech as addressed to the infant.

How does the child know what object is being spoken about? Clearly he can guess if he himself has drawn attention to something that is then followed by an adult remark. But there are also gestures at the adult's disposal that the child can interpret reliably enough. The two main ones we investigated were offering an object and pointing to it. Without any doubt, offering an object drew the child's attention to it, because he nearly always took it. This was true even of the very young children who were addressed in a language that was, to them, incomprehensible. There is also much evidence from common experience as well as from our observations that pointing to an object draws a child's attention to it. Often when the tester pointed, the child looked at the object pointed to (scored as no response), or he himself pointed at it (scored as a wrong response if it was the wrong object), or repeated the object's name (wrong response). So even though he did not respond correctly by our criteria, he did attend to the object. Interestingly, it seems that it is very difficult, if not impossible, to lead any animal other than a human to interpret the significance of pointing, and it seems quite easy to get a child to do it.

How does the child know that it is the object as a whole, and not just one of its properties, that is referred to? Of course there are all sorts of cues, provided he has already made some classifications of objects in the environment. "Sitting down," for example, is unlikely to be the name of the object, *Daddy*, simply because *Daddy* is nearly always called "Daddy," but very often he is "standing up," or "gone," or "reading," instead of "sitting down." And other objects besides *Daddy* are "sitting down" from time to time. In our observations we believe that phrases that accompanied the gesture of offering probably denoted the object as a whole for the child; he nearly always took the object, and one cannot take an object's properties without taking the object.

How does the child know whether an utterance is a command, a question, or a statement, to take only the three most basic speech acts? We had hoped that a rising intonation pattern might signal a question as distinct from a statement or command. We found no evidence that it does. Several friends have pointed out to us that rising intonation frequently signals a command in adult speech to infants. The point is well made, but it must not be forgotten that all the signals we studied are ambiguous. Even the gesture of holding out an object may express various intentions: look at it, take it, I am removing it from my person, if you touch *this* again you will be punished, etc. All we can conclude is that the rising intonation did not seem to convey much to the children in our experiment; or it was not as salient as other signals.

This is not to deny that in appropriate circumstances rising intonation indicates a question to small children, or that other intonation patterns are unimportant. Presumably an utterance that is made in a very loud voice is likely to be interpreted as a command. And presumably any signs of annoyance, in gesture or facial expression, are likely to indicate that the accompanying utterance is a command.

Of the two gestures we examined, that of offering seems to have been taken as a command to take the offered object, and so may have indicated that the accompanying sentence was a command. When an object was pointed to, the child generally did not take it. Perhaps he interpreted the accompanying sentence as giving a name to the object, which would explain why several children repeat the name in this condition.

There must be other clues which we did not study. For example, if a child is looking at a picture book, utterances are likely to be treated as naming ones. On the other hand, if the child is doing something he knows he shouldn't, or not doing something he knows he should, he can expect that utterances will be commands.

It is important to repeat that none of the signals we studied was unambiguous as to the signaler's intention, and to add that all the signals were equally involved with intentions. The first of these points merely reiterates Quine's (1960) observation that events never adequately determine intentions. We do not go on with Quine to deny the existence or usefulness of intentions. With Katz (1966) we see a need for a set of constructs that, depending on one's purpose, may be called ideas or intentions. Fortunately, that point is easier to make today, with the development of artificial intelligence studies, than it was 10 years ago. However, the second point is perhaps less generally appreciated. Many still believe that learning theory might explain, by means of associations, the process of *naming* objects, though they would not necessarily claim that the process of relating speech acts (such as affirming, commanding, questioning, doubting) to sentence forms was so simple. This is due to a confusion. Names relate to objects as a whole, rather than to their qualities, say, only through the intentionality of the namer. Learning a name presupposes the correct assessment of the speaker's intention to name an object as a whole. This is just as much an assessment of intention as the process of identifying speech acts. All we have done is to explore some "teaching links" (the term is David Pear's, 1971), not just between an utterance and its use, but between an utterance and its accompanying intention.

REFERENCES

Brown, R. *Words and things*. New York: Free Press of Glencoe, 1958.
Ekman, P., & Friesen, W. V. Nonverbal language and cues to deception. *Psychiatry*, 1969, *32*, 88–106.

Ekman, P., Sorenson, E. R., & Friesen, W. V. Pan-cultural elements in facial displays of emotion. *Science*, 1969, *164*, 86–88.

Katz, J. J. *The philosophy of language.* New York: Harper and Row, 1966.

Lieberman, P. *Intonation, perception, and language.* Cambridge, Mass.: MIT Press, 1967.

Macnamara, J. The cognitive basis of language learning in infants. *Psychological Review*, 1972, *79*, 1–13.

Pears, D. *Wittgenstein.* Fontana/Collins, 1971.

Quine, W. V. *Word and object.* New York: Wiley, 1960.

Shapiro, J. G. Agreement between channels of communication in interviews. *Journal of Consulting Psychology*, 1966, *30*, 535–538.

Shapiro, J. G. Relationships between visual and auditory cues of therapeutic effect. *Journal of Clinical Psychology*, 1968, *24*, 236–239.

Shapiro, J. G., Foster, C. P., & Powell, T. Facial and bodily cues of genuineness, empathy, and warmth. *Journal of Clinical Psychology*, 1968, *24*, 233–236.

Snow, C. E. The language of the mother–child relationship. In S. Rogers (Ed.), *They don't speak one language.* London: Edward Arnold, 1976.

3

What Does It Take to Bootstrap a Language?

ZENON W. PYLYSHYN

University of Western Ontario

The main substance of my remarks will be that in order to account for language acquisition one is led, along with Macnamara, to posit that a more primitive conceptual system is already available. In addition, however, I want to suggest that one should distinguish between a manifest system that serves to communicate intentions (which is a form of nonverbal signaling system and need not presuppose that for its development still more primitive intention signals are available) and an entirely internal symbol system. The latter is a system of concepts through which the child perceives the world and onto which both the intention signals and the later verbal language can be attached. For this to occur, however, a considerable amount of innate structure is necessary (such as that which leads to inducing that a reference relation holds between two percepts). Furthermore, to obtain an optimum match between organism and environment, the system of interfaces must have considerable autonomy in their development and function—they must be partially separable.

To help establish a general framework for these remarks, let me begin by setting down what I believe to be three major preconditions for the development of a language. At this stage we need make no assumptions concerning the order in which these various conditions develop or become operative.

1. Sensory experience must be structured. The "blooming, buzzing confusion" of William James must be susceptible to segmentation, analysis, and reconstruction. Some aspects must be foregrounded relative to others so that the environment becomes articulated or differentially noticed in some fashion.

2. Communication codes (both verbal and nonverbal) must likewise be structured. The stream of vocal or gestural behavior must be perceived as segmented and a distinction between signifying and nonsignifying variation must be made (in generation and/or perception).

3. The occurrence of a speech act must be recognized. This is perhaps the most important but most neglected aspect of preconditions for language acquisition. Not only must a child attend to the appropriate aspects of his environment, but he must do it within the context of what Merleau-Ponty would call (loosely) an "intention to mean." This is a subtler notion than what linguists sometimes refer to as the "context of communication," since communication (at least in the usual sense of transmitting information to someone else) need not be involved. Without the recognition that an event is a speech act with a *meaning potential*, there would be no impetus to map from a linguistic event to a nonlinguistic event—and indeed no basis for distinguishing the two.

The first of these preconditions takes us into the study of how patterns are cognized by humans: how humans build up what Quine would call their "quality space" and how percepts are analyzed, decomposed, and assigned to equivalence classes. Such studies of assimilation and accommodation between perceptual events and human cognitive systems may be examined in relation to biological conditions, cultural conditions, and semiotic functions.

The second precondition—that linguistic signs be cognized as such—is studied by scholars interested in the development of phonological, gestural, and other sign systems. Clearly, before any act can become signifying, it must first be discriminable and/or reliably performable. It seems to me further that there must be some perceptual basis for identifying and grouping qualities independent of the linguistic function of the signal. What I mean by this is that it seems to me highly unlikely that the units of signaling and the distinction between free and significant variation is entirely conventional. Thus, although there is cultural variation with respect to which discriminable characteristics of speech (or gesture) are linguistically signifying (i.e., phonemic), such variation is remarkably narrow, especially when described appropriately—for example, in terms of articulatory distinctive features. Were this not the case, and were there not some biological basis for the qualitative groupings of sounds, the already difficult process of learning a language by infants might never get launched. I need not remind you of the research showing infants' abilities to discriminate intonation profiles, prosodic patterns, and so on, since this is not the primary concern of these comments.

But I do want to make the general point that although learning to make linguistic distinctions is evidently dependent upon the norms of a particular linguistic community and, to some extent, upon the way in which that community determines how its members carve up their experiences (as Whorf has argued) there must, at least on the outside layers of these interacting systems, be a measure of autonomous activity or *decoupling*. Thus I am arguing that in order to drive the thin edge of the language acquisition wedge, there must at the outset be a reasonable degree of autonomous development of reality partitioning independent of language and a reasonable degree of development of speech code perception independent of language.

Now these speculative remarks have glossed over one of the most important of the preconditions for language: that which I referred to as the recognition of the speech act. Supposing that (say toward the end of his first year), the child's experience has some conceptual order. The events in his perceptual field and that subset of events that are potentially linguistic (i.e., gestures, vocalizations) contain enough similarity-structure to form the basis for language induction. What more is needed?

Many people have recognized that something more *is* needed. For why should the child construct a mapping from one set of conceptualized events to another? The behaviorist answer is simple: An accidental pairing brings reinforcement. But, though this no doubt does occur, it does not solve the basic puzzle, which, put in behavioral terms, is: What is the relevant operant and how does the child recognize what is being reinforced? Consider again the case of naming. Surely the relevant operant (if I may continue to use this word) is neither the utterance nor the child's orienting response to the object but rather the establishment of a very special kind of asymmetrical irreflexive relation (which we might call reference or signification) between them. True, we can obtain what in many ways appears to be "naming" behavior without this last step—animals can learn to produce behaviors (or, as Skinner calls them, MANDS) that are instrumental for obtaining specified objects. But this is only a small part of what is involved in naming. To name an object implies that the object has been conceptually singled out or wrenched from its context and is available for arbitrary cognitive activity—including recombination into novel arrangements.

Bronowski and Bellugi have proposed

> that the human practice of naming parts of the environment presupposes and rests on a more fundamental activity, namely, that of analyzing the environment into distinct parts and treating these as separate objects. That is, there is implied in the structure of cognitive sentences a view of the outside world as separable into things which maintain their identity and which can be manipulated in the mind, so that even actions and properties are reified in words. In this philosophical

sense, predication is not merely putting together words in syntactical patterns, nor even the manipulation in the mind of ready-made objects and categories. Rather, predication is in the first place a way of analyzing the environment into parts, and only after that can they be regrouped in new arrangements and new sentences. [Bronowski & Bellugi, 1970]

Thus, for a child to acquire even something as apparently simple as the name of an object is already a highly cognitive activity. What seems to give this relation a status distinct from that of simple "association" between events is that it is formed in a special context: a context in which an event is being attended to *as a sign* or in which attention is being focused on a referential relationship. I believe that the observation that something more than mere co-occurrence of events is necessary for language development is central to understanding the phenomenon of language. I am belaboring the point at this time because I believe that it is closely related to the reason why Macnamara found it necessary to introduce the notion of inferred intentions as a factor in language acquisition. I am suggesting that perhaps the most fundamental of the inferred intentions is the "intention to mean." Without this the task of building language would never begin. There are, in addition, many other types of intentions that the child soon learns to recognize independent of adult language. What follows is an informal attempt to examine some of the types of intentions a child may learn to infer at an early age and which might serve as a way of bootstrapping further language development.

Although this taxonomy is very tentative, it may be useful to distinguish among the following:

a. The intention of establishing a signaling relation with another individual. What I mean is that prior to any communicative act a person needs to obtain the attention of another person in a special sense. The two participants must not only attend to one another but must attend in what might be called a *communicative mode*. There is reason to believe that one of the main ways of indicating this intention is through eye contact and that this probably occurs even at a very early age. For example, M. C. Bateson (1971) has shown that when an adult and an infant of a few weeks of age were face to face, one to two feet apart with intermittent episodes of eye contact, they tended to wait for one another to finish vocalizing during vocal interaction. Bullowa, Fidelholtz, and Kessler (1973) observed a film sequence of a 28-day-old infant crying on his father's lap and concluded that a communicative relationship existed because eye contact was mutually sought. It is generally felt that eye contact is a sufficient, though not necessary, condition for tagging accompanying activity as communicative (in the broad sense). It is not surprising that the first lesson in behavior modification technology is to establish eye contact with the patient.

b. Communicative–functional intentions. This includes such things as the functional categories posited by M. A. K. Halliday. Halliday (1975) studied the functional origins of language in his son Nigel from the age of about 9 months. With the very beginnings of Nigel's language he identified expressions with functions he called *pragmatic* for which a response was required. These included *instrumental* expressions glossed as "I want" or *regulatory* expressions glossed as "do such-and-such." A second category of nonpragmatic types of expressions he refers to as *mathetic*. These do not require a response and are generally used by the child to explore his nonlinguistic environment. Initial mathetic expressions include *interactional* ones glossed as "me and you," *personal* ones glossed as "here I come" or "that's nice." Later, Nigel added other mathetic categories such as *heuristic* (glossed as "tell me why" or "let's look at this together," and *imaginative* (glossed as "let's pretend").

I mention Halliday's taxonomy because I believe it represents roughly the kinds of intention-contents that a child might be expected to perceive or to signal prior to the development of a linguistic system recognizable as such. Indeed Halliday proposed this system to try to study the developmental sequence of "meaning potentials." Thus, his research bears on the question of whether perception of meaning or intention precedes the development of a linguistic code.

Some important findings of his study, as they pertain to the present discussion, are:

i. Expressions in the first four categories (instrumental, regulatory, interactional, and personal) arose between the ages of 9 and $10\frac{1}{2}$ months. At this point the expressions appeared to be clearly linguistic, as evidenced by their meeting the criterion that each must be observed in at least three unambiguous instances in relation to a content interpretable in functional terms.

ii. The form of the expressions owes nothing to English. The sounds made by the child were spontaneous, holophrastic, and not appropriately captured in a phonetic alphabet—the latter being too specific and insufficient to capture generalized postures and prosodic values. As Halliday remarks, however, although the expression owes nothing to English, the content probably does insofar as English embodies meanings such as "I want that" and the adult hearer recognizes and responds to such meanings. Such meanings may be cultural, biological, or linguistic universals (or all of these).

iii. There is no evidence that the pragmatic utterances precede the mathetic ones, as would be expected from a behavioral perspective. The validity of the pragmatic/mathetic distinction was confirmed later when Nigel ($19\frac{1}{4}$–$19\frac{1}{2}$ months) introduced a systematic opposition between rising and falling tone that distinguished pragmatic from mathetic expressions. Here also is a clear example where a distinction that is linguistically significant in English is adopted by the child to express a functional distinction present in his own semantic system, but which is *not*, one must note, the same semantic distinction that opposition expresses in adult English since the latter distinction is not yet available to the child.

c. To complete this picture of types of intentions one must add a long list of attitudinal and social intentions signaled by a variety of gestural, postural, and paralinguistic variables (such as studied by Birdwhistell, 1970) as well as a set of fascinating intention-signaling devices used in dialogue (e.g., Scheflen, 1964, and Kendon, 1972, have studied the role of major postural shifts in signaling beginning and end of discourse as well as change of topic). Far less work has been done in relation to communication between infants and their caretakers but what is known clearly points to the importance of nonlinguistic intention signals. The only reason for drawing your attention to the existence of this complex network of nonlinguistic intention signals is to make the point that it would be most surprising indeed if young children did not learn to perceive or to use gestural signals in parallel with language. This does not, of course, argue that the gestures have a primacy in setting up the linguistic context during language acquisition. We shall return to this point later.

Let me now turn to the research reported by Macnamara. In these studies Macnamara sets out to explore the view (as expressed in Macnamara, 1972) that the child learns a language by determining the speaker's intention independent of language and then using this knowledge as a clue to understanding the language. To be able to do this, Macnamara correctly notes, the child must have the ability to use nonlinguistic objects, events, gestures, etc., as clues earlier and more reliably than he can use language. Thus, the experiments are aimed at establishing that children 11–20 months of age are able to interpret correctly such clues as eye-to-eye contact, and gestures such as pointing and offering, and to establish the relative potency of these signals when they conflict with one another or with linguistic signs. Macnamara did succeed, not surprisingly, in showing that children in this age range were, by and large, able to interpret such nonlinguistic signs appropriately—or at least that they can be misled by conflicting gestures. In the latter case it appears that when words and gestures conflict or when the child does not understand the words, he prefers to rely on the gestures. Within the non-linguistic signs some are more potent than others in certain specific situations; for example, eye-to-eye contact was less important than *offering* or *pointing* in eliciting an orienting response (e.g., taking, indicating, or "doing something to" the appropriate object); the gesture of offering led to more correct responses than pointing, and so on. But given the rather unusual situation that confronted the child in these experiments, it is difficult to know how to interpret these results. Imagine the child's consternation when the experimenter switches to an unknown language at the start of testing, offers objects to the child while looking and/or addressing the mother, and then doing the reverse. While reading the description of the experiments, I sometimes found myself wondering what sort of game the child saw this experiment to be that would prompt him to reach for an item being offered to his mother by the experimenter who is directing his attention to the mother and speaking to her in an alien language (the child did reach for the object 30% of the time in Experiment 2, and 60% of the time when the English object-name was mentioned). In view of such odd moves, I am not sure what the child was up to and therefore cannot guess whether the child reached for the offered object more often than the pointed-to one simply because it was closer or because the experimenter appeared pleased the last time the child did so. I need not belabor these methodological questions since the main thesis—that young children are quite capable of reading certain nonlinguistic intention cues—seems secure. More important than the fine points, such as which gestures are more potent, is the general issue of how this type of investigation bears on the original proposal concerning the basis for language acquisition.

Let us assume that infants can be shown not only to interpret nonlinguistic signs appropriately but also to give them preference over linguistic utterances when the two are not in harmony. This does not yet establish a causal relation. But that is not the main difficulty. To my mind, one of the problems with this thesis (and here I am only partly playing the devil's advocate) is to understand precisely what is being claimed when it is asserted (Macnamara, 1972) that "a speaker's linguistic system and his intentions are distinguishable." It seems obvious to me that a speaker's intentions and the utterances he uses to express them are distinguishable. But it is not nearly so obvious that those intentions that are at issue in language learning are distinguishable from all over acts that can be called linguistic (or semiotic). This is no longer the problem of whether we are dealing with "ethereal entities." Even if we accept the reality of intentions, it is not clear how this will help the language acquisition problem. Either the speaker's intentions are manifest (in which case one can ask whether this is not already some form of linguistic system and hence how *it* was acquired) or they are not (in which case the only way they can be relevant is if both child and adult have them independently and in parallel). Both alternatives, one must admit, require much more explication, and at least one of them may lead us to postulate a highly complex system of innate perceptual categories. I personally am hoping for a primitive linguistic (though not creative nor possessing a multilevel structure) signaling system that can be founded on biological principles and that can be shown to form the first level of a scaffolding on which a full language can be erected.

This, at least in part, is Halliday's view. The conclusion he draws from his investigations is

> that the child already has a linguistic system before he has any words or structures at all. He is capable of expressing a range of meanings which at first seem difficult to pin down, because they do not translate easily into adult language, but which become quite transparent when interpreted functionally, in the light of the question "what has the child learned to do by means of language?"

Admittedly this does not solve the basic puzzle but it does change its shape. Presumably we do not need to posit a still more basic linguistic system to underly the preverbal one: The carving up of reality occurs at the same time as concepts are being formed for the preverbal system. What this says is that intention inferring goes on because there is present, in effect, a developing primitive expressive preverbal language system. This language can be studied in its own terms as Halliday has done. His work can be viewed in a sense as the converse of Macnamara's. While the latter tried to see what gestural (i.e., preverbal) cues the child could perceive as containing meaning potential, Halliday searched for expressions of meaning potential in the child's preverbal (but predominantly articulatory) gestures. It might be useful to try to bring the two approaches together in an attempt to characterize the developing preverbal linguistic (i.e., meaning signaling) system of the child. What we need are ways of learning about this early system—which features are universal, which directly linked to biological structures, which ontogenetically evolving, etc.—and ways of relating this system to the overt, lexical, syntactically structured adult speech.

My own view diverges somewhat from Halliday's when it comes to the nature of what he calls the prelexical linguistic system of the child. For Halliday, as for many linguists, this symbolic system is inextricably tied to *expression*, that is, the only "meaning potentials" existing in this system are ones for which the child has some overt communicative expression—whether it be vocal, gestural, or some other behavioral form. In my view this ties meaning too closely to communication. Why should we not consider, say, the concept "graspable" to be a meaning potential assigned to a certain class of perceptual events by virtue of a common operation that is recognized as performable on certain perceived objects. In other words, why should we not consider that an internal naming or referencing act is performed when a set of objects is cognized as susceptible to common actions as well as to those to which we ascribe a common overt linguistic expression. What I am arguing for is an extension of the notion of prelexical language to concepts formed on the basis of their potential for action as well as their potential for expression. Such an extension opens the way for recognizing a unity among verbal and nonverbal thought, a trend to which I am wholly sympathetic.

REFERENCES

Bateson, M. C. The interpersonal context of infant vocalization. Quarterly Progress Report No. 100, Research Laboratory of Electronics, Massachusetts Institute of Technology, January 1971, 170–176.

Birdwhistell, R. L. *Kinesics and context*. Philadelphia: University of Pennsylvania Press, 1970.

Bronowski, J., & Bellugi, U. Language, name, and concept. *Science*, 1970, *168*, 669–673.

Bullowa, M., Fidelholtz, J. L., & Kessler, A. R. Infant vocalization: Communication before speech. Paper presented at the Ninth International Congress of Anthropological and Ethnological Sciences, Chicago, 1973. To appear in the published proceedings (The Hague: Mouton).

Halliday, M. A. K. Learning how to mean. In Eric Lenneberg and Elizabeth Lenneberg (Eds.), *Foundations of language development*. Vol. 1. New York: Academic Press, 1975.

Kendon, A. Some relationships between body motion and speech. In A. Seigman and B. Pope (Eds.), *Studies in dyadic communication*. Elmsford, N.Y.: Pergamon Press, 1972.

Scheflen, A. E. The significance of posture in communication systems. *Psychiatry*, 1964, *27*, 316–331.

4

On the Acquisition
of Phonology

PAUL KIPARSKY
LISE MENN

Massachusetts Institute of Technology

In acquiring the phonology of a language, the child accomplishes two feats. First, the child must master the phonetic repertoire of the language. Second, the child learns the phonological rules that represent the regularities governing the variation of its words and morphemes. Each accomplishment involves both perceptual and productive ability. Learning the phonetic repertoire of the language involves both learning to pay attention to its relevant acoustic cues and achieving articulatory control over its sounds and sound combinations. Learning the phonological rules involves both the ability to recognize word identity across rule-governed phonological differences, and the active internalization of at least some phonological rules for purposes of production, such as those accounting for the inflectional morphology of English, which are learned productively by the primary school stage.

The learning of the phonetic repertoire and the later learning of the more abstract phonological regularities are often considered to be quite distinct in nature. It is of course true that the learning tasks that the child faces are very

This work was supported in part by a grant to Paul Kiparsky from the National Institute of Mental Health, 2P01 MH13390-09, and in part by NSF Dissertation Grant NSF SOC 74-22167 to Lise Menn.

different in the two cases. In the following, we shall argue that the linguistic means by which he/she solves these tasks are nevertheless the same. At every stage on the long road from the child's first utterances that attempt to match the segmental phonemes of adult models, to the adolescent's learning of the fine details of morphology, the same basic learning principles and the same kinds of internalized linguistic systems come into play.

THE LEARNING OF THE PHONETIC REPERTOIRE

We shall begin by reviewing the well-known theories of Jakobson and Stampe. Both of these view the child's speech as the result of a filtering of the adult speech, where the filter is a reflex of a set of constraints in universal grammar.

On Jakobson's account, there is a universal hierarchy of features arranged in a strict pattern of successive dichotomous branchings. The unfolding of a child's phonemic system is governed by this hierarchy: At any given stage, distinctions corresponding to branches lower than a certain set of nodes on this hierarchy "tree" are not manifested in his/her speech. We may illustrate by considering a portion of the hierarchy set forth in *Kindersprache*, and in Jakobson and Halle (1956). The hierarchy is complicated by the existence of relations among some branches: High vowels, for example, are claimed to show a palatal–velar (front/back) distinction before low vowels do.

For this reason, actual representation of the hierarchy as a tree is confusing, and Jakobson and Halle choose a "decimal" coding of the hierarchy, assigning to each contrast a number sequence chosen so that if dichotomy A presupposes dichotomy B, then the sequence of numbers for A contains the sequence of numbers for B. A portion of the table reads:

Consonants:	dental versus labial	0.1
Vowels:	narrow versus wide	0.11
Narrow vowels:	palatal (front) versus velar (black)	0.111
Wide vowels:	palatal versus velar	0.1111
Consonants:	velo-palatal versus labial and dental (anterior)	0.112
Consonants:	palatal versus velar	0.1121
...	(No firm predictions are made about glides or liquids.)	

This embodies predictions such as: The child will not have a phonemic contrast between /k/ and /t/ (0.112) before contrasting low and non-low vowels (0.11), but a phonemic contrast between dentals and labials (0.1) will precede or be simultaneous with any contrast among vowels.

This hierarchy also determines the phonemic systems of the languages of the world: The use by a language of any contrast in the hierarchy presupposes the presence in that language of all those contrasts ordered above it.

Jakobson does not put forth a theory of children's perception of words. He remarks that perception is in advance of production, but that at the time production begins, the child may still fail to pay attention to certain acoustic cues.

Interpreted as a predictive theory, Jakobson's schema has some odd properties. It seems to make very strong predictions, and has not yet been strictly falsified, so that it has remained widely accepted (McNeill, 1970). Yet careful examination shows that one reason for its durability is that it is very difficult to falsify. The small corpuses that can be gathered, even by diary methods, for children at the early stages of speech, are often too small to establish whether the subject has command of certain contrasts. Furthermore, Jakobson's theory is explicitly only a theory of the acquisition of contrast, not a theory of the mastery of phonetic targets.

In assessing the phonetic predictions made by Jakobson's theory, we must keep in mind that he views features not as absolute, but as relative properties of phonemes, defined within a network of oppositions, whose phonetic value thus is allowed a certain latitude. For example, contrary to what is sometimes asserted by other authors, Jakobson does not say that the child will have bV before gV (using b, d, g, to stand for labial, dental/alveolar, and velar stops, respectively); what he claims is that there will not be a phonemic opposition bV/gV or dV/gV before the appearance of the opposition bV/dV. In order to falsify this claim, a child must show both the *absence* of a bV/dV opposition and the *presence* of an opposition between gV and the members of the other set. Absence of an opposition like bV/dV can be shown only if the child attempts to say adult words containing labials and words containing dentals and then fails to distinguish those sounds in output. A child may have no dentals, at a time when he/she has both bV and gV, and yet fail to be a counterexample to the Jakobson schema if there is no evidence that labials and dentals are merged (Daniel, described in Menn, 1971). Absence of dentals from the child's output is no evidence of merger if the absence is achieved by the child's not attempting adult words that have dental stops.

To illustrate Jakobson's schema, we construct six hypothetical examples of corpuses. The first corpus would be a perfect example for showing development according to the two predictions (mentioned above): (A) "a phonemic contrast between dentals and labials will precede or be simultaneous with any contrast among vowels"; (B) "the child will not have a phonemic contrast between /g/ and /d/ before contrasting low and non-low vowels." The second hypothetical corpus is one type that is compatible with the Jakobson schema but which might better be approached by some other theory. The third and fourth hypothetical corpuses would falsify prediction A, and the fifth and sixth would falsify prediction B.

Good Case, Hypothetical Corpus 1 (hypothetical total output corpus; predicted by A and B)
time 1: [pa]   (regardless of the model word)
time 2: [pa], [ta]   dentals versus labials
time 3: [pa], [ta], [ti]   low versus non-low vowels
time 4: [pa], [ta], [ti], [ka]   velar versus labials and dentals

Hypothetical Corpus 2 (does not contradict A or B) (total output corpus)
time 1: *pa* → [pa]   *tea* → [ti]   (complementary distribution)
time 2: *pa* → [pa]   *tea* → [ti]   *cup* → [kʌ]   (complementary distribution)

Hypothetical Corpus 3   Hypothetical Corpus 4 (both falsify A)
pa, ball, doll → [ta]   [ta] ~ [pa]   [ti] ~ [pi]
bee, tea → [ti]   (regardless of the model word)
(vowel heights contrast, but dentals do not contrast with labials)

Hypothetical Corpus 5   Hypothetical Corpus 6 (both falsify B)
cat, kiss → [ka]   [ki] ~ [ka]   [ti] ~ [ta]
toy, tea → [ta]   (regardless of the model word)
(vowel heights do not contrast, but velars contrast with dentals)

For testing Jakobson's schema, we depend on evidence from merger of adult contrasts or from free variation in the child's speech. The latter phenomenon is relatively uncommon, and so we rely heavily on the former, a test that requires consideration of both input and output levels of child speech.

Here we face a problem in interpretation of Jakobson, for we must bear in mind that he is almost entirely concerned with the internal phonemic structure of the child's speech, and not with its behavior as a representation of adult language. Jakobson speaks almost exclusively in terms of contrasts "appearing" and "failing to appear" in the child's speech. What exactly do we mean by saying that a contrast *fails to appear*? If we speak of a contrast that fails to appear, it is necessarily defined with respect to something outside the child's speech. We must be defining it either by a universal phonetic description or by a description of the ambient adult language, or by both. Suppose we refer only to universal phonetics, and suppose we have a child like Jacob Hankamer (Menn, 1976) who has dental and velar stops, but no labials, for a certain period. When Jacob has only *d* and *k*, then it is certainly true that in one sense, the *b/d* contrast "failed to appear" prior to the appear-appearance of the *d/k* contrast. On what grounds do we then claim that such a case fails to test (and falsify) the Jakobson schema? What is the basis for our interpretation of Jakobson? Does it rest on explicit statements by him?

It does not; an intermediate step of reasoning is required which will certainly be obscure to those who have not dealt directly with the small corpuses that can be obtained from even the most intensive diary study of children at the threshold of speech. In a small total corpus, accidental gaps are everywhere. Only recent work, not available to Jakobson (see Ferguson & Farwell, 1973; also below), has shown that many gaps in a corpus may be nonaccidental and due to phonological selection by the child. Certainly we do not wish to interpret Jakobson's schema in a fashion that would make it trivially falsifiable by a child who happened not to be interested in naming any objects whose names began with labials at a time when his/her total vocabulary consisted of, say, ten words, such as (a hypothetical example) *hi, no, down, daddy, kitty-cat, nanna, ta-ta, doll, toast, light.* If all gaps are accidental and we wish to avoid trivial falsification, we must require that a putative falsification of the Jakobson schema show that the child in question really does not have the ability to make an output distinction, e.g., between labials and dentals at a time when he/she does make the output distinction between dentals and velars. The only positive evidence that a child cannot maintain a certain distinction is phonemic merger of adult phonemes which do make that distinction.

Let us next consider Stampe's approach, which he calls a theory of "Natural Phonology." Stampe, a generative phonologist, deals explicitly with adult words as forms underlying the child's output forms, relating adult word to child word by a set of rules. His theory is primarily concerned with the properties of these rules, which he considers to be innate. Again we have a filter simplifying adult speech, but it is not a static hierarchy like Jakobson's. It is, rather, a dynamic system consisting of innate rules or "natural processes," each of which reflects some property of the articulators that we might characterize as some "inertia" that must be overcome with effort. The processes are held to apply initially in unordered fashion wherever their structural description is met, and if all the processes apply, essentially all phonemic distinctions are lost.

Some natural processes are context-free replacements and others are context-dependent. Learning adult phonology requires the child to inhibit the application of some of these processes. There are three mechanisms by which this is done: suppression, limitation (context-dependent suppression), and ordering. Processes may, and often do, conflict. For example, there is considered to be a context-free denasalization process (loss of the nasal/oral distinction in favor of the oral phonetic realization) and on the other hand a nasalizing process that appears in the neighborhood of nasal consonants. The possibility of varying resolutions of conflicting processes can account for the wide phonetic range of treatment of adult forms that we find in children, and this is then one source, for natural phonology, of the richness necessary in any adequate theory of child phonology.

In principle, the postulated natural processes are identifiable independently of child language in two main ways. The processes should first of all follow from the structure of the speech mechanism under an adequate theory of phonetics. At present, this is more in the nature of a promissory note. There is as yet no theory which accurately predicts a wide range of phonological facts from physiological or acoustic facts, though phoneticians have been chipping away at it since Sievers, and some success has been achieved in certain subdomains (for two recent attempts, see Lindblom & Liljencrantz, 1972; Ohala, 1974). Secondly, examination of enough cases of language change and synchronic phonological systems should reveal the recurring operation of the processes. The lack of systematic surveys of phonological processes in the languages of the world which is delaying progress here is now beginning to be remedied (Greenberg, 1970; Bhat, 1973; Bell, 1971; and other contributions to the Stanford Language Universals Project). In the case of segment systems, on which more information is accessible (Trubetzkoy, 1949; Hockett, 1955), some testing of the theory of natural phonology has been done (Miller, 1972).

Contrary to Jakobson, Stampe claims that the input to the child's system—the child's lexical representation—by the time he/she starts to speak is "the" adult surface form. Stampe's approach, however, would not lose its essential character if it were modified to allow for incomplete perception of the adult phonetics at the onset of speech.

We may exemplify Stampe's analysis with the derivations from his 1969 paper:

		Channing	*candy*
		/čǣnɨŋ/	/kǣndi/
(a)	*nd → nn*	—	kǣnni
	degemination	—	kǣni
(b)	flapping of *n*	kǣn̆ɨŋ	kǣn̆i
	flap deletion	kǣɨŋ	kǣi
	desyllabification	{kǣɨ̯ŋ}	{kǣi̯}

"Later, 'candy' became {kǣni}, by ordering (b) after (a)." (Details of representation of nasalized vowels and vowel off-glides are not worked out, being peripheral to the discussion, as is the rule velarizing the initial palatal.) Central to Stampe's position is the resolution, exemplified here, of phonological rules into minimal steps. Above, *nd* is not regarded as being deleted, but as undergoing, in some sense, four separate reductions in strength: *nd →* *nn → n → n̆ → ∅* in the course of deletion. The postulated "natural processes" are those that bring about these and similar minimal changes.

We see that in Stampe's theory, the approach to adult competence via suppression, ordering, and limitation of rules corresponds in a certain sense to the elaboration of the feature hierarchy in Jakobson's theory. However, an important difference not made fully explicit by Stampe is that his theory predicts the phonetic outcome of each process: The merger of nasal and oral sounds referred to earlier is not only a loss of opposition, but is also specified as a loss of nasality; the output must be oral, not nasal. Jakobson, because of his focus on phonemic contrast, does not deal with such "allophonic" facts.

According to Stampe, then, early phonology is an ever shrinking system of ordered processes that reduces the forms of adult speech to the child's ever growing phonetic repertoire. This view allows Stampe to make an interesting connection between child and adult phonology. He draws a sharp distinction within the adult system between *processes* and *rules*. The flapping of *t, d* in American English *matter, madder*, or the devoicing of obstruents in German *Land, Weg* are typical processes. Processes, unlike rules, do not admit exceptions or morphological conditioning, and they are inevitably extended to foreign words adopted into a language. Typical examples of rules are those which take *k* to *s* or change the vowel in words like *opacity, electricity* (cf. *opaque, electric*). Stampe claims that while the rules of the adult system are learned, the processes are not. The adult processes are, in his theory, simply those of the child's innate processes which are not suppressed by contrary data in the course of language acquisition.

There is a misleading aspect to this formulation, however: The relation between the child's modifications of adult words and the allomorphy found in adult language cannot be so direct. The modifications introduced by children, regardless of whether they are innate, as Stampe holds, or discovered by the experimenting child, as we shall propose, are purely phonetic adjustments. After all, in these very early stages of language acquisition, there is no allomorphy, each morpheme having a unique phonetic shape.

In most of the languages of the world, except for the strict isolating languages, the major role of phonological rules is to describe the relations between allomorphs. This is true of those rules that are considered to be "processes" by Stampe as well as of those which he considers "learned rules." Learning such rules involves the conceptual task of discovering allomorphies.

For example, let us suppose that we have a language which devoices final obstruents, as many do. By all available evidence, final obstruent devoicing is very common among children, regardless of how they start to use it; this rule—or process—is one of the best candidates for a "natural" rule of child phonology and of adult phonology.

It is quite possible that a child learning a language that devoices final obstruents will never learn how to articulate voiced obstruents preceding word boundary; he/she may be spared learning this rule *as an articulatory task*. But the conceptual task of linking up allomorphs remains: $[V_i C_{i + \text{voice}} + X]$ will still have to be recognized as containing an allomorph of $[V_i C_{i \triangle \text{voice}} \#]$. We have no reason to assume that this conceptual task of decoding the allomorphy is any easier than it would be for the child if the language happened instead to have the opposite, antinatural rule of final obstruent voicing.

It should be noted that these arguments do not apply where allomorphic variation is not involved. In those restricted cases where a rule of the sort that children typically have functions in a language *only* as a redundancy rule (only as a descriptor of surface patterns), and where there is no allomorphy to be decoded, then a language which has that natural rule might be easier for most children to learn than one which had an antinatural redundancy rule. The speakers of a language that has a natural redundancy rule not involving allomorphy may probably be spoken of in Stampe's fashion as not having suppressed processes of child phonology, but this is a very special case.

Stampe (1969) distinguishes phonological from purely phonetic manifestations of final devoicing (and, by implication, of other rules/processes):

> English-speaking children must suppress this process if their pronunciation is to conform to standard, but German children need not, because German permits this devoicing. *hunt*/*hunde* 'dog/dogs'. As the example shows, the devoicing process governs only the phonetic representation of German words, since the phonological representation of *hunt* is *hund*. In other languages it governs the phonological representations as well, since there is no voicing opposition in morpheme-final obstruents. [p. 445]

But by implication and example, he would not agree with our arguments based on the distinction between cognitive and articulatory learning. From his basic procedure of "factoring" all possible rules of adult phonology into natural steps, in the same fashion as his treatment of *candy* → [kǽj] and *Channing* [kǽĩŋ] exemplified above, it would seem that he holds precisely the opposite view: that the procedure of abstraction from surface to underlying forms runs most easily along "natural" path increments, and that the *conceptual* task of decoding allomorphy should be easier if the allomorphs are related by a phonetically natural rule such as final obstruent devoicing rather than by an antinatural rule such as a hypothetical final obstruent voicing.

We can construct one sort of possible test concerning the distinction of articulatory from cognitive learning, if Stampe's view on this matter is taken in conjunction with some other tenets of his theory. Let us consider the implications of the following quote from Stampe (1969):

> In languages which, for example, lack morpheme-final consonants altogether, the process of final-obstruent devoicing stays in the system but has no overt manifestation. This claim . . . appears to be supported by the pronunciation, in such languages, of foreign words with final voiced obstruents, which, if they are pronounced at all, are characteristically devoiced.

(Stampe has not cited sources for the claim that loanword final consonants, if they are pronounced as such in a language that generally permits no final obstruents, are devoiced, but we will assume, for the sake of the argument, that he is right on this point.)

Let us consider three hypothetical native speakers of, respectively, Japanese, which has no final obstruents, English, which has both voiced and unvoiced final obstruents, and Russian, which has a phonological rule of final obstruent devoicing. Let us have these three persons attempt to learn German without textbook instruction. Since all three speakers have a voicing contrast in their native language, let us assume that they all perceive the phonetic difference between *Tag* [tāk] and *Tage* [tāgə]. They might, however, face problems in the phonetic task of learning to pronounce them and in the cognitive tasks of learning that they contain the same morpheme and of learning the devoicing rule by which the allomorphs [tāk] and [tāg] are related. For the Russian, who has essentially the same rule in his/her native language, we would predict, and so would Stampe, that the phonetic task will be automatic and the cognitive task of discovering the allomorphy may be facilitated by transfer of the principle underlying the corresponding allomorphy in Russian: Assuming there is such transfer, on hearing the plural *die Tage*, the Russian would expect the singular to be pronounced [tāk], and on hearing a singular [hunt], he/she would assume that the inflected forms might show up with either /d/ or /t/ at the end of the stem, and would be on the outlook for evidence as to which might be the case. For the native speaker of English, who according to Stampe has suppressed the natural process of final obstruent devoicing, and who according to us may have once invented such a rule as a child but has long since discarded it, both the phonetic and conceptual tasks will be novel and therefore harder than for the Russian speaker. The differentiating case between our position and Stampe's will be the case of the speaker of Japanese. On Stampe's theory, the Japanese is in the same position as the Russian. Since the Japanese speaker has not suppressed the innate process of final obstruent devoicing, he/she should find it easier than the English speaker to learn the German rule not only in its phonetic aspect but even in its cognitive aspect; the discovery that [tāgə] and [tāk] contain the same morpheme should pose less of a problem to the native speaker of Japanese than to a native speaker of English. Our conjecture is, on the contrary, that while the Japanese speaker may spontaneously devoice final obstruents like the Russian, he or she is in exactly the same position as the speaker of English when it comes to figuring out German patterns of allomorphy. (Note: This is a hypothetical case to make clear in principle the empirical nature of the disagreement between natural phonology and our discovery-oriented approach to the acquisition of phonology. If it is not the case that final obstruent devoicing is generally found among speakers of languages without final obstruents when they start to learn a second language with voiced final obstruents, an example to illustrate the same point could be constructed around some other natural process.)

As seen by both Jakobson and Stampe, the early stages of the acquisition of phonology are rather different from the later stages, when morphophonemic relations are being learned. In the later stages the child behaves as an active grammar-constructor. The child is faced with the problem of remembering, producing, and recognizing variant forms of morphemes and solves it by devising a system of rules and underlying representations that represent the general and predictable aspects of this variation.

The pattern of rule learning in children on the schema "special case–overgeneralization–learning of exceptions" is well known from the work of Berko, Anisfeld and Tucker, and Bogoyavlenskiy (reprinted in Ferguson & Slobin, 1973). As a schematic illustration, learning the past tense of *bring* might involve the following stages:

   I   *bring* ∼ *brought* (present and past tense forms of verbs are learned
                separately in the lexicon)

  II   *bring* ∼ *bringed* (the child learns the regular dental suffix, and
                overgeneralizes it)

 III   *bring* ∼ *brought* (*brought* is relearned as an exception to the general
                rule)

  IV   *bring* ∼ *brang*   (the child learns the ablaut rule $i \rightarrow æ$ and
                overgeneralizes it)

   V   *bring* ∼ *brought* (*brought* relearned)

(We do not claim, of course, that this whole sequence will occur for this particular word in each child; merely that such a pattern of bracketing out successively finer generalizations is typical.)

It is clear, also, that the child's speech development cannot simply be viewed as a monotonic approximation to the adult model. Linguistic structure occasionally drags red herrings across the trail of the learner. Consequently, progress may be interrupted by false hypotheses, which include not only overgeneralizations but entire rules which must later be discarded. For example, Zwicky (1970) reports his daughter Elizabeth at age 4.6 invariably producing "doubly regular" participles of strong verbs like *aten, gaven, roden, sawn, shooken, tooken,* and *wroten.* According to Zwicky, "six subsequent months of frequent corrections by her parents had no noticeable effect." Elizabeth had devised the two promising but, alas, wrong rules of English:

(A) The participle has the same stem as the past.
(B) The strong participle is formed by the suffixation of *-n.*

She applied them conjunctively to produce the doubly marked participles.

Compared to what we know about later acquisition, the picture we get from Jakobson and Stampe of early acquisition seems rather deterministic: There is no "discovery," no experimentation, no devising and testing of hypotheses. The child's problem, in their view, contains a built-in solution— for Jakobson, unwrap the features; for Stampe, get rid of processes.

We shall argue here that, on the contrary, phonology acquisition is a "problem-solving" activity from the earliest stages. The child has a goal— learning to talk—and a subgoal with which we are concerned—saying recognizable words. This is a difficult task, and the child must discover ways to circumvent the difficulties. These discoveries are made through experimentation, guided by the child's innate hypothesis-forming capacity and a complex feedback toward the goal of speaking.

Different children exclude definable classes of output by different means. When we observe such repeated "exclusion," we conclude that these classes of outputs (clusters, certain co-occurrences, the "third position," etc.) represent difficulties to the child, and that the various rules of child phonology (substitutions, deletions, etc.) as well as selective avoidance of some adult words, are devices the child finds for dealing with those difficulties. For extensive consideration and exemplification of rules of child phonology, the reader should consult Ingram's (1974) basic article "Phonological Rules in Young Children." We shall discuss here a few examples of classes of outputs that children are known to avoid, and their means to that end. Note that not all children avoid all of these difficulties; we present these as general tendencies rather than as universals.

We take as our first example the "third position" problem. We use this term for a phenomenon reported in a more general case by Ferguson and Farwell (1973) and actually found, although not generally noted as a typical occurrence, in several corpuses: Children learning English who have output control of two of the three principal stop positions often have few or no output words manifesting the remaining one.

If there has been phonemic merger of dentals with velars, and absence of velars (or dentals) results, the child is progressing as predicted by Jakobson. However, in several cases the child does not give any evidence of merger, but instead selectively avoids input words using one stop position—dentals for Daniel Menn, labials for Jacob Hankamer. Substitutions of several kinds, avoidance of different positions, and possibly deletions of disfavored stops are all means toward the end of restricting output words to only two stop positions for a period of time. The same problem is solved by different means in each "third-position-avoiding" child studied. Selective avoidance is a phenomenon of great theoretical interest, as has been noted by Ferguson and Farwell and by Drachman. It requires that the child be aware that some phonetic targets are difficult for him/her, and is entirely outside the scope of theories, such as

Jakobson's and Stampe's, which are concerned with the child's failure to mark distinctions made by the ambient language.

Similarly, there are several ways of dealing with consonant clusters: deletion of all but one of the phonemes (in a stop-X or X-stop cluster, the one preserved is *not* always the stop), conflation of some of the features of the elements of the cluster (eg., *sm* > *M*, *fl* > *w*), insertion of a vowel to break up the cluster, metathesis (*snow* > *nos*), etc. (see Greenlee, 1974).

The very diversity and "ingenuity" of these devices might indicate that early phonology should be regarded as the result of the child's active "problem solving," rather than merely of an intrinsic filter acting on the target forms. Stronger evidence for this position comes from the earliest stages of speech. There is first the well-known although imprecise observation that children often manifest a "presystematic" period before they begin the orderly discarding of sounds by information-reducing rules (Nakazima, 1972). We also find what A. Moskowitz has called "phonological idioms," those occasional words that children say which transcend their usual output limitations and come much closer to the adult model than would be expected. Phonological idioms are frequently found in the presystematic period. (Actually, the onset of phonemic systematization is probably gradual and not restricted to a "period." This topic is difficult and has not been well studied.) Our claim is that during this "period," the child is inventing rules for simplifying his/her lexical representation of words in order to be able to say them fluently.

One of the examples studied by Moskowitz (1970) is one of Hildegard Leopold's first words, *pretty*. She said it essentially correctly, with the /pr/ cluster and the medial /t/ following it. Yet as the next of her words came in, Hildegard had no consonant clusters, and in fact, for months after the acquisition of this word had no other output words in which there were two different stops (cf. Ferguson & Farwell, 1973). The consonant harmony, consonant deletion, and cluster reduction rules that Hildegard used and that resulted in her restricted output seem not to have been available at the time she acquired *pretty*, and thus not to have been automatic, but to have been invented slightly after that time.

Again, consider the general avoidance of sequences $C_1VC_2(V)$ (C_1 not homorganic with C_2) found in many children. The "open syllable" children, those who prefer $CV(CV)$ canonical form, like Hildegard Leopold, may avoid mixed sequences of consonants by whole-syllable reduplication or by deletion of a final stop in a C_1VC_2 model. The closed-syllable children (Smith, 1973; Menn, 1971) tend to assimilate the stops according to several rule types. Yet in the Daniel Menn corpus, for example, the first 29 words, a few of which were CVC output and many of which were CVC input, showed no consonant harmony, and then consonant harmony quite suddenly appeared, as the cornerstone of the child's system of phonological rules.

Phonological idioms may also occur after phonemic systematization seems established, by what we take to be a process comparable to lexicalization in adult phonology. Jonathan Kiparsky substituted dentals for velars systematically, for example, [ato] *Michael*, [dæts] *catch*; later (at about age 1.8) substitution began to be restricted to initial positions [teyk] *cake*, [tuki] *cookie*; but even then the [t] was retained as an archaism in his rendering of *Michael*, [ato], and persisted even in its improved rendition, [maito].

Significantly, even some of the most plausible natural "processes" may give evidence of having been discovered by a child, rather than being automatic results or inherent constraints on the speech mechanism. Daniel Menn's second and third words were the phonological idioms [hay] *hi* and [hwow] *hello*; at a later stage he added /h/ deletion to his phonology.

As Ferguson and Farwell note, Jakobson's approach cannot (and in general, no "filter" approach can) very well be modified to allow for a stage in which a contrast is controlled followed by a stage in which the same contrast is neutralized, as is the $h:\emptyset$ contrast in this example. (Jakobson himself did not fail to notice such cases, cf. 1968, p. 23.) Taking the more "cognitive" view which we advocate, these are simply the expected cases of apparent regression reflecting the addition of new rules, comparable to morphological regression of the standard *brought* → *bringed* type.

A further argument for our view is that many of the characteristic rules of child phonology that are used to simplify words for output are not "low-level" rules, such as deletions and contact assimilations. We have mentioned the more sophisticated kind of simplification found when the child uses consonant harmony, as in [gɔg] for *dog*, (Menn, 1973; Stampe, 1969; Smith, 1973) or reduplication, as in [be:be:] for *biscuit* (Waterson, 1971). Such rules increase the redundancy of the articulatory instructions in the word; we may assume that [gɔg] is easier than *dog* in the same way that *101* is easier to type than *103*, for example. Metathesis over intervening vowel ([nos] for *snow*), discussed by Ingram (1973) as being one of the most powerful arguments for the child's preference for a small set of canonical output forms, is sometimes found as a way of avoiding consonant clusters. It is difficult to see how such a rule could arise from the operation of automatic articulatory processes.

A third type of simplification of this type, found in older children, is achieved by stereotyping the surface inventory by the use of dummy syllables. Here the simplification does not necessarily involve reducing the number of articulatory features that have to be produced per word; instead the repertoire of output word forms is reduced. Ingram (1973) has discussed such cases in terms of phonological redundancy rules (Stanley, 1967). We may illustrate it continuing with the analogy used in the preceding paragraph: If we know that all the sequences that we will be called upon to type have *O* as the second character, and we have access to this knowledge while typing, then we have less information that must be kept in mind about each individual sequence while typing. Smith's son used the dummy syllables *ri:* or *ri* for virtually all unstressed initial syllables: *attack* [ri:tæk]; *arrange* [ri:reinz]; *guitar* [ri:'ta]. The child has actually increased the number of articulatory instructions required for the word *attack*, *arrange*, and he has departed from his normal treatment of velars in *guitar*, but he has sharply decreased his repertoire of pretonic unstressed syllables. Avoidance of clusters by metathesis over vowels, discussed above, and other devices for restricting the output to a few canonical forms, also increase the repertoire without necessarily reducing the number of articulatory features that have to be produced per word.

One interesting consequence of a "problem-solving" view of phonology acquisition is that one might expect the child's previous solutions to be extended to new problems. A child's learning could thus show a certain amount of overall patterning attributable to the repeated use of certain strategies for devising rules.

Consider from this point of view the observation of Branigan (1974) that his subject shows a "focus" on the initial segment of a word in two distinct ways: The child uses initial stops to copy from in reduplication, and the word-initial position is the locus of experiments with and mastery of new phonemic distinctions. (A restricted version of this observation is made in Moskowitz, 1970.) For Daniel Menn, we see almost the mirror image of this case; final consonants are the ones he prefers to assimilate to, and word-final position is the place where new or complex phonemes (fricatives, affricates) and consonant clusters make their first appearance.

We suggest that here we see two children who have devised similar strategies, "pay attention to/try to match the beginnings of words" and "pay attention to/try to match the ends of words." If we assume that the child is capable of learning from his successes, we can account for those two "syndromes" by saying, for instance, that Branigan's subject has learned to deal with one problem, say the avoidance of $C_1VC_2(V)$, by focusing on C_1, and that this focusing then guides his attempts to deal with phonetic complexity of other sorts.

A further consequence is that Stampe's distinction between learned rules and innate processes loses its ontogenetic basis, at least in its present form. If we are right, then *all* phonological rules are in some sense acquired. The actual diversity observed among children's phonologies also tends to cast doubt on the idea that some adult phonological processes might be retentions of innate processes operating in child language. We are not aware of any longitudinal studies that bear on this claim. However, it seems to be falsified by children who do not exhibit a given process even though it is compatible with the target speech (cf. Braine, 1974, for discussion). For example, among his earliest words, Jonathan Kiparsky had a splendid *t* in [ata] *daddy*, contrary to *both* the flapping process and the flap of the adult speech he heard. In fact, the distinction between rules and processes does not emerge altogether clearly in the grammars of the languages either. Even quite "low-level" rules may have lexical exceptions or morphological and/or syntactic conditioning (in particular, there are analogs to "phonological idioms" in adult language). On the other hand, morphologically conditioned rules can be quite as exceptionless as phonologically conditioned rules. In our view of the acquisition of phonology, there is reason to expect just this to be the case.

The development of the child's perception and classification of phonetic categories is a notoriously difficult area to study. It would be consonant with our general approach to find an element of learning here as well. Though there are some indications that the child must discover how to attend to linguistically relevant distinctions in perception (Edwards, 1974; Garnica, 1973) and how to classify them (Menn, 1973; Halliday, 1973) there is very little that can be said on this subject with any confidence.

In summary, we propose the following framework:

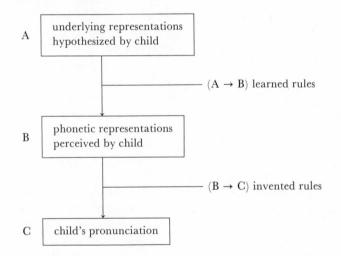

Each of the representations in the three boxes has a different status. A is constituted by the child's hypotheses about the underlying representations of the adult language he/she is learning. B is constituted by the child's perceptions of the phonetic representations of the adult language he/she is learning (to repeat, it is possible and even likely that these are distinct in some respects from the adult phonetic representations, though there is little concrete data on this point). And C is the child's ("intended") pronunciation (*Lautabsicht*), which may in turn be different in certain ways from the physical output, as when a purely *physical* limitation (say, a lisp) merges segments that the child may believe he is in fact distinguishing.

In the early stages of language acquisition, A and B coincide, while B and C are maximally distinct. As the child masters more of the phonetics, after the initial period of rule invention, C approaches B and the system of rules (B → C) shrinks. The process normally terminates when C becomes identical with B. Independently, and surely concurrently in part, though continuing well into adolescence, a second learning process goes on. As the child keeps discovering the phonological relationships of his language, A becomes increasingly different from B and the system of rules (A → B) becomes increasingly elaborate. This process terminates when A and A → B develop into the adult lexicon and rule system.

This picture can only in part be compared to Jakobson's, for Jakobson's goals were different. He presented a theory of the child's learning of the *phonemic* system, not of the morphophonemic system. Within this domain, however, a difference between his view and ours is that we differentiate between inherent phonetic limitations and linguistic, "invented" devices for coping with them, whereas for Jakobson there is only an inherent "filter." Therefore, the actual diversity in the child's solutions becomes somewhat problematic for Jakobson, whereas it is expected on our account.

Of course, if we are right about the inventive and diverse character of even the first steps in phonology acquisition, the difficulties of testing some of the best-known predictions of Jakobson's theory, and the need to take into account more than just the acquisition of contrasts, what we take to be Jakobson's central claim may perfectly well still hold true: namely, that whatever implicational laws hold for the languages of the world also hold for each stage in a child's acquisition of phonology. For it is quite possible that these implicational laws (presumably expressed by markedness principles of some sort) establish a hierarchy of features that is only partial but that does hold in both domains. For example, there seems to be no strict hierarchical relation between the major points of consonant articulation either developmentally or cross-linguistically, so that there is neither a single fixed order in which the *p, t, k* series are learned, nor an implicationally fixed distribution (that is, any of the series can show a gap: Hawaiian has *p, k* but no corresponding dental; the velar position can be missing, as is commonly the case for nasals; and labials can also be lacking, either for a particular manner of articulation, or altogether, as in Iroquoian and Tlingit). On the other hand, it may well be true that plain consonants are implied by palatalized, pharyngealized, aspirated, glottalized, and so on, consonants *both* in acquisition and across languages. Work now in progress by Myrl Solberg (M.I.T.) on the acquisition of Quechua phonology so far tends to confirm the hypothesis, for features of the latter type. How far this kind of correspondence goes remains a matter for further investigation.

Stampe's idea of the learning of "processes" resembles Jakobson's in that the differentiation between inherent limitations and invented devices is not made, although he does allow for an aspect of "invention" (insufficient, in our view) in the possibility of selecting between different inherent processes by their selective suppression. Stampe's theory is the first to account for both the learning of the phonetic repertoire and of the phonological relations. Our main difference with Stampe in this respect is that we see the two as separate, so that all phonological rules are learned, and there is no basis in language acquisition for any distinction one might wish to draw in the adult system between "rules proper" and "processes" (with the possible exception, noted above, of certain types of redundancy rules, viz., those that are natural and produce no allomorphy).

THE LEARNING OF MORPHOPHONEMICS

The question of how morphophonemics is acquired is complicated from the outset by some basic uncertainties about the nature of what is learned. Generative grammar holds that what is learned is a system of rules of a certain form, which apply to underlying phonological representations in order, and whose output is the set of phonetic representations. Contemporary phonological theories fall more or less within this ballpark; in the forefront of ongoing theoretical debate are such questions as whether the types of ordering or the abstractness of underlying phonological representations might be limited in some ways, whether intermediate levels of some sort should be assumed to exist, and where morphology fits in.

Recently, the psychological reality of generative phonology has been questioned on the grounds of experimental results by Ohala (1972) and Krohn, Steinberg, and Kobayashi (1972). They elicited pronunciations of made-up morpheme combinations to see whether speakers would apply to them such morphophonemic rules as trisyllabic laxing and velar softening. They found that in most responses, no changes were made in the stem, and what changes were made were rather heterogeneous and mostly not predicted from the morphophonemic rules. This shows at best that these rules are not fully productive, a fact that could have been discovered more simply by noticing that they do not automatically apply to new words that are formed in English.

However, there seems to be a more fundamental problem with these experiments. Neither Ohala nor Krohn, Steinberg, and Kobayashi included the control case of productive rules in their experiment. As a matter of fact, in the one experiment (of which we are aware) in which this has been tested in adults (Haber, 1975), their performance on English plurals was generally poor. On a Berko-type setup, the percentage of correct responses ranged from 100% (on one item /wuwǰ/) to 53% (/rowməz/). The commonest deviant responses were (1) no change, e.g., /dɔ́piš/ → /dɔ́piš/; (2) devoicing, e.g., /frawg/ → /frawks/; (3) voicing, e.g., /blif/ → /blivz/. Less common were (4) misplaced /əz/, e.g., /blif/ → /blifəz/; (5) internal vowel change, e.g., /fowθ/ → /fayθ/. Several other even more exotic formations occurred marginally. It seems clear that errors of this type do not occur, at least in such numbers, in ordinary speech. (Derwing and Baker's [this volume] replication of Berko's experiments with adult subjects has now confirmed Haber's results.)

These rather surprising findings cast some doubt on the interpretation of the Ohala and Krohn–Steinberg–Kobayashi experiments, and suggest that there may be something about the experimental situation, a "strangeness effect," which causes subjects' performance to deteriorate relative to their normal speech. (Compare the well-known pitfalls in obtaining grammaticality judgments of sentences in isolation—Labov, 1971; Spenser, 1973.) Producing pieces of language out of context—especially, perhaps, single words—may well be a task of a special sort, comparable in its artificiality to that of making love to an arrangement of rubber and electrodes under the watchful eyes of Masters and Johnson, which reportedly also has a negative effect on some subjects' performance. (Our comparison is only in part facetious; there may well be a real effect from the severe feelings of insecurity about language that most people have. More on these and other experimental designs, and on different kinds of "productivity" that they might be used to test, can be found in Kiparsky, 1975.)

Moskowitz's (1973) study on the learning of English vowel shift by children also relies on production tasks. Her subjects "were required to learn two front vowel alternations and then were tested for generalization to a third front vowel alternation as well as two kinds of back vowel alternations, the surface ones and the rule-predicted ones." This paradigm was run three different ways: Under Condition I, subjects were given pairs with two of the three front vowel alternations of the actual English pattern (sīyp ~ sĕpity, pāyp ~ pĭpity). Under Condition II, they were given two kinds of pairs differing in tenseness and diphthongization but no vowel shift (sēyp ~ sĕpity, pīyp ~ pĭpity). Under Condition III, they were given two kinds of pairs with an incorrect vowel shift pattern (sĕyp ~ sĭpity, pīyp ~ pĕpity). On the learning of the two given kinds of vowel pairs, she found (for 9–12-year-olds) that "Condition I was considerably easier then either II or III. There also seems to be a tendency for III to be easier than II on all three measures, i.e., whether or not the subject learned to criterion, the number of trials completed before the ten criterion trials, and the number of errors made" (p. 241). Correct generalization to the third type of front vowel pair ($\bar{e}y \sim \breve{æ}$, $\bar{a}y \sim \breve{æ}$, and $\bar{a}y \sim \breve{e}$, respectively) was also highest for Condition I, and somewhat better for III than for II (pp. 242–243). Transfer to back vowels was equally bad for all three groups (pp. 244).

Moskowitz (p. 248) sums up that "there is no doubt that these children have knowledge of vowel shift, since the data are almost overwhelming." But "it seems at first mysterious that at an age when children are relatively unfamiliar with much of the relevant vocabulary, they not only are able to manipulate vowel-shift patterns well but also are strongly resistant to other patterns in such an easy task. Likewise it seems mysterious that an incorrect vowel-shift pattern is easier than a phonetically simpler pattern involving no shift", i.e. that Condition III is easier than Condition II. She concludes, somewhat obscurely, that their competence is derived from their literacy, which may be true but does not follow from her findings (the near-impossibility of varying literacy while holding other cultural/social variables constant should not excuse investigators from caution in claiming that a certain behavior is due to literacy).

Moskowitz's remark about the late acquisition of the relevant vocabulary really applies only to the *context* of trisyllabic laxing, the knowledge of which this experiment did not test in any way. The vowel shift *pattern* itself, whose knowledge was at issue, is of course contained in quite basic vocabulary, notably in the inflectional morphology of verbs: *hide* ~ *hid*, *bite* ~ *bit*, *feed* ~ *fed*, *keep* ~ *kept*, and so on. It is therefore not so surprising that children know it, and there is certainly no need to invoke spelling as a necessary source of this knowledge. Indeed, the poor performance on the back vowels is evidence against doing so. Spelling should have led the children to respond to *spōwb* with *spɔbity*, for example, since they presumably learn these two values for orthographic *o* just as they learn two values for the other vowels. The fact that the children failed to respond correctly with back vowels could, however, be explained on the assumption that the children know the vowel pairings from the verb morphology, for there are in fact no back vowel verbs like *bāwt ~ *bʌt, corresponding to *hide* ~ *hid*, and the pattern [ūw] ~ [ɔ], corresponding to front *feed* ~ *fed*, is also rare (*shoot* ~ *shot* is the only example in inflection). Generalization from the front vowels might be difficult because the back vowel inventory is different—there are only two short back vowels, with no ɔ/o contrast. Besides, the orthography hypothesis also fails to predict the difference between Condition II and Condition III.

Moskowitz concludes from the failure of subjects to perform well on Condition II that "the vowel-shift rule is not separable from the rules of tensing and diphthongization" (p. 249). Again, we think that this may well be true but in no way follows from her results. If anything, these tend to suggest just the opposite. For if Moskowitz's line of argument from production tasks to grammatical form is taken seriously, her experiment would actually have to be interpreted as supporting not only the separation of Vowel Shift and Trisyllabic Laxing, but even the actual formulation of Vowel Shift in *Sound Pattern of English* (SPE).[1] We hasten to add that in spite of note 1, we do not consider Moskowitz's results as particularly compelling support for the SPE analysis. Our own prejudices, for the record, run somewhere close to hers. We differ from her in being more skeptical about the ability of production tasks to show much of anything, at present, about the form of internalized

---

[1] Vowel shift is there formulated as a *two-part* process:

$$\begin{bmatrix} + \text{ tense} \\ V \end{bmatrix} \rightarrow \left\{ \begin{array}{l} [-\alpha \text{ high}] \Big/ \begin{bmatrix} \alpha \text{ high} \\ - \text{ low} \end{bmatrix} \\ [-\beta \text{ low}] \Big/ \begin{bmatrix} \beta \text{ low} \\ - \text{ high} \end{bmatrix} \end{array} \right. \qquad \begin{array}{l} \text{(a)} \\ \\ \text{(b)} \end{array}$$

The Vowel Shift pattern (Condition I in Moskowitz's experiment) is derived as follows:

		/ī/	/ē/	/ǣ/
Underlying forms		/ī/	/ē/	/ǣ/
(Trisyllabic Laxing, if applicable)		(ĭ	ĕ	ǽ)
Vowel Shift, if Trisyllabic Laxing has not applied	(a)	ē	ī	ǣ
	(b)	ǣ	ī	ē
Other rules		āy	īy	ēy

Obviously, Moskowitz's findings on Condition I would follow from the assumption that her subjects knew this process, in addition to the Trisyllabic Shortening rule. They would then recognize pairs presented to them (*skīyg ∼ skĕgity, kāyč ∼ kĭčity*) as instances of these processes, correctly take the third case (*zēyg*) as underlying /zǣg/, and produce *zagity*. To produce the alternation pattern of Condition II (*skēyg ∼ skēgity, kīyč ∼ kĭčity, zāyg ∼ zăgity*), subjects would have to either drop both parts of Vowel Shift (entering the stimulus words as underlying /skēg/, etc.) or reorder both parts of Vowel Shift ahead of Trisyllabic Laxing (with underlying /skǣg/, etc.). The alternation pattern of Condition III (*skīyg ∼ skăgity, kēyč ∼ kĭčity, zāyg ∼ zēgity*) is the result of a smaller modification of the grammar. We apply part (b) of Vowel Shift before part (a):

	/ǣ/	/ī/	/ē/
(Trisyllabic Laxing)	(ǽ	ĭ	ĕ)
Vowel Shift (b)	ē	ĭ	ǣ
(a)	ī	ē	ǣ
Other rules	[īy]	[ēy]	[āy]

yielding the pairing of tense and lax vowels in Condition III. Both Moskowitz's principal findings (viz., (1) that Condition I is by far the easiest, and (2) that Condition III is somewhat easier than Condition II) then follow if we assume that her subjects analyzed English vowel alternations literally as in SPE, and were trying to accommodate the unfamiliar alternation patterns of Conditions II and III by modifying this analysis. Furthermore, no other hypothesis with which we are familiar accounts for Moskowitz's finding (2)—in particular, her own hypothesis that Vowel Shift and Trisyllabic Laxing are learned together as a single indivisible alternation pattern incorrectly predicts that performance on Conditions II and III should be the same.

linguistic knowledge, given the near-total obscurity surrounding the question of whether and how this knowledge is used in speech. It is for this reason that we cannot see these results as support for Moskowitz's final conclusion that the learning process involved in acquiring Vowel Shift is very different from other phonological learning.

The contrary conclusion is in fact indicated by what seems to us the most systematic and exciting work to date on speakers' knowledge of the marginally productive patterns of English derivational morphology: Rosemary Myerson's as yet unpublished doctoral thesis at the Harvard Graduate School of Education. Myerson used production tasks to elicit trisyllabic laxing, palatalization, and stress shift in 8-, 11-, 14-, and 17-year-olds. In this task she replicated the Krohn–Steinberg–Kobayashi results. She also probed with a task that proved to be far more sensitive, which she devised along lines suggested by work on memory by Piaget and Inhelder and work reported by Olson (in Moore, 1973). Myerson's recall task shows that children do learn some of the nonproductive patterns described by SPE as they become adolescents. A pattern of results emerged for the acquisition of derivational morphology which is highly consonant with the pattern we already have of the emergence of inflectional morphology in younger children.

The recall task was to learn word pairs, where each pair consisted of a nonsense stem which was given meaning as a noun, verb, or adjective, and a derivative made with an appropriate member of the set *-ic, -ity, -ion*. For example:

> *romal, romal + ic*
> *inclort, inclort + ion*
> *grice, grice + ity*

All of the derivatives met the structural description of one of the rules in question, but only half of the derivatives were presented to the subjects in accordance with the applicable rule; the other half of the derivatives were taught to the subjects with the endings merely "tacked on."

Thus one set of subjects might have seen

> *romal,* [rómʌlɨk]
> *grice,* [grɨsɨtiy]
> *inclort,* [ɨnklɔrtiʌn]

while the other might have seen

> *romal,* [romǽlɨk]
> *grice,* [grájsɨtiy]
> *inclort,* [ɨnklɔršʌn]

It should be noted again that the "tacked on" forms were of the same nature as the subjects' own output on production (Berko-type) tasks.

For the younger children, in recall, the words were either retrieved as taught or had their endings replaced by endings like -*ness*, -*ty* which produce no allomorphy (*griceness*, *gricety*) and which are mastered earlier by English-speaking children. However, at age 11 or later, the phonological rules operated in recall: Derivatives like [ɨnklɔrtiʌn] which had been originally learned as preserving the surface phonetic form, and derivatives like [ɨnklɔršʌn] which had been learned as obeying the phonological rule, were eventually recalled as if they had been presented according to the phonological rules: [ɨnklɔrtiʌn] was recalled as [ɨnklɔršʌn].

Myerson found that, at age 14 and 17, certain subjects were able to transcend the rules and to recall the forms exactly as they had been taught, but such subjects also displayed a metalinguistic awareness that forms like [ɨnklɔrtiʌn] were strange.

We see that a recall task, then, taps a level at which some phonological rules operate, even when a production task may not, and that the pattern "special case–overgeneralization–learning of exceptions" emerges for such rules as stress shift and palatalization in English, apparently during early adolescence. The "dips in learning curves" which, as Bever (1970) has noted, are the surface symptoms of a discontinuous leap in the developing system from an initial analysis of low generality to a functionally superior, but (at first) observationally less adequate one, thus seem to occur throughout language acquisition at increasingly fine points of linguistic structure.

This view of language acquisition suggests an interpretation of certain types of analogical change. The commonest cases involve simply the elimination of arbitrary restrictions on rules. For example, *brethren* > *brothers* is the extension of the regular plural rule to a word that hitherto has been an exception to it. In more concrete terms, the exceptional plural of this word began not to be learned by increasing numbers of speakers some hundreds of years ago. (As often happens, the irregular form survived where lexicalized in special uses, e.g., in reference to members of religious or fraternal organizations.)

Of course this does not answer the question of how innovations of individual speakers become general changes of language. The mechanism of this process has begun to be studied for sound change (Labov *et al.*, 1972); whether analogy spreads the same way is not presently known. There are some considerations that may be of relevance in this connection. First, the frequently observed tenacity with which children hang on to their early speech forms against even explicit correction could be a factor (see Kornfeld & Goehl, 1974, p. 216, for a recent example and a tentative explanation for the phenomenon). The extreme case is the occasional retention of stylized baby talk by siblings as a secret language (Applegate, 1961; Forchhammer, 1939). It is also worth noticing that many childhood forms may persist as *optional* variants into adult language, where they become dominant by selection (Haber, 1975). A further factor may be an active favoring of analogical forms as "simple" by the adult community. Whatever the mechanisms, they will presumably have to be invoked also to account for the substratum effects long known to historical linguists, whereby features of the original language of immigrant and conquered populations may persist for generations in the new language, even in monolingual speakers.

What we have said so far pertains only to the learning of individual rules. However, a basic insight of modern linguistics is that linguistic regularities are interdependent. In work on generative grammar, substantial evidence has been accumulated that the formal relationships between rules are of the specific type representable by means of ordering. In both syntax and phonology, derivations work by applying the first rule to the input and each successive rule to the output of the preceding one.

There is evidence that rule ordering is required in children's grammars at a rather early stage. The well-known phenomenon of *displaced contrast* must usually be described in these terms. For example, Smith's (1973) son Amahl pronounced *puzzle* as *puddle* but *puddle* as *puggle*. In his speech, therefore, the rules

$$1.\ d \rightarrow g/\underline{\quad}l$$
$$2.\ z \rightarrow d/\underline{\quad}l$$

had to apply in that order. What is interesting is that the *g* in the child's rendering of *puddle* is retained even though he can pronounce *d* there, as shown by his version of *puzzle* (cf. L. Anderson, 1975).

Applegate (1961) has reported an interesting "sibling dialect" of two brothers, who were 4 and $5\frac{1}{2}$ years old. According to Applegate, "it was the only language spoken by them, and they used it in communicating with the adults of the community, who spoke English, as well as in communicating with each other and with their playmates." A third brother, then $8\frac{1}{2}$ years old, who Applegate was told had earlier spoken the same way, "understood the speech of his brothers and served as a translator for them in situations in which they could not communicate effectively with adults." The principal difference between the sibling dialect and the (New England) speech of their parents and community was constituted by two additional rules in the children's speech:

A. The second of two identical stops within a word is replaced by a glottal stop.

E.g., [dayʔ] *died*, [teykiʔ] *taked* 'took', [dæʔiy diʔit] *daddy did it*, [baʔiy] *Bobby*, [peyʔər] *paper*, [pəʔiy] *puppy*, [keyʔ] *cake*, [kiʔ] *kick*, [beyʔiy] *baby*

B. Fricatives and affricates are replaced by homorganic stops.

E.g., [wakt] *walks* (both 3. sg. of the verb and pl. of the noun), [mænd] *mans* 'men', [kænd] *cans* 'can'

These two rules applied only in the order given, as shown by two independent facts. *Fact 1:* The *t*'s and *d*'s derived from *s, z, č, ǰ* by Rule B did not become glottal stops by Rule A even if preceded by an identical stop within the same word—[takt] *talks*, [teykt] *takes*, [dagd] dogs, [dəd] *does*. *Fact 2:* The *t*'s and *d*'s derived from *s, z, č, ǰ* by Rule B did not trigger replacement of a following dental by a glottal stop in spite of Rule A—[tuwt] *suit* (contrasting with [tuw?] *toot*).

Applegate's observations support the claims to psychological validity of theories countenancing (extrinsic) rule ordering. Theories with only intrinsic ordering (e.g., feeding, see below) cannot express the connection between Fact 1 and Fact 2, and indeed are unable to treat either, that is, cases like [dəd] *does* or those like [tuwt] *suit*, as anything more than exceptions to Rule A. This is of course the standard argument for rule ordering. This argument is elsewhere sometimes countered with the proposal that the relevant regularities are sufficiently explained by the historical chronology of the corresponding sound changes, and that speakers are in reality learning surface forms without apprehending the regularities that depend on ordering. This objection cannot be made here, since the rules and their output are "invented" by the children themselves.

We know of no systematic work on the actual process by which the ordering of phonological rules is learned. However, it is possible to draw some conclusions indirectly, with due caution, from examination of the way ordering functions in synchronic and historical phonology.

There are two sorts of elementary ordering relations between rules.

1. *Feeding.* When a rule A creates potential inputs to another rule B, A and B are in the *feeding relation.* When, in such a case, A is ordered before B (so that B applies to the output of A), we have *feeding order.* If A creates potential inputs to B, but A is ordered after B, then A and B are in *nonfeeding order.* For example, the English rule that simplifies a sequence of consonants with identical place of articulation feeds the "flap" rule which turns *t* and *d* into a voiced flap *D* between a stressed and unstressed syllabic, for example, *gotta, what does (he do?)*:

/wat	dəz/	
wat	əz	consonant simplification
waD	əz	flapping

2. *Bleeding.* When a rule A removes potential inputs to another rule B, A and B are in the *bleeding relation.* When A is ordered before B (i.e., B fails to apply in the cases to which A applies), we have *bleeding order.* For example, the (optional) rule that deletes the vowel of certain unstressed auxiliary verbs in

English bleeds (and therefore precedes) flapping:

/wat dəz/
wat   əz   consonant simplification
wat   z   ə-deletion
(inapplicable) flapping

While it is convenient to examine the logic of ordering in terms of such pairs of individual rules, an additional important consideration is that each rule forms part of a system in which the ordering relation is, apparently, transitive; that is, rules can be arranged in a single sequence where all necessary pairwise ordering relations are preserved. (This has, however, been contested by S. Anderson, 1974.) We would like to claim that in the case of both the feeding and bleeding relations, the two possible orderings of rules which fall into each relation are asymmetrical from a language learner's point of view. Feeding and bleeding order are preferred ("unmarked") compared to nonfeeding and nonbleeding order. Examination of phonological rule systems shows that instances of bleeding order tend to outnumber instances of nonbleeding order, and instances of feeding order generally outnumber instances of nonfeeding order in a quite dramatic way. The closer we move to the lower end of the sequence of phonological rules, the more pronounced this preference for feeding and bleeding order becomes. In fact, *all* rules of English phrase phonology studied in Selkirk (1972) are in feeding or bleeding order.

There is a historical phenomenon that is probably related to this synchronic observation. Cases of the far from common, but very interesting, type of change where nothing but the order of two rules changes show (unless certain other factors, to be discussed shortly, happen to intervene) a consistent directionality toward feeding and bleeding order. In line with our earlier reasoning, this directionality of reordering is interpretable as the historical reflex of a language acquisition strategy of the following sort: Given no evidence to the contrary, assume that rules apply in the "unmarked" feeding and bleeding orders.

We hypothesize, therefore, that a child who has learned two rules without encountering evidence for their mutual ordering will set up the hypothesis that they apply in unmarked order. This hypothesis should be verifiable by a study of children's mistakes. Where the adult language shows unmarked ordering, the child should not, if we are correct, make mistakes attributable to marked ordering. Suppose, for example, that a child has mastered the rule determining the choice of plural suffixes in English. Let us assume that the underlying form of the suffix is /z/ and that *i* is inserted before it after "hissing" and "hushing" sounds by the rule:

$$i\text{-}insertion\colon\ \emptyset\ \rightarrow\ i/\check{c},j,\check{s},\hat{z},s,z\ +\ \underline{\quad}\ z\#.$$

Suppose now the child speaks a dialect in which final dentals are deleted before consonant and word boundary, e.g. *toas'* but *toaster, toasting.* That is, he has the phonological rule

$$t\text{-}deletion: \text{dental} \rightarrow \emptyset / \underline{\quad} \begin{cases} C \\ \# \end{cases}$$

Our prediction is that when a child who has never happened to hear the plural form of a word like *test* (or even if he has heard it, has not registered its form) has occasion to use it, he will pronounce it [tesɨz] even if forms like *testing* have caused him to enter it in the lexicon with the underlying representation /test/. The reason is that this form results from the unmarked (in this case, feeding) order. (Subsequent encountering of the "correct" form *tests* might of course then lead the child to reorder the rules.) Plurals like [tesɨz] are in fact reported for Black English (Labov, 1972), where dental-deletion rules of this family exist.

Notice that this prediction is made independently of how the relevant rules are formulated. Suppose that (as is sometimes claimed) the underlying form of the plural suffix is /ɨz/ and the *ɨ* is deleted in the complement of the left-hand context of the insertion rule. (The *t*-deletion rule must be made more complicated in that case, in order to make it apply before the now vocalic plural suffix /ɨz/.) The point to note is that the unmarked ordering of the two rules is still the one which outputs [tesɨz], this time because it is a bleeding order. This invariance under rule reformulation is a general property of ordering asymmetry.

A suggestion for formalizing these ordering asymmetries and at the same time relating them to other phenomena has been to introduce the concept of *opacity* (converse: *transparency*) as a (*quantitative*) property of rules, defined as follows:

A rule (R) of the form
$$A \rightarrow B/C\underline{\quad}D$$

is opaque to the extent that there are phonetic representations of the form

(i)   A in the environment C__D, or
(ii) B (not from R) in the environment C__D
(cf. Kiparsky, 1973).

Both cases are quite straightforward. According to (i), a rule is made opaque by forms that look as if they should have undergone it, but did not; according to (ii), it is made opaque also by forms that look as if they should not have undergone the rule, but did. Transparency is thus related to the concept of recoverability in syntax. The unmarked orders can now be characterized as those which maximize transparency. The marked nonfeeding and nonbleeding orders will always lead to one rule being opaque by (i) and (ii) respectively. The advantage of this formulation is that we can now consider opacity as a general property of rules that may have other sources than marked ordering. For example, all exceptions make a rule opaque by case (i). It now turns out that opaque rules as a class, whatever the source of opacity, have certain properties in common. For example, only opaque rules are known to be lost historically from grammars.

What we have done is essentially to distinguish two sorts of linguistic difficulty: one, complexity, (hopefully) measured by the number of symbols in the grammar, the other, opacity, measured as just proposed. As a simple illustration of their independence, let us consider an arbitrary rule P and ask how it might be made harder to learn. One way would be to add more conditioning factors to its structural description. This would increase its complexity but not its opacity. Another way would be to order other rules after it in marked order. This would increase its opacity but not its complexity. A third way would be to mark certain items as exceptions to it. This, the worst case of all, would both make the rule opaque and add complexity to the grammar.

The status of these two sorts of linguistic difficulty is furthermore rather different, from the viewpoint of the language learner and the viewpoint of the theory we are proposing. Complexity is assigned by the evaluation measure to grammars as abstract objects. Opacity is a property of the relation between the grammar and the data. An opaque rule is not more complex, merely harder to discover. Consequently, we do *not* predict that the rules of early phonology, which are not hypotheses about data but figments of the child, should show the same preference for transparent order. In fact, opaque orders are quite common in this domain. The examples of displaced contrast cited earlier are cases in point.

The preferred ordering among the invented rules may depend on other functional considerations than learnability, however. In general, feeding order reduces contrasts and nonfeeding order preserves them. For example, if the $d \rightarrow g$ and $z \rightarrow d$ rules operate in that order, as they did in Amahl Smith's grammar (see above), the contrast between *puzzle* and *puddle* is preserved (albeit in altered form). The reverse order of application would merge them both as *puggle*. If the child seeks to represent as many adult contrasts as possible given his phonetic resources (which seems plausible but has admittedly not been demonstrated so far—for discussion, see L. Anderson, 1975), then a useful strategy for deploying rules would be the following: *Put the rules in nonfeeding order if possible.*

In the learning of morphophonemics proper, it may also happen that transparency is at odds with other functional requirements on the grammar

(Kisseberth, 1973; Kaye, 1975). One such factor is paradigmatic leveling, probably the best-known type of analogy in both child language and linguistic change. Kazazis (1969) has described a case in the speech of his daughter Marina at age 4.7. Marina was trilingual, and the example concerns her Greek. In this language, the fricatives [x] (back) and [ç] (front) are in complementary distribution; in the cases under consideration, the choice between them is determined by whether the following vowel is back of front. In nonderived environments, Marina pronounces [x] or [ç] with the correct distribution. In the verbal paradigm, however, she generalized [x], for example, 3.Sg. *exete* for adult *eçete*.

A good example of the way in which paradigmatic leveling is connected to bleeding order is Canadian Raising, the change of the diphthongs *ay, aw* to *әy, әw* before voiceless consonants, as in *write* versus *ride*. The rule that does this interacts with another rule which makes *t* voiced intervocalically in words like *eating*—let us denote the output of this rule simply as *d*. In words like *writing*, the *t*-voicing rule has the effect of potentially depriving—bleeding—the raising rule of some of its inputs. If the *t*-voicing rule precedes, *writing* will retain its open *ay*, contrasting with the *әy* of *write*:

System A :		/rayt ɨŋ/	/rayt/
	t-voicing	rayd ɨŋ	—
	Raising	—	rәyt
	Output	[rayd ɨŋ]	[rәyt]

However, if raising precedes *t*-voicing, we have instead:

System B :		/rayt ɨŋ/	/rayt/
	Raising	rәyt ɨŋ	rәyt
	t-voicing	rәyd ɨŋ	—
	Output	[rәyd ɨŋ]	[rәyt]

The ordering of System B is opaque, since the output of Raising there appears on the surface in environments in which the rule is inapplicable. Nevertheless, this opacity appears to be offset by the fact that in System B the stem of *write* and similar words appears with a fixed vocalic nucleus. In Canada, System B appears to have ousted System A in the last 30 years (Chambers, 1973). The corresponding directionality of change can be observed in other cases of the same type.

The example is instructive in yet another respect. Notice that if we adopt a very "concrete" analysis, with /ay/ and /әy/ as separate phonemic entities, the change from System A to System B can be represented as a straightforward simplification of the grammar. We should then need, at the stage described above as System A, a lowering rule that changes /әy/ to /ay/ before the voiced segments resulting from *t*-voicing. The change that took place in the language can then be understood as a loss of this (opaque) lowering rule.

In general, an attentive examination of historical change suggests in many cases that the underlying representations constructed by speakers are shallower than many current phonological theories would have it. In particular, nonderived (morpheme-internal) outputs of sound change seem to be characteristically restructured by speakers in a form that is close to their phonetic form.

However, sometimes we get indications in the child's error pattern of a more "abstract" analysis of a surface form if it is one that looks as though it could have been produced by a rule the child knows. If the rule involved is optional, like flapping and some parts of vowel reduction in English, but of very high probability, we may get "back formations" in which an opposition almost always neutralized on the surface appears because the child fails to apply an optional rule. *Raisins* with [ʌ] instead of [ɨ] in the second syllable, and *recorder* (flute) with [t] instead of [d], resulted from such cases where insufficient surface information allowed Stephen Menn to hypothesize the wrong underlying forms (a non-high vowel in *raisin*, /t/ in *recorder*). Drachman and Malikouti-Drachman (1973) present material on the reanalysis of the voiced allophone of /p/ in Modern Greek (occurring after nasals), which suggests that the child's ability to recover the allophony follows his/her acquisition of the voicing rule when it appears productively across the article–noun boundary. We do not yet know what the conditions are under which a child will "dig beneath" the phonetic surface.

Let us summarize our conclusions. The child is faced with two distinct problems in learning phonology: in the early stages, the quasi-physiological problem of his own limited phonetic capabilities, to which the adult output must be fitted; later (though doubtless in part concurrently) the cognitive problem of learning the abstract regularities of the phonological system, whether in order to remember, understand, or speak his language. We have suggested that the *form* of the child's solution to both problems is the same. It is a "cognitive" form that is determined by the child's ability to construct grammars. The child devises a system of underlying representations and general rules, which operate on phonological features, to derive the output form. In both systems, the rules allow lexical exceptions. In both systems, the rules may apply in extrinsic order. The child's speech reveals, in both cases, a highly plastic, active process of acquisition, with many signs of restructuring of underlying representations and addition and discarding of rules. On the other hand, it remains an open question as to what extent, if at all, there is a *substantive* connection between the two systems, in the sense of rules being continued directly from one into the other.

ACKNOWLEDGMENTS

We thank Charles Ferguson, Dan Kahn, Michael Kenstowicz, and Charles Kisseberth for noticing errors of omission and commission in our first draft. The blame for remaining errors is ours.

REFERENCES

Anderson, L. Learning your language or another's. Ditto, preliminary version, 1975.

Anderson, S. *The organization of phonology*. New York: Seminar Press, 1974.

Anisfeld, M., & G. R. Tucker. English pluralization rules of six-year-old children. In Ferguson and Slobin (Eds.), *Studies of child language development*. New York: Holt, 1973.

Applegate, J. Phonological rules of a subdialect of English. *Word*, 1961, *17*, 166–193.

Bell, A. Some patterns of occurrence and formation of syllable structures. Working Papers in Language Universals, No. 6. Stanford University, 1971.

Berko, J. The child's learning of English morphology. *Word*, 1959, *14*, 150–167.

Bever, T. G. The cognitive basis for linguistic structures. In J. R. Hayes (Ed.), *Cognition and language learning*. New York: Wiley, 1970.

Bhat, D. N. S. Retroflexion: An areal feature. Working Papers in Language Universals, No. 13. Stanford University, 1973.

Bogoyavlenskiy, D. N. The acquisition of Russian inflections (translated). In Ferguson & Slobin (Eds.), *Studies of child language development*. New York: Holt, 1973.

Braine, M. O. S. On what might constitute learnable phonology. *Language*, 1974, *50*, 270–299.

Branigan, G. Syllabic structure and the acquisition of consonants. Mimeo, Boston University, 1974.

Chambers, J. K. Canadian raising. *Canadian Journal of Linguistics*, 1973, *18*, 113–125.

Drachman, G. Generative phonology and child language acquisition. In W. V. Dressler and F. V. Mares (Eds.), *Phonologica 1972*. München: Finck, 1975. Pp. 235–251.

Drachman, G., & Malikouti-Drachman, A. Studies in the acquisition of Greek as a native language, I. Ohio State University Working Papers, No. 15, 1973.

Edwards, M. L. Perception and production in child phonology: The testing of four hypotheses. *Papers and Reports on Child Language Development*, 1974, *7*, 68–84. Committee on Linguistics, Stanford University.

Ferguson, C. A., & Farwell, C. Words and sounds in early language acquisition: English initial consonants in the first 50 words. *Papers and Reports in Child Language Development*, 1973, *6*, 160. Committee on Linguistics, Stanford University. (Also *Language*, 1975, *51*, 419–439.)

Ferguson, C. A., & Slobin, D. I. (Eds.). *Studies of child language development*. New York: Holt, 1973.

Forchhammer, E. Uber einige Fälle von eigentümlichen Sprachbildungen. *Archiv für die gesamte Psychologie*, 1939, *104*, 395–438.

Garnica, O. K. The development of phonemic speech perception. In T. E. Moore (Ed.), *Cognitive development and the acquisition of language*. New York: Academic Press, 1973.

Greenberg, J. Some generalizations concerning glottalic consonants, especially implosives. *International Journal of American Linguistics*, 1970, *36*, 123–145.

Greenlee, M. Interacting processes in the child's acquisition of stop-liquid clusters. *Papers and Reports on Child Language Development*, 1974, *7*, 85–100. Committee on Linguistics, Stanford University.

Haber, L. The muzzy theory. *Papers from the Eleventh Regional Meeting*. Chicago Linguistic Society, 1975.

Hockett, C. *Manual of phonology*. Indiana University Publications in Linguistics, 1955.

Ingram, D. Phonological analysis of a developmentally aphasic child. Mimeo, Institute for Childhood Aphasia, Stanford University, 1973.

Ingram, D. Phonological rules in young children. *Journal of Child Language*, 1974, *1*, 49–64.

Jakobson, R. *Child language, aphasia, and phonological universals*. A. Keiler, Trans. The Hague: Mouton, 1968.

Jakobson, R., & Halle, M. *Fundamentals of Language*. The Hague: Mouton, 1956.

Kaye, J. A functional explanation for rule ordering in phonology. *Papers from the Parasession on Functionalism*. Chicago Linguistic Society, 1975.

Kazazis, K. Possible evidence for (near-) underlying forms in the speech of a child. *Papers from the Fifth Regional Meeting*, Chicago Linguistic Society, 1969.

Kiparsky, P. Phonological representations. In O. Fujimura (Ed.), *Three dimensions of linguistic theory*. Tokyo: TEC Co., 1973.

Kiparsky, P. What are phonological theories about? In D. Cohen and J. Wirth (Eds.), *Testing linguistic hypotheses*. Washington & London: Hemisphere, 1975. Pp. 187–210.

Kisseberth, C. W. *The interaction of phonological rules and the polarity of language*. Mimeo, Indiana University Linguistics Club, 1973.

Kornfeld, J., & Goehl, H. A new twist to an old observation: Kids know more than they say. *Papers from the Parasession on Natural Phonology*. Chicago Linguistic Society, 1974, Pp. 210–219.

Krohn, R., Steinberg, D., & Kobayashi, L. R. The psychological validity of Chomsky and Halle's vowel shift rule. XXth International Congress of Psychology, Tokyo, 1972. Abstract Guide, p. 1905.

Labov, W. *Sociolinguistic patterns*. Philadelphia: University of Pennsylvania Press, 1972.

Labov, W., Yaeger, M., & Steiner, R. *A quantitative study of sound change in progress*. Philadelphia: U.S. Regional Survey, 1972.

Leopold, W. F. *Speech development of a bilingual child*. Evanston, Ill.: Northwestern University Press, 1939–1949.

Lindblom, B., & Liljencrantz, J. Numerical simulation of vowel quality systems: The role of perceptual contrast. *Language*, 1972, *48*, 839–62.

McNeill, D. *The acquisition of language*. New York: Harper and Row, 1970.

Menn, L. Phonotactic Rules in Beginning Speech. *Lingua* 26:225–251, 1971.

Menn, L. Origin and growth of phonological and syntactic rules. *Papers from the Ninth Regional Meeting*. Chicago Linguistic Society, 1973.

Menn, L. Pattern, control, and contrast in beginning speech: A case study in the development of word form and word function. Unpublished doctoral dissertation, University of Illinois, 1976.

Miller, P. Some context-free processes affecting vowels. Ohio State University Working Papers in Linguistics No. 11. February 1972.

Moore, T. E. (Ed.). *Cognitive development and the acquisition of language*. New York: Academic Press, 1973.

Moskowitz, A. Acquisition of phonology. Working Paper No. 34, Language-Behavior Research Laboratory, University of California, Berkeley, 1970.

Moskowitz, A. On the status of vowel shift in English. In T. E. Moore (Ed.), *Cognitive development and the acquisition of language*. New York: Academic Press, 1973.

Myerson, R. A developmental study of children's knowledge of complex derived words of English. Mimeo, Harvard Graduate School of Education, 1975.

Nakazima, S. A comparative study of the speech development of Japanese and American children (Part Four)—The beginning of the phonemicization process. *Studia Phonologica*. 1972, *6*, 1–37. University of Kyoto.

Ohala, J. J. On the design of phonological experiments. Paper presented at Linguistics Society of America Winter Meeting, Atlanta, 1972.

Ohala, J. J. Phonetic explanation in phonology. *Papers from the Parasession on Natural Phonology*. Chicago Linguistic Society, 1974.

Selkirk, E. The phrase phonology of English and French. Doctoral dissertation, Massachusetts Institute of Technology, 1972.

Shibatani, M. The role of surface phonetic constraints in generative phonology. *Language*, 1973, *49*, 87–106.

Skousen, R. An explanatory theory of morphology. *Papers from the Parasession on Natural Phonology*. Chicago Linguistic Society, 1974.

Slobin, D. I. Cognitive prerequisites for the development of grammar. In Ferguson and Slobin (Eds.), *Studies of child language development*. New York: Holt, 1973.

Smith, N. V. *The acquisition of phonology: A case study*. Cambridge: Cambridge University Press, 1973.

Spenser, N. J. Differences between linguists and nonlinguists in intuitions of grammaticality-acceptability. *Journal of Psycholinguistic Research*, 1973, *2*, 83–98.

Stampe, D. The acquisition of phonetic representation. *Papers from the Fifth Regional Meeting*, Chicago Linguistic Society, 1969.

Stampe, D. What I did on my summer vacation. Manuscript, Ohio State University, 1972.

Stanley, R. Redundancy rules in phonology. *Language*, 1967, *43*, 393–435.

Troubetzkoy, N. S. *Principes de Phonologie*. (J. Cantineau, Trans.) Paris: Librairie C. Klincksieck, 1949.

Velten, H. V. The growth of phonemic and lexical patterns in infant language. *Language*, 1943, *19*, 440–449.

Waterson, N. Child phonology: A prosodic view. *Journal of Linguistics*, 1971, *7*, 179–221.

Zwicky, A. M. A double regularity in the acquisition of English verb morphology. *Papers in Linguistics*, 1970, *3*.

5

Is the Child Really a "Little Linguist"?

BRUCE L. DERWING

University of Alberta

Kiparsky and Menn's chapter consists of two loosely connected sections, the first a theoretical critique of the Jakobson and Stampe "innate filter" approaches to the acquisition of phonemic oppositions and low-level "allophonic" (or phonotactic) rules, respectively, and the second a statement of various linguistic principles thought to be operative in the acquisition of "underlying forms" and "phonological" (or morphophonemic) rules in morphology. What links these two sections together is described as a "discovery-oriented" approach to language acquisition, which views the child as an "active grammar-constructor" who is engaged in " 'problem-solving' activity from the earliest stages on."

I am in general sympathy with the first section of Kiparsky and Menn's chapter. The literature on the acquisition of phonetics (to which I would add Olmsted, 1971, as a basic source) suggests to me, too, that there is simply too much variability and uncertainty involved to lend much credence to the Jakobsonian view of a strict hierarchy of universal unfolding of phonemic oppositions, and I have a similar reaction to Stampe's notion of a "built-in" set of specific linguistic "processes." I would go farther than Kiparsky and Menn, however, in also questioning the value of any linguistic theory that attempts to invoke "innateness" as an explanatory vehicle. For to maintain that some cognitive or behavioral skill is "innate" does not provide any positive insight into either its nature or development, but is rather tantamount to an admission of a *failure* to explain it. "Innateness" is a purely negative notion; it means that something has *not* been learned, hence that it can *not* be explained in terms of any known principles of learning. Explanation does not consist in substituting one unknown for another, but rather in accounting for what puzzles in terms of some general principle which *is* known and which *is* understood. And how, in any event, does one ever propose to demonstrate that some particular aspect of human language has, in fact, *not* been learned? (Is he to set out to prove the null hypothesis that "something did not happen?") The search for "innate" linguistic principles, therefore, strikes me as more of a weakness than an attractive alternative to looking for answers in terms of psychological or physiological capacities that human beings have been shown to possess (see Derwing, 1973, pp. 63–77, 188–218, 239–243).

To illustrate the contrast, it is no doubt true that the intrinsic makeup of the human vocal apparatus and the real-life exigencies of normal speech production have their effects on both phonetic acquisition and the learning of phonological rules. It seems clear, for example, that, in production, the fricative consonants present a much more formidable articulatory problem than do the stops, as evidenced by their later acquisition. But it is also clear that considerably more delicacy is required in motor control in order to "almost close off the air stream" than to close it off altogether. The result is a "universal" linguistic tendency, to be sure, yet one which is explained not by invoking some mysterious set of formal constraints on "universal grammar," but which is rather a very natural consequence of a developing coordination with respect to the particular motor skills involved. By the same token, many of Stampe's "processes" likely have a natural physiological or "ease of articulation" basis as well. Take the case of vowel nasalization, for one. It is a virtual physiological impossibility, I should think, to articulate a vowel plus nasal sequence without an intervening pause such that some of the nasalization does not spill over onto the vowel. Similarly, the tendency toward the final devoicing of obstruents might also be explained in quite straightforward articulatory terms (cf. Chomsky & Halle, 1968, p. 301), and so on.

It is considerations of this kind, therefore, which leave me largely dissatisfied with the second part of Kiparsky and Menn's paper, for the particular "learning principles" the authors develop in that section are largely hypothetical "linguistic" notions and not well-established psychological or physiological ones at all.[1] What Kiparsky and Menn do, in short, is to view the child as a kind of "little linguist," who "solves problems" in his language and "constructs a grammar" for it in much the same way, and in accordance

---

[1] See Ferguson and Garnica (1975) for a more balanced survey of phonological development, and Kornfeld (1976) for a paradigm example of a proposed *empirical* explanation in child phonology.

with much the same sort of formal principles, as the professional linguist might. But as Baker observes in his discussion of Moeser (this volume), it is hardly obvious that the child ever sets out intentionally to learn a "language system" at all, much less to go about his task with anything like the assiduousness, systematicity, or comprehensiveness of the linguist. The linguist's task in analyzing a language seems qualitatively different from the child's task in learning one. In particular, the linguist is typically preoccupied with the search for formal patterns and regularities exhibited by speech forms, while the child's concern is rather one of simply understanding what is said to him and making himself understood by others. Hence we should not really be very surprised if the language learner were to "miss a generalization" now and again! Spencer (1973, p. 87) puts the matter this way:

> The linguist views language in a highly specialized way, and perhaps is influenced by a perceptual set. The resulting description may not be an ideal representation of linguistic structure. It may be an artifactual system which reflects the accretion of conceptual organization by linguists.

(See also Derwing & Baker, 1976.) One especially unsettling consequence of Kiparsky and Menn's heavily linguistic orientation to the problem of language acquisition is their apparent underestimation of the extent of the "basic uncertainties about the nature of what is learned." They seem to take for granted many "facts" which are in reality matters that are still very much open to question and debate. What, to begin with, is the status of "grammars as abstract objects?" Can we sensibly talk about "the regularities of the phonological system" as known quantities of any language, even prior to the question of what it is that the child actually learns? My perspective is that since the "language system" exists only in the minds of language learners, we must therefore explore these minds—and not merely samples of their verbal output, which admit of numerous alternative interpretations—in order to ascertain what that system is actually like (see Derwing & Baker, this volume). Is it really a "fact" in the Applegate illustration, for example, that the adult forms constitute the "input" to the child, who then "derives" various phonetic forms from these by "applying" various phonological rules? The only facts involved here (if reliable; we must trust a single observer who has recorded his *own* interpretation of a select few speech forms of two of his children) are that certain phonetic correspondences appeared among the adult forms and the child's forms; nothing more. We know nothing *factual* either about how the child actually construed the adult forms (i.e., in his own mind) or what mechanisms he used to alter them. Why do Kiparsky and Menn believe implicitly that children actually learn "underlying forms" and the specific phonological rules they describe? What does it even mean, psychologically, to claim that such forms and rules are learned, and how do we go about testing the claim? (See Linell, 1974, for a thorough critique of the generativist's notion of "morpheme-invariant underlying forms.") It seems strange indeed that the same scholar who has already argued so convincingly that the "clever" linguistic analysis is not necessarily the psychologically valid one (Kiparsky, 1971) should now see the child behaving like a linguist once again, even to the extent of "ordering" his rules in various "feeding" and "bleeding" relationships.

The specific evidence that Kiparsky and Menn present in support of rule ordering in child phonology is hardly unequivocal. In the first example, taken from Smith (1973), we have a child who can evidently hear the difference between the words *puzzle* and *puddle* (otherwise, why "displace the contrast"), but cannot yet reproduce it accurately. If this account is to be internally consistent, however, it must be recognized that, for the child, at least, the [d] (= /z/) of his own speech is *distinct* (and hence not to be confused with) the [d] (= /d/) of his parents' speech. Since it is only this latter *d* that appears on the left side of Kiparsky and Menn's "rule," however, we should hardly expect that rule to *reapply* to the other, even if the rules operated with an unordered "output condition" (Derwing, 1973, 1975) or "phonotactic filter" (Braine, 1974) framework.

The same kind of argument also holds for the Applegate example. In that case, too, Kiparsky and Menn's own theory implies that the first [t] of [tuwt] *suit* represents the child's playful /s/, but the second [t] of that word, as well as both the [t] and the [ʔ] of [tuwʔ] *toot*, his /t/. As far as the child is concerned, in other words, [tuwt] *is* /suwt/ and [tuwʔ] *is* /tuwt/, so why should we expect him to apply Kiparsky and Menn's Rule A to the first word at all? The word /suwt/ (= [tuwt]) "acts like an exception" to Rule A because it *is* an exception to it!

So while data such as these *can* be described by making use of a general convention of extrinsic rule ordering, it is not *necessary* to do so, even under the kind of "rule" interpretation that Kiparsky and Menn choose to place upon this rather special kind of problem. Both the simultaneous application and "output condition" theories may sensibly be construed to be at work in these examples as well, and all three approaches are equally "verifiable" (to use Kiparsky and Menn's term) on the basis of precisely the same set of data. Like Jakobson's theory of phonemic development, therefore, it seems that the durability of the rule-ordering hypothesis, too, is largely a consequence of the difficulty of exposing it to potential falsification. The hypothesis in question, like the general notion of the grammatical transformation itself, is an extremely flexible and powerful descriptive tool, and if some particular investigator is intent upon finding an "explanation" for some set of linguistic data by invoking it, he may surely do so. But the finding of it, though it may tax his ingenuity, will not necessarily increase our knowledge and understanding of either natural language or its acquisition. What we lack is the crucial ingredient: the facts. We do not know very much at all about the kinds of rules actually learned by speakers and actually used by them in the production and perception of speech. In fact, we do not even know how "ordered" rules might conceivably be learned in principle, since we have no clear precedent in psychology for this type of learning. Finally, and most fundamentally, we do not even know how to go about looking for answers to this last question, since the kind of phonological theories that countenance rule ordering have not yet been formulated in psychological terms (cf. Derwing, 1974). The same is also true, of course, of the notion of a syntactic or phonological "derivation" in generative grammar, and Crystal (1974, p. 303) points out that transformationalists are "ready to argue about specific derivations . . . , but not, it seems, about the very notion of derivation." It is difficult to know, then, what to make of a linguistic theory that maintains that language learners "order their rules" to "derive forms," when we are given no clear idea at all what either of these phrases mean in either psychological or physiological terms. As Prideaux (1975, p. 3) has put it, "The reason is not that the rules are difficult to understand or formulate within a given grammatical theory, but rather that such rules are designed to represent formal syntactic [or phonological] relations among constituents of the language *product*. They have nothing at all to say about language as a *process* or about the psychological states or operations that the language user knows or executes when he produces or understands a sentence."

If we could interpret "ordered rules" to mean that speakers *use* their rules in some particular sequence in *real time*, either to produce or to comprehend speech forms, that would be an entirely different matter (cf. Cook, 1974). In that case we would have at least a partial model of linguistic *performance* which we could in principle proceed to test, develop, and modify in accordance with normal scientific procedures. But not only have such interpretations been explicitly rejected by advocates of the kind of "competence" theories in question, they have also refrained from suggesting any viable alternative interpretations and tests. As a result, we have no *psychological* theory at all—just a "generative grammar" or "competence model" which, beyond the simple description of language output, embodies no particular factual claims about who knows what. Unless or until these issues are satisfactorily dealt with, therefore, I simply fail to see how such theories can be of any possible scientific interest or use.

In the meantime, the best advice I have been able to find has been offered to us by Ferguson and Garnica (1975):

> At the present time, the greatest contributions to the development of more satisfying theories of children's acquisition of phonology will come not from elaborate speculation, no matter how sophisticated linguistically, nor from large-scale data collection without reference to particular problems, but from principled investigations focused on specific hypotheses and questions of fact. [p. 176]

In other words, we need to do more controlled experiments!

REFERENCES

Braine, M. D. S. On what might constitute learnable phonology. *Language*, 1974, *50*, 270–299.

Chomsky, N., & Halle, M. *The sound pattern of English.* New York: Harper & Row, 1968.

Cook, V. J. Is explanatory adequacy adequate? *Linguistics*, 1974, No. 133 (August 1), 21–31.

Crystal, D. Review of R. Brown's *A first language: The early stages. Journal of Child Language*, 1974, *1*, 289–307.

Derwing, B. L. *Transformational grammar as a theory of language acquisition.* London: Cambridge University Press, 1973.

Derwing, B. L. English pluralization: A testing ground for rule evaluation. Paper presented at the meeting of the Canadian Linguistic Association, Toronto, May, 1974. To appear in G. D. Prideaux, B. L. Derwing, and W. J. Baker (Eds.), *Experimental linguistics.*

Derwing, B. L. Linguistic rules and language acquisition. *Cahiers Linguistiques d' Ottawa*, 1975, No. 4, 13–41.

Derwing, B. L., & Baker, W. J. On the re-integration of linguistics and psychology. Paper presented at the Psychology of Language Conference, University of Stirling, June, 1976.

Ferguson, C. A., & Garnica, O. K. Theories of phonological development. In E. H. Lenneberg and E. Lenneberg (Eds.), *Foundations of language development: A multidisciplinary approach.* Vol. 1. New York: Academic Press, 1975.

Kiparsky, P. Historical linguistics. In W. O. Dingwall (Ed.), *A survey of linguistic science.* College Park: Linguistics Program, University of Maryland, 1971.

Kornfeld, J. R. Implications of studying reduced consonant clusters in normal and abnormal child speech. Paper presented at the Psychology of Language Conference, University of Stirling, June, 1976.

Linell, P. *Problems of psychological reality in generative phonology: A critical assessment. Reports from Uppsala University Department of Linguistics*, 1974, No. 4.

Prideaux, G. D. An information-structure approach to syntax. Paper presented at the University of Ottawa, March, 1975.

Olmsted, D. L. *Out of the mouth of babes.* The Hague: Mouton, 1971.

Smith, N. V. *The acquisition of phonology: A case study.* London: Cambridge University Press, 1973.

Spencer, N. J. Differences between linguists and nonlinguists in intuitions of grammaticality-acceptability. *Journal of Psycholinguistic Research*, 1973, *2*, 83–98.

6

The Psychological Basis for Morphological Rules

BRUCE L. DERWING
WILLIAM J. BAKER

University of Alberta

INTRODUCTION

It is an obvious fact that children learn language or, at least, "bits and pieces" of the linguistic system of their native language. They acquire these "bits and pieces" gradually over time as a result of exposure to language data in meaningful situations which permit them, somehow, to relate the data to significant things and events around them. They observe, they learn, and, eventually, they begin to produce utterances that are not only in general conformity with the linguistic system but also appropriate to the situation at the time of the utterance. They begin to demonstrate not so much that they know the language as that they know how to use the linguistic system in a meaningful way.

This last distinction is critical since it is a category mistake to believe that children attempt to learn language per se. They are strongly motivated to learn to communicate, to control and manipulate things and people in their environment to satisfy their felt needs, and they will seize upon any device, linguistic or otherwise, that enhances their ability to do this. After they discover that others in their immediate environment are responsive to their needs—once they learn to make them known—children are powerfully motivated to find any and every means to express themselves. Language provides one of the easiest and most flexible means to this end. Thus, why they learn seems quite clear, but how they learn and what they learn are not. The latter are two of the great imponderables of current cognitive psychology.

The simpler conditioning or association theories of learning have been found to be conceptually inadequate to account for the productive or "creative" use to which language learning is put. Rather than learning specific instances of language, it is fairly evident that the child learns generalizations about the language system, generalizations he can then apply in relatively novel situations which are different from his specific learning experiences. He can produce and understand, as a result of these generalizations, specific utterances he has never encountered before.

Linguists, in looking at samples of language data, also search for generalizations, descriptive statements that will be true of the data and that will capture interesting general or recurring features that will hold for instances of the language not necessarily included directly in the data at hand. It has become common practice to refer to these generalizations as "linguistic rules." Similarly, in cognitive psychology, it has become common to refer to productive (essentially, nonimitative) behavior as being "rule-governed" (Segal & Stacy, 1975). But are these two notions of "rule" referring to anything like the same thing? Specifically, for the case at hand, are the "rules" the linguist writes "psychologically real," that is, are they the same rules that the naive language learner extracts from his experience and which are then employed by him so that they govern (i.e., in some sense, account for) his language behavior? Chomsky has strongly implied that they are the same (Chomsky, 1964, 1965, 1966, and elsewhere) but offers no empirical support for such a sweeping claim. Unfortunately, the simple fact that a generalization can be made about language data is not sufficient to warrant a claim that it is psychologically real (Kiparsky, 1968, p. 172).

Obviously, what is required in order to cope sensibly with these questions is the development of a precise notion of the concept of "rule" and of an experimental paradigm capable of empirically demonstrating that naive language learners employ just that "rule" in some nonimitative or productive mode of behavior. The first part of the problem is attacked in this paper by an explicit development of the concept of "morphological rule." The second part is covered by describing an experiment that significantly extended and improved upon the Berko (1968) technique, which was one of the first to aim specifically at demonstrating "rule-governed behavior" in the use of English inflectional and derivational morphology. In the last section, a brief report is also given of some recent research on "morpheme recognition," with emphasis on the development of experimental techniques for measuring and relating the critical variables involved.

SOME POTENTIAL MORPHOLOGICAL RULES

The term "morphological rules" is not a widely used or generally accepted one in either linguistics or psychology, so we must clarify this term in order to delineate the scope of the research to be described below. For purposes of the present discussion, we shall impose a very broad interpretation upon this term: A morphological rule (or M-Rule) will be regarded as any linguistic regularity that relates either to the constituent or phonological structure of a word.[1] Under this interpretation, each of the following four types of linguistic statements will qualify as M-Rules: (I) word-level syntactic rules, (II) lexical generalizations, (III) morphophonemic rules, and (IV) phonotactic rules. A few illustrations may be useful at this point to clarify each of these distinctions:

Type I M-Rules: Word-Level Syntactic Rules

Word-level syntactic rules are rules that describe how the minimal meaning-bearing units of a language, that is, its morphemes, are combined into larger constituents, such as stems and words. Such rules differ from other "higher-level" syntactic rules only insofar as the word is the largest constituent involved, omitting the phrase, the clause, the sentence, and so on. Examples of word-level syntactic rules for English are the following:

1. The plural form of a Noun is regularly formed by adding a Plural suffix to the Noun Stem (i.e., Npl = Ns + Pl), for example, *cats, dogs*.

2. The past tense form of a Verb is regularly formed by adding a Past suffix to the Verb Stem (i.e., Vpast = Vs + Past), for example, *helped, walked*.

3. The possessive form of a Noun is formed by adding the Possessive suffix to the Noun Stem (i.e., Nposs = Ns + Poss), for example, *cat's, dog's*.

4. The progressive form of a Verb is always formed by adding the Progressive suffix to the Verb Stem (i.e., Vprog = Vs + Prog), for example, *helping, walking*.

---

[1] The concept of the "word" is mainly an intuitive one and is not particularly well defined formally. Marchand attempts a definition which combines Bloomfield's notion of a "minimal independent unit of utterance" (1926) with the criterion of susceptibility to transposition in sentences (Marchand, 1969, p. 1).

5. The present tense form of a Verb is formed by adding the Present suffix to a Verb Stem (i.e., Vpres = Vs + Pres), for example, *helps*, *walks*.[2]

6. An agentive Noun is regularly formed by adding the Agentive suffix to a Verb Stem (i.e., Nagt = Vs + Agt), for example, *teacher*, *helper*.

7. An affectionate–diminutive Noun is regularly formed by adding the Diminutive suffix to a Noun Stem (i.e., Ndim = Ns + Dim), for example, *doggie*, *horsie*.

8. An Adverb is regularly formed by adding the Adverbial suffix to an Adjective Stem (i.e., ADV = ADJs + Adv), for example, *quietly*, *slowly*.

9. An Adjective can be regularly formed by adding the Adjectival suffix to a Noun Stem (i.e., ADJ = Ns + Adj), for example, *dirty*, *watery*.

10. A Compound Noun can be regularly formed by joining two Noun Stems together in sequence (i.e., Ncom = Ns + Ns), for example, *birdhouse*, *airplane*.

The first five of these rules are traditionally regarded as describing "inflectional" processes, while the last five are referred to as "derivational."[3] In both cases, however, what is involved at this level of analysis are certain specific *patterns of concatenation* among morphemes within words. In order to learn Type I M-Rules, therefore, the child must presumably come to realize that words may sometimes be morphologically complex and, further, to identify the specific concatenation pattern that is involved in each particular case.

Type II M-Rules: Lexical Generalizations

Lexical generalizations are rules that relate particular semantic concepts or "meanings" to a set of one or more arbitrary "vocal symbols," which are the sequences of phonemes employed in a given language to represent these concepts. Berko used the term "morphological rules" in this sense when she described the regular plural, possessive, present tense ("third person singular") and past tense forms of English in the following way:[4]

> The productive allomorphs of the plural, the possessive, and the third person singular of the verb are phonologically conditioned and identical with one another. These forms are /-s ~ -z ~ -əz/, with the following distribution: /-əz/ after stems that end in /s z š ž č j/, e.g. *glasses*, *watches*;

---

[2] The "present tense" of English verbs is normally marked only in the third-person singular form.

[3] See Nida (1949, p. 99) for a summary of the major differences between these two types of morphological processes.

[4] See Derwing (1974) for a variety of alternative ways of describing these forms.

/-s/ after stems that end in /p t k f θ/, e.g. *hops, hits*;
/-z/ after all other stems, viz. those ending in /b d g v ð m n ŋ r l/, vowels, and semivowels, e.g. *bids, goes.*
The productive allomorphs of the past are /-t ~ -d ~ -əd/, and they are also phonologically conditioned, with the following distribution:
/-əd/ after stems that end in /t d/, e.g., *melted*;
/-t/ after stems that end in /p k č f θ s š/, e.g. *stopped*;[5]
/-d/ after stems ending in voiced sounds except /-d/, e.g. *climbed, played.* [Berko, 1958, p. 151]

Lexical generalizations may also be morphologically conditioned or "irregular," as in the following examples for English:

1. The morpheme meaning 'knife' has two allomorphs, /nayf/ and /nayv/. The former variant is the more common one, while the latter occurs only in conjunction with the Plural morpheme:

$$(knife) \rightarrow \begin{Bmatrix} \text{nayv} \text{ / } \underline{\hspace{1cm}} + \text{ Pl} \\ \text{nayf} \text{ / elsewhere} \end{Bmatrix}$$

2. The morpheme meaning 'sit' also has two phonemic variants, namely, /sɪt/ and /sæt/, where the latter occurs only in the past tense or prefective aspect:

$$(sit) \rightarrow \begin{Bmatrix} \text{sæt} \text{ / } \underline{\hspace{1cm}} + \text{ Past, Perf} \\ \text{sɪt} \text{ / elsewhere} \end{Bmatrix}$$

The last and most trivial kind of lexical generalization is a rule which simply associates a single, specific (i.e., invariant) phonological representation with a particular semantic representation, as in the following examples for English:

3. The Progressive morpheme is always symbolized by the phonemic sequence /ɪŋ/ (i.e., (Prog) → ɪŋ), for example, *singing, helping, walking.*)

4. A postulated "basic" or "underlying" lexical representation for the morpheme meaning 'plural' is the phoneme /z/ (i.e., (Pl) → z), for example, *cats, dogs, horses.*[6]

Notice that no distinction is being made here between lexical representations that are in fact invariant (such as the progressive -*ing* suffix of English[7]) and lexical representations for those morphemes that do vary in form (such

---

[5] We have added the phoneme /s/ to this list, which Berko inadvertently omitted.

[6] See Derwing (1974, pp. 10–17) for one analysis of the English plural that incorporates this rule.

[7] We are ignoring so-called "free" or stylistic variation here, as between the forms *sitting* and *sittin'* (i.e., /ɪŋ/ ~ /ɪn/).

as the English plural suffixes), but the variation is accounted for as the result of the operation of certain morphophonemic or phonotactic rules, as discussed below.

In psychological terms, however, these various kinds of Type II M-Rules ought perhaps to be distinguished. In the learning of the simplest kind of lexical generalization, for example, the child must presumably learn to associate a particular semantic concept with a particular, arbitrary phonological shape. This process is often called "symbolization" in the linguistic literature (cf. Chafe, 1970, pp. 15–23), and though the inherent complexities of this task have probably tended to be underestimated in such discussions, the appropriate learning paradigm in psychology would nevertheless seem to be that of simple *association learning*. But when allomorphic variation is involved, as in the other examples, the child is presumably faced with at least two additional kinds of tasks. For one thing, the child must learn either that the same concept has more than one formal manifestation or, alternatively, that various forms that he originally construed to be morphologically distinct are actually nothing more than alternative symbols for the same concept. The first process would be an example of *differentiation*, the second of *generalization*. In addition to this, the child must presumably also learn to associate each alternative manifestation of a morpheme with some particular feature or set of features of its immediate linguistic environment or context, whether phonological (as in Berko's example above) or morphological (as in the 'knife' and 'sit' examples). These would all be illustrations of *contingency learning*, where the relevant patterns of variation are all restricted to specific morphemes. The psychological status of rules such as (4) above, which involve postulated "underlying" forms, is very uncertain at best (but see Derwing, 1974, 1975, for some discussion).[8]

Type III M-Rules: Morphophonemic Rules

Morphophonemic rules are rules which, in formal grammar, take lexical representations as input and yield phonemic representations as output; these rules characteristically involve morphological conditioning and so do not ordinarily express general phonotactic constraints.[9] Since such rules typically

---

[8] A thorough critique of the linguistic notion of "morpheme-invariant underlying forms" is provided by Linell (1974).

[9] See Cearley (1974, p. 32) for a concise summary of the major characteristics that distinguish morphophonemic ("morphological") rules from phonotactic ("phonological") rules, and see Skousen (1974) for a general theoretical approach to morphology that seems largely compatible with the one outlined here.

have numerous exceptions, they are often also called "minor" rules (as in Lakoff, 1970; and Lightner, 1968).[10]

Morphophonemic rules represent one descriptive alternative to morphologically conditioned lexical generalizations. To illustrate this by means of the examples introduced in the preceding section, the following morphophonemic rule has been proposed for English to account for the /f/ ~ /v/ alternation exhibited by nouns such as *knife, wife, loaf, shelf, leaf, calf*, and so on:

(1)   f → v / —— + Pl, for a list of /f/-stem nouns.

Notice that this rule is not completely general, since there are a number of /f/-stem nouns in English that do not conform to it (e.g., *cough, oaf, chief, staff, cliff*, etc.).

Similarly, the vowel alternations exhibited by the various classes of "irregular" or "strong" verbs in English can also be described by means of such rules. The alternation between /ɪ/ and /æ/ exhibited by verbs such as *sit, swim, sink, sing, ring*, for example, can be accounted for by the following morphophonemic rule:

(2)   ɪ → æ / —— + {Past, Perf}, for a list of verbs containing the vowel /ɪ/.

This rule, too, is not completely general, since there are some verbs in /ɪ/ that exhibit different vowel alternations (such as *dig, win, stick, fling, swing*, etc., for which /ɪ/ alternates with /ə/; and *bring*, for which /ɪ/ alternates with /ɔ/, with concomitant changes), others that exhibit no change at all in their past or perfective forms (e.g., *hit, quit, slit*, etc.), and still others that are competely "regular" throughout the paradigm (e.g., *slip, wish, rig, trim, pit*, etc.).

Another kind of morphophonemic rule proposed for English is one in which the morphological conditioning is covertly expressed by means of a special "phonological" boundary, as in the following example:

(3)   ə → ø/[−sibilant]# —— [+sibilant]##.

This rule states that the vowel /ə/ is deleted between a sibilant and a word-final nonsibilant, provided that the /ə/ in question is also the first segment of a morpheme that belongs to a particular class of affixes marked by the word (#) boundary (see Miner, 1975, and Derwing, 1974, for further details).

Type III M-Rules, as characterized here, are much like Type II M-Rules of the kind that involve morphological conditioning. The only substantive difference is one of generality: While a lexical generalization is restricted to a single, specific morpheme, a morphophonemic rule represents a pattern or

---

[10] Our "morphophonemic" rules are called "morpholexical" in Anderson's (1975) taxonomy, a term that nicely reflects their essentially "irregular" character.

regularity that is shared by a list of at least two morphemes. The acquisition of such rules would presumably involve contingency learning, once again, except in this case more would be involved than simply observing the co-occurrence of a regularity with some aspect of its immediate phonetic environment. The learner must now recognize that the *same regularity* is involved for more than one morpheme, and he must remember the arbitrary *list of morphemes* that are involved in each specific case.

Type IV M-Rules: Phonotactic Rules

Phonotactic rules are rules that express completely general phonotactic constraints in a language, that is, constraints on the kinds of sound sequences the language allows. Such rules are distinguished from morphophonemic rules on the basis of their complete generality or phonological conditioning. To learn a phonotactic rule is to learn a regularity involving phonetic co-occurrences which is without exception in normal speech and which therefore cuts across all relevant morphological classes.[11] Such rules have been interpreted by Whitaker (1971), Derwing (1973, 1974, 1975), Braine (1974), and others to represent neuromuscular patterns or articulatory habits of the speakers of a language. An example of such a rule for English is the following:

$$(1) \qquad \begin{bmatrix} +\text{obstruent} \end{bmatrix} \rightarrow [\alpha \text{ voiced}] / \begin{bmatrix} +\text{obstruent} \\ \alpha \text{ voiced} \end{bmatrix} \underline{\qquad} \#\#$$

Rule (1) above states that word-final obstruents always exhibit the same quality of voicing ($\alpha = +$ or $-$) as that exhibited by an immediately preceding obstruent. Thus, in English, for example, the word-final /ts/ of *cats* consists of obstruent sounds that are both voiceless, while the final /gz/ of *dogs* (= /dɔgz/) consists of obstruents sounds which are both voiced, but no words end in clusters such as */tz/ or */gs/. As illustrated in Derwing (1974), rules of this kind provide a further alternative to lexical generalizations in the description of such forms as the English regular plurals.

Other examples of phonotactic rules for English dialects are rules which "automatically" aspirate syllable-initial voiceless stops before stressed vowels, which nasalize vowels before nasal consonants, which "flap" dental stops intervocalically if the first vowel is stressed, and which delete a nasal before a

---

[11] As defined here, this category includes many rules often referred to elsewhere as "morphophonemic" (where the conditioning is phonological rather than morphological), as well as rules sometimes referred to as "phonetic" or "allophonic" (as in Moskowitz, 1973.) Anderson (1975, p. 43) distinguishes two types of phonotactic rules, one which he calls "phonological" and a second called "phonetic." It is quite possible that such a distinction may prove necessary, though we have adopted a more simplified scheme here.

voiceless consonant (see Derwing, 1973, pp. 201ff., for further discussion of these rules.)

In a model of language *production*, it is hypothesized that M-Rules of Types I–III above will all be utilized prior, *in real time*, to M-Rules of Type IV. This is proposed on the ground that the former all represent part of the cognitive "assembly" phase of an utterance, while the latter constitute part of a purely mechanical "output filter" which is the speech articulation mechanism itself.[12]

SOME EXPERIMENTS IN PSYCHOLOGICAL PRODUCTIVITY

In contradistinction to the admittedly oversimplified "instantaneous" models espoused by Chomsky (1964) and Chomsky and Halle (1968), we shall assume that language acquisition takes place via a long series of small steps or "stages," and that the only "data" that the child has available for consideration and comparison at any one stage are limited to whatever specific information he has learned and retained in memory from the preceding stages. Expanding somewhat on McCawley's (1968) proposals, therefore, the kind of schematic model of the language acquisition process that emerges is the following:

	Stage I		*Stage II*		*Stage III*	
D1 →	LS	→ I1 → D2 →	LS	→ I2 → D3 →	LS	→ I3 … etc.

In this still grossly simplified model, language acquisition is viewed in terms of a sequence of discrete developmental stages. At the initial stage it is assumed that a certain highly restricted body of linguistic (and other) data (D1) provide the input to the model, whose basic component consists of a set of particular native capacities or learning strategies (LS) which the child employs to infer, extract, and store some specific body of tentative information about the structure of his language (I1). At each subsequent stage it is this stored information, together with any new or repeated data (D2), which provides the potential input for the next stage, the original data no longer being available as such.[13] It is also possible, and even quite likely, that the

---

[12] The question of the possible interpretation and role of M-Rules in a model of language comprehension is not discussed in this paper, which, like the associated experiments described below, deals only with the production phase of linguistic performance.

[13] We use the term "potential input" here in order to emphasize the point that it is the *child* who determines what the nature of the data is which actually get inside the model, and that these data may be incomplete, faulty, or even completely wrong from the standpoint of the adult or trained linguistic observer.

child may periodically change his own basic strategies for coming to grips with his language, in which case it would be appropriate to distinguish the LSs which appear in the successive stages as well. This would seem to be a major thrust of the Piagetian view of development.

In any event, the crucial theoretical questions that arise in connection with this model all relate to the specification of what these various LSs may be: (1) How does the child manipulate the data available to him at each stage in order to extract, organize, and store the particular information from them that he does; and (2) what external (or internal) factors motivate him to modify or amplify his stored representation of the language at each stage? It seems to us that the primary goal of language acquisition research is to find answers to these two fundamental questions. Unfortunately, however, in order to answer either of these questions, we require a large body of systematic knowledge about the facts of language acquisition which is simply unavailable at the present time. Before we can even broach the question of *how* the child comes to acquire the linguistic knowledge which he does, and certainly long before we can ever hope to learn the main reasons *why* the child chooses to adopt one course of linguistic development rather than some other, we must first find out just *what* the child does in fact learn at each particular stage. Information is particularly lacking when it comes to the question of what linguistic *rules* are learned, whether by children or by adults, largely because the appropriate kind of research has only begun to be carried out. The taxonomy presented in the previous section outlined a range of theoretical alternatives for morphological rule learning, but provided no basis for choosing among them, apart from considerations of relative descriptive simplicity. But as Skousen (1972, p. 567) has pointed out:

> A simple analysis might be better than a complex analysis, but only if it is true that speakers would account for the data by means of the simpler analysis. By just looking at static data, there is no way at present for a linguist to determine what regularities speakers will capture.

In the research reported below, therefore, we were interested in trying to find out what some of the English-speaking child's creative linguistic capacities were with respect to these various kinds of potential "morphological rules," and thus to ascertain which of these alternatives, if any, had an empirically defensible claim to "psychological reality."

The first component of our research thus involved a series of production experiments designed to yield information about the acquisition of each of the ten morphological processes described on pp. 87–88 that is, the plural and possessive noun inflections, the progressive, past tense and third-person singular present tense inflections of the verb, and the agentive, affectionate–diminutive, adjectival, adverbial, and noun compound derivational constructions.

Our surest evidence that a speaker has extracted a linguistic regularity as a behavioral rule occurs when he extends that regularity in formulating utterances that are novel to his linguistic experience. On this ground, Berko (1958) proposed the forced manipulation of nonsense words as a useful test for knowledge of morphological rules (see also Bloomfield, 1933, pp. 274–275). The present study adopted Berko's technique and extended her original work across a much broader age range and to a phonologically much more representative sample of real and nonsense stems for English. The main focus of this study was to increase our understanding of the ways in which certain of the language learner's rules change as he passes from one developmental stage to the next, and thus hopefully to contribute to our limited understanding of those particular factors most crucial to the acquisition of linguistic rules in general.

Brief Description of the Experiments

In the inflections study, two lists of English-like nonsense words were created such that corresponding items on these lists shared only a common stem-final vowel nucleus, consonant, or consonant cluster. A total of 67 distinct stem-final phoneme classes and clusters were represented on each of these lists, which largely exhausted the set of allowable possibilities for English. These nonsense words were combined in random order with a variety of real English nouns and verbs, each selected to represent a particular irregular class of plural forms (for nouns) or past tense forms (for verbs), and with a few additional real, but regular, nouns and verbs to fill out the test. This test was administered to 112 children, all monolingual English speakers residing in Edmonton, Alberta, and ranging in age from 3 through 9 years, with 8 boys and 8 girls in each age group. Half of these children were given the first list of nonsense words as nouns and the second list as verbs, while the other half were assigned the nonsense words in reverse fashion. All responses were tape recorded for subsequent verification.

The presentation sequence for each item consisted of a series of sentences or sentence frames designed to introduce the stimulus item and to elicit the plural and singular possessive form of each noun and the progressive, past tense and third-person singular present tense form of each verb, much as in Berko's original study (1958).[14] We deviated from Berko's procedures in three main respects, however. (1) We did not always accept the child's first response as the definitive response, but allowed our subjects a second and sometimes a third attempt under certain well-defined circumstances. (2) We eventually

---

[14] The procedures for the construction, presentation, and scoring of our test are outlined only briefly here, as are the results. For full details, see Derwing and Baker (1974).

abandoned Berko's two-way "correct" versus "incorrect" scoring system in favor of a three-way system in which responses were scored as "irrelevant" (0), "incorrect" (1), or "correct" (2). For the 67 nonsense stems common to all five inflectional tasks, therefore, our "percent correct" figures were calculated on the basis of a maximum score of 134 ($= 2 \times 67$). A response was scored as "irrelevant" if it failed to include the defining characteristics of each stimulus word, specifically, its stem-final vowel nucleus, consonant or consonant cluster, and which thus failed to supply us with information as to how that subject might productively inflect a stem of that particular type (e.g., $*/\theta r \partial mps/$ for $/\theta r \partial mpfs/$, $*/skyuks \partial z/$ for $/skyusks/$, etc.) (3) We also departed from Berko in regard to our *standard* for correctness of a response. Berko (1958, p. 158) chose a variable standard based on an elicited set of adult responses, whereas we chose instead a completely invariant standard that could be applied to both children and adults alike.[15] Our standard of correctness for *nonsense* stems was based upon those forms which would be appropriate if the stems involved were all to be assimilated into the class of real, regular words, such that the form of the suffix added was phonologically rather than morphologically conditioned (as in Berko's formulation of the rules given on p. 88). An inflected form of a *real* word was evaluated according to the preferences indicated in the Webster's *Seventh New Collegiate Dictionary*, with the qualification that if a word had *both* a regular (e.g., *fishes*) and an irregular (e.g., *fish*) form, the latter was always adopted as the standard.

It seemed appropriate to begin the study of the acquisition of English derivational rules by looking first at those processes that would most likely emerge in the earliest stages, together with at least some of the rules for the inflections. The five derivational constructions investigated were thus selected on the basis of an examination of the available word lists for preschool children (e.g., Horn, 1925; and IKU, 1928), which revealed them to be the only derivational patterns represented with sufficient frequency (i.e., more than one or two word-types each) to suggest any possibility of rule learning at this early age. Presentation frames were thus constructed for each of these patterns, again as in Berko's original study (1958), and at least one nonsense stem and one real, regular stem was selected for presentation in each of these frames; where possible, a common real, irregular stem was also included.[16] The result was a test consisting of 15 items, which was randomized and pre-

---

[15] One reason for departing from Berko's "adult-standard" scoring system was a rather surprising degree of variability we found in the responses of a small adult sample which we tested. In particular, it seems that the adults were much more prone than the children to treat nonsense stems as exemplars of the various *irregular* morphological classes, as well as more inclined to treat them as "pure nonsense," and hence to provide totally nonsensical responses. A much larger sample of adults is now being tested in order to verify these preliminary findings.

[16] See Derwing (1976) for a more detailed discussion of the methods and results of this study.

sented to subjects in either forward or reverse order. The subject sample in this study consisted of 40 children (aged 8–12), 28 adolescents (aged 13–17), and 27 adults, all of whom were native speakers of English but none of whom had had any prior training in formal morphological analysis.

Summary of Results

Both the inflectional and derivational studies provided convincing evidence of rule-governed behavior, as indicated by an ability to manipulate many of the nonsense stems in a consistent and systematic way, even on the part of the youngest subjects in our samples. Among the five inflections investigated, performance on the progressive was the most successful overall (83% standard responses on the 67 nonsense stems included in the study), followed by the plural (78%), the past tense (77%), the possessive (75%) and the present tense (71%). Attempts are made in Derwing and Baker (1976) to explain these results in terms of such variables as formal rule complexity, perceptual saliency, and pattern frequency, but our attention will be restricted here to the issue of "alternative rules," as discussed in the following section.

All but one of the derivational constructions also proved to be psychologically productive for the majority of subjects tested, including both the "agentive" (e.g., *teacher*) and "instrumental" (e.g., *eraser*) versions of the *-er* suffix.[17] The only derivational construction tested for which productivity failed to be exhibited, in fact, was the one involving the affectionate–diminutive *-y* or *-ie* suffix, and even in this case the result seems to have been due to a flaw in our methodology, rather than to a lack of knowledge of the rule. Specifically, the presentation frame we employed to elicit this particular construction did not suffice to elicit it even with the real noun stems that we employed, and thus would not appear to have been a suitable frame to use for this construction in general. The learnability of at least these very general kinds of Type I M-Rules, therefore, does not appear to be a matter of serious debate.

Which Rules Are Learned? The Example of the English Plural

While the status of word-level concatenation rules seems fairly secure, there still exists considerable controversy related to the question of the learnability of M-Rules of Types II–IV, which often provide descriptive alternatives with respect to identical sets of "static" or "primary" linguistic data. Although the

---

[17] There were interesting and significant differences in our subjects' performance on these latter two subpatterns, however, which are also discussed in Derwing (1976).

results of our productivity experiments provide a sufficient basis to explore this issue for all five of the inflectional morphemes investigated, we shall restrict our attention here to the English plural inflection, largely following the line of argument developed in Derwing (1974), to which the reader is referred for details.

Brown has observed that rules such as those that describe the allomorphs of the regular English plural (cf. p. 88) "predict behavior with such detailed accuracy that one cannot doubt that the rules are, in some sense, inside the heads of speakers of the language" (Brown, 1964, p. 250). But which particular set of pluralization rules is Brown referring to here? It is quite clear that "the allomorphs of plurality for English" can be described in a great variety of different ways, and many alternative rules have been formulated that make precisely the same set of predictions about these forms. In fact, were it not for data of a kind reported in the section above, we would not be forced by the mere presence of regularities in adult speech to conclude that mastery of the English plural inflection need necessarily involve any rule learning at all. Since the number of pluralizable noun stems in English is finite, it is possible in principle that each occurring plural form might be learned and stored as an idiosyncratic, indivisible whole. Such a thoroughgoing "list" hypothesis was the first analysis outlined in Derwing (1974) but shown to be inadequate even on the basis of Berko's original, limited results. Berko (1958) demonstrated that both adult English speakers and young children were able to form the plurals of many novel, unfamiliar noun stems in a remarkably consistent and systematic way; she thus demonstrated that the learning of the English plural must involve more than the simple memorization of forms to which the learner had been previously exposed. This discovery that English pluralization involves a genuine "productive" or "creative" linguistic capacity also attests to the inadequacy of the "whole stem" theory described in Derwing (1974), which claims that although a generalization might be learned with respect to the three regular "allomorphs" of the English plural, the choice between them is nonetheless conditioned by knowledge of a particular list of familiar, learned stems. Our data serve to confirm Berko's earlier finding that even the young child of age 4 or 5 can pluralize many stems which are, by all accounts, completely unfamilar to him as wholes.

Berko's original data, however, have virtually nothing to say about four of the five remaining alternative theories of English pluralization which Derwing reviews. The first of these (Derwing's Analysis III) suggests that English plurals might be learned on the basis of a *rhyming analogy* with familiar English plurals, a strategy quite compatible with Berko's data. Two other familiar possibilities suggest that the English plural endings might be predicated upon either the final phonemic segment of the stem (Analysis IV—and also the analysis Berko herself accepted, though giving no empirical basis for her choice) or merely upon certain intrinsic phonetic features of that segment (Analysis V), and both of these theories, too, are in full accord with Berko's results. It should be noted that all of these alternatives represent competing versions of a Type II or "lexical generalization" analysis.

An alternative theory, widely espoused by generative grammarians in particular, is that the English plural involves the learning of only a single basic "lexical" representation, namely /z/, and that all regular deviations from this standard are consequences of the operation of one or another of two particular Type IV or "phonotactic" rules, one which assimilates final obstruent clusters as to voicing, and another which inserts a vowel to break up combinations of sibilant segments within the same syllable (Analysis VI). This theory, too, is consistent with all of Berko's productivity data, on the reasonable assumption that her youngest subjects had simply not yet acquired any strategy for dealing with the sibilant stems, or else treated them as forms already marked for plurality. Finally, some linguists have also argued for a theory somewhat like the preceding, but in which the single "underlying" representation proposed for the plural is /əz/, rather than /z/, and where the completely general rule of vowel insertion of the previous analysis is replaced by a morphologically conditioned or Type III rule of vowel deletion, affecting only the vowel /ə/ within a particular class of morphemes (the so-called "neutral suffixes") which includes the plural (Analysis VII; see also p. 91). Under the psychological interpretation proposed by Derwing for this analysis, this theory seems to imply that the /z/ allomorph of the plural ought not to be used productively by the language learner until after the /əz/ allomorph has already been mastered, since the latter serves as the only derivational source for the former within the language. Furthermore, all early "overgeneralization" errors ought to involve the /əz/ allomorph, rather than the /z/ or /s/, a situation which clearly did not obtain with the real, irregular words in our study. In Berko's study, too, the /əz/ allomorph was clearly the last of the three regular plural allomorphs to be employed productively with unfamiliar stems, a finding that has already cast this last theory into grave doubt.

The new data collected in our study, which involved a much larger and more representative set of nonsense stems than that employed by Berko (1958), Koziol (1970), and others, permit us to carry our conclusions considerably farther with respect to all of the alternative theories considered. Berko's finding with respect to the "list" and "whole stem" analyses is merely replicated and strengthened: Some rule learning of *some* kind must definitely be involved in the mastery of the English plural inflection. We can now add to this the new information that the "rhyme" hypothesis is an inadequate formulation of what the rule in question might be. Approximately half of our nonsense stems had no real-word rhymes at all, yet our subjects invented plurals for these in the same consistent and systematic manner as for the rhyming stems. Furthermore, we also failed to find a significant list effect on more than a handful of our nonsense items, a finding which demonstrates rather conclusively that it is only the stem-final segment or consonant cluster that plays a significant role in the child's developing rule for pluralization in English.

We are also in a position to conclude at this time that Berko's own "segment" hypothesis is probably false. We found that the development of the child's capacity to pluralize novel stems in English was much too regular and systematic to be compatible with the view that the stem classes involved are learned on an item-by-item basis, as a function of their particular final phoneme or consonant cluster. Our data strongly indicate instead that mastery of the plural for one particular stem-type (such as stems ending in the vowel /i/, for instance) is highly correlated with mastery of all other stem-types whose final segments are highly similar phonetically (such as stems ending in any other vowel, or even in a resonant consonant). Our data thus provide rather strong support for some form of the "feature" hypothesis outlined above (see also Innes, 1974, who presents further detailed evidence in support of this view).

Our data, however, are also reasonably consistent with a "phonotactic" analysis in which the voiceless (/s/ or /t/) and vocalic (/əz/ or /əd/) allomorphs of the plural, possessive, present, and past tense morphemes are all described as consequences of a pair of general "articulatory habits," one which results in the voicelessness of these suffixes after voiceless nonsibilant obstruents, and another which inserts a /ə/-vowel to eliminate certain difficult word-final consonant clusters. We did find a disturbing morpheme-by-allomorph interaction in our data which seemed initially to militate against the theory that all four of the morpheme categories in question might be subject to any common set of general rules such as the ones proposed, but a more detailed analysis has led us to the conclusion that certain confounding variables were most likely responsible for this result (see Derwing & Baker, 1976, for details).

These findings leave us with the conclusion that the psychological process of pluralization in English is a productive or rule-governed one even from a very early age and, furthermore, that the rules that are learned at every stage seem on the evidence to take some notion of the subsegmental phonetic feature into account. Our data also continue to permit the view that the rules involved might be of a very general phonotactic nature, and hence operative across more than one morphological category. All of the other alternatives investigated have been shown to be inadequate on the basis of firm and crucial empirical evidence, some of which has been collected and identified for the first time in the research described here.

MEANING, SOUND, AND MORPHEME RECOGNITION

The area of derivational morphology is beyond doubt one of the most diffi-cult and least understood of all the areas of linguistic description (cf. Lightner, 1968, p. 71). A central difficulty is the question of lexical identity or morpheme recognition itself. Just what does it take to identify a morpheme, and how much do individuals vary in their ability to perform this task? Many of the morphological rules that appear in formal linguistic descriptions, whether morphophonemic or phonotactic in presumed character, are posited pri-marily, if not solely, in order to capture certain kinds of supposed "lexical redundancies," that is, systematic variations that appear in the phonological form of the "same morpheme" when that morpheme occurs in different syntactic constructions. The psychological viability of all such rules is thus directly contingent upon the assumption that the native speaker has recog-nized that there is a common norpheme involved. Macnamara (1972, pp. 9–10) presents a suitable example from the inflectional morphology of Irish, while Chomsky (1964, p. 90) provides some rules for a proposed analysis of the derivational morphology of English. The Irish child must presumably "use the fact that the referent is constant to arrive at the appreciation that . . . there are three surface manifestations of the same underlying morphophonemic form" (Macnamara, 1972, p. 10). In Chomsky's examples, too, both the morphophonemic rule that changes a /d/ to an /s/ before the suffix /ɪv/, and the phonotactic rule that changes a /d/ plus /i/ or /y/ into a /ž/ before a vowel, are largely motivated by the presumed fact that the English words *decisive* and *decision*, for example, contain in their "underlying" or "lexical" representa-tions the common morpheme *decide*. But how does one decide whether this claim is justified for ordinary native speakers of the language, particularly in some of the more problematical cases discussed in Derwing (1973)? Are words such as *decisive* and *decision* even treated as morphologically complex by such speakers? And even if we knew the answer to these first two questions, how could we determine whether the speaker ever goes so far as to learn rules of the kind described, rather than simply settling for less elegant but quite adequate "lexical generalizations," whereby, for example, the morpheme *decide* might be thought simply to have a nonpredictable or "irregular" variant in final /s/ before the morpheme /ɪv/, and the same for other verbs like *deride*, *conclude*, and so on, without the learner's ever taking note of the fact that there is a generalization involved which actually cuts across all of the verbs in this set? In sum, to what extent is the linguist's penchant for detailed morphemic analysis realized psychologically by the ordinary lan-guage learner?

It is widely and naturally assumed that the psychological recognition of morphological relatedness is critically dependent upon the degree of semantic and phonetic similarity of the word-pairs involved. It is an easy matter to recognize a common morpheme in word-pairs such as *teach–teacher*, which are highly similar both in meaning and in sound, but more difficult to do so when either the connection in meaning is rather less than straightforward (as with the pairs *slip–slipper* or *awe–awful*), or when the words are more extensively different in sound (as with the pairs *cup–cupboard* or *hand–handkerchief*); or both (as with the pairs *price–precious, moon–month*, or *lace–necklace*). An experiment was envisioned which might serve to clarify the role of these two variables in morpheme recognition.

Before such a study could be seriously entertained, however, we need first to establish some empirical measure of semantic and phonetic similarity, since these were the two independent variables proposed. For this purpose a list was constructed of 115 potentially related word-pairs, representing a broad range of estimated semantic and phonetic similarity (e.g., *dirt–dirty, hunger–hungry, message–messenger, fable–fabulous, break–breakfast, spin–spider, beard–barber, lean–ladder, holy–Halloween*, etc.). Each of these word-pairs was then rated by 129 adult subjects as to the extent of their similarity in meaning, and by 127 adult subjects as to the extent of their similarity in sound. The lists were randomized and counterbalanced for order, and subjects who received one list for the semantic similarity test were given the other list for the phonetic similarity test. Data were also obtained from subjects on the following control variables: age, sex, class (all subjects were students in introductory linguistics courses at the University of Alberta), education level, and foreign language competence.[18] On the basis of the results of these two scaling experiments, 50 items were selected from the original list of 115 which best represented the full range of semantic and phonetic similarity involved. These word-pairs are listed in Table 6.1. These items were next randomized and presented in a test for "morpheme recognition" which employed another technique originally proposed by Berko.

Berko's Test for Morpheme Recognition

To assess whether or not a child recognized the derived character of a word, Berko (1958, p. 157) proposed asking him why a particular word has the name that it does. In response to this type of question from a sample of children ranging from 4 to 7 years of age and for a list of 14 compound nouns, Berko got essentially three different types of answers: (1) an *identity* response (e.g., "a blackboard is called a blackboard because it is a blackboard"); (2) a

---

[18] For a more complete description of this study and analysis of the results, see Derwing (1976).

TABLE 6.1

Semantic and Phonetic Similarity among Selected Word-Pairs

Semantic Similarity	Very low (0.0–1.5)	Slight (1.5–2.5)	Moderate (2.5–3.5)	Very high (3.5–6.0)
Clear (3.5–4.0)	kitty–cat puppy–dog wilderness–wild	lawyer–law shepherd–sheep numerous–number	messenger–message strawberry–berry hungry–hunger	eraser–erase teacher–teach doggie–dog dirty–dirt quietly–quiet
Probable (2.5–3.5)	barber–beard weather–wind precious–price	month–moon holiday–holy heavy–heave	cupboard–cup birdhouse–bird lousy–louse	handle–hand cookie–cook wonderful–wonder
Uncertain (1.5–2.5)	Halloween–holy feather–fly timid–tame	breakfast–break spider–spin fabulous–fable	handkerchief–hand necklace–lace awful–awe	sweater–sweat slipper–slip skinny–skin
Dubious (0.0–1.5)	ladder–lean carpenter–wagon muggy–mist	gypsy–Egyptian cranberry–crane hideous–hide	Friday–fry rubber–rub bashful–bash	liver–live buggy–bug eerie–ear

Phonetic similarity

functional response (e.g., "a blackboard is called a blackboard because you write on it"); and (3) an *etymological* response (e.g., "a blackboard is called a blackboard because it is a board and because it is [sometimes] black"—or "Thanksgiving is called Thanksgiving because the pilgrims gave thanks," etc.). Only the last case of the "etymological" response provided positive evidence that the child was aware of the derived nature of the word in question.

A replication of Berko's study was attempted, using the 50 items just described and employing the same subjects ($N = 95$) who also took the derivational productivity test, as described earlier (p. 96). The percentage of relevant "etymological" responses was then tabulated for each item, taking such responses to express morphological relationships that were psychologically valid for the particular subjects involved. The result was a set of data that resisted all our attempts at a sensible, consistent interpretation. There were a few cases in which words that shared a high degree of both semantic and phonetic similarity with their supposed roots (such as *teacher–teach* and *eraser–erase*) for which the percentage of relevant responses was also relatively high (87% and 83%, respectively), but other cases in this same category for which the relevant response rate was extremely low (such as 15% for the word-pair *dirty–dirt* and 4% for *quietly–quiet*). For the 50 items overall, the correlation of the rate of relevant responses to degree of semantic similarity was only .57, with an even lower, nonsignificant correlation of .17 to degree of phonetic similarity. In neither case were any discernible patterns evident from the scatter diagrams.

The main source of difficulty in this initial attempt to assess a capacity for "morpheme recognition" in our subjects appears to have resided in Berko's proposed test itself. We can sympathize with Berko's position that an appropriate etymological response is a valid indicator of morpheme recognition in this type of study. It is much less obvious, however, that a subject's *failure* to provide such a response is likewise indicative of his *lack* of cognizance of morphological relationships. It is extremely difficult to believe, for example, that only about 4% of our subjects were able to see the rather obvious morphological relationship between the words *quietly* and *quiet*, for example. It is much more resonable to assume instead that our subjects preferred, by and large, a paraphrase rather than an "etymological" response to this item because such a response provided a more natural reply to the particular question asked. Thus, for example, the fact that *quietly* had something to do with *quiet* was in this situation something that was perhaps thought to be too obvious even to consider mentioning. (For some reason, subjects were much more inclined to provide etymological responses for some classes of derived words, such as the *-ie* diminutives, *-er* words, and noun compounds, than for others, such as the *-ly* adverbs and the *-y* adjectives. Perhaps this says something about the relative obviousness or "transparency" of the particular morphological patterns involved.) The major defect in Berko's technique, it seems, is that it allows for far too much variety in the types of responses it can quite sensibly elicit and thus does not necessarily require subjects to look for morphological relationships at all. To the extent that this is true, therefore, Berko's technique fails to tap the "morpheme recognition" issue, and is hence invalid as a technique for doing so. We believe that it was this flaw in the technique that was mainly responsible for the failure of the first study to reveal any coherent relationship between either semantic and phonetic similarity and the ability of subjects to identify morphological relationships between words in a variety of derivational categories.

A Revised Test for Morpheme Recognition

In an attempt to correct this defect in methodology, an alternative technique was sought in order to test for a capacity to "identify morphemes." One suggestion was that we simply ask each subject directly whether the first ("derived") word in each pair "came from" the second ("base") word. The morpheme recognition study was subsequently repeated on this basis, using the same 50 word-pairs as before, with 65 adult students in a beginning linguistics course as subjects, none of whom had had any prior exposure to formal morphological analysis. For each word-pair, the subjects were asked the following two questions, using the pair *teacher–teach* as an example here:

1. Do you think that the word *teacher* comes from the word *teach*?
2. Have you ever thought about this before?

The first question was intended to focus the subject's attention upon a specific morphological issue, and he was asked to rate his response on the following five-point scale: (4) NO DOUBT ABOUT IT; (3) PROBABLY; (2) CAN'T DECIDE; (1) PROBABLY NOT; (0) NO WAY. The second question was introduced in order to furnish additional information potentially useful in assessing whether the particular morphological relationships which were being focused upon in the test were of a kind which the subjects had become aware of naturally as a result of their prior linguistic experience, or whether the possibility of such relationships was something which was being brought to their attention for the first time in the test situation itself. Subjects were asked to rate their responses to this second question on the following three-point scale: (A) YES; (B) NOT SURE; (C) NO.

The results of this study show that morpheme recognition (as measured by the "comes from" test) is very highly related to semantic similarity ($r = .79$, $p < .00001$), but less so to phonetic similarity ($r = .40$, $p < .002$), taking all 50 word-pairs into account. The partial correlations between the "comes from" means and the two similarity measures are an even higher .80 and .47, respectively, controlling for the opposite similarity measure in each case. An inspection of the scatter diagram relating the "comes from" mean and semantic similarity revealed a near-linear function, spoiled only by a small number of off-diagonal points which represented word-pairs involving a quite low rating for phonetic similarity, such as *puppy–dog, carpenter–wagon, weather–wind, kitty–cat*, and *hideous–hide*.

Another way of viewing the interaction between these two variables is presented in Table 6.2, which provides the mean "comes from" rating and (in parentheses) the mean percentage of subjects who supplied NO DOUBT (4) and YES (A) ratings for those word-pairs which filled each of the 16 cells defined in the semantic by phonetic similarity matrix of Table 6.1. As can be seen by inspection of Table 6.2, morpheme recognition increases quite regularly on both measures as either semantic similarity or phonetic similarity increases, but the semantic dimension is the much more important of the two. In order to achieve a NO DOUBT rating from the majority of our subjects, for example, the phonetic similarity between the word-pairs could be *slight* (1.5–2.5), but only if the semantic similarity was *clear* (3.5–4.0); on the other hand, even if the phonetic similarity was *moderate* (2.5–3.5) or *very high* (3.5–6.0), a comparable majority pattern of NO DOUBT ratings could only be

TABLE 6.2

Morpheme Recognition as a Function of Semantic and Phonetic Similarity among World-Pairs

		Very low	Slight	Moderate	Very high
	Clear	2.42 (34%; 38%)	3.68 (76%; 68%)	3.57 (75%; 64%)	3.94 (95%; 69%)
Semantic Similarity	Probable	2.14 (17%; 14%)	3.17 (45%; 39%)	3.51 (65%; 57%)	3.41 (54%; 40%)
	Uncertain	2.13 (20%; 25%)	2.61 (29%; 31%)	2.97 (40%; 43%)	2.70 (26%; 28%)
	Dubious	1.09 (5%; 4%)	1.63 (10%; 10%)	1.11 (4%; 15%)	1.39 (11%; 11%)

Phonetic similarity

achieved if the semantic similarity between the words was at least *probable* (2.5–3.5). These patterns corresponded to mean "comes from" ratings of approximately 3.40 or above.

The "recall ratings" which resulted from the second question in the revised test sequence correlated very highly with the "comes from" ratings which resulted from the first question; the overall correlation was .90 for the 50 items. This indicates that subjects who saw clear morphological relationships between particular word-pairs also believed rather strongly that they had also thought about these same relationships previously, while it was largely the unclear or strained relationships they believed they were considering in the test for the first time. In almost every case, however, the mean recall ratings were lower than the mean "comes from" ratings, indicating that the subjects showed a bias in the direction of *accepting* a specific, proposed morphological relationship, even though they might never have considered the possibility on their own in any of their prior linguistic experience.

Since it seemed that both parts of the revised test for morpheme recognition yielded important and relevant information, our tentative conclusions regarding the morphological relatedness of the word-pairs studied take both the "comes from" and the recall ratings into account. We can suggest that a word-pair involves a *probable* morphological relationship if the majority of our subjects expressed no doubt about such a relationship on the "comes from" test and if, generally speaking, they also felt certain that they had thought about this relationship prior to the test. That is, the criterion proposed in this case is %YES > 50 on both parts of the test. In general, the word-pairs that satisfied this criterion were those which had a mean of 3.00 or greater on the "comes from" test. At the other extreme, there was another set of word-pairs that seemed to involve only very *improbable* morphological relationships. For these pairs, more of our subjects provided a NO WAY than a NO DOUBT response on the "comes from" test, and the majority were also certain that they had *not* previously thought about the possibility of their being related. All of the items that satisfied these criteria had a mean rating of less than 2.00 on the "comes from" test. The remaining word-pairs seemed to involve morphological relationships of a very *uncertain* nature, in that the majority of our subjects were less than certain of their ratings on both parts of the test. In general, these were the word-pairs which had a mean "comes from" rating between 2.00 and 3.00.

The results of this revised test for "morpheme recognition" are very encouraging. Combined with the scaling techniques for semantic and phonetic similarity, this test now appears to provide a measuring instrument adequate for the experimental exploration of a whole new domain of interesting theoretical questions.

SUMMARY AND CONCLUSIONS

All of the research described in this paper has been concerned with the question of the empirical evaluation of linguistic knowledge in the language learner. Both in the areas of inflectional and derivational morphology, our results confirm the view that a variety of kinds of surface regularities (M-Rules) are extracted by language learners and productively employed by them in producing novel speech forms. As illustrated here for the plural inflection, we have also found developmental and other data that help to determine which of a variety of possible alternative surface regularities are in fact the specific ones that serve as the basis for the English-speaking child's productive linguistic capacities with respect to this particular morpheme. Finally, we have also begun to explore experimentally the ability of native speakers to identify morphemes in their language, and to relate this skill to such experimentally derived dependent variables as semantic and phonetic similarity ratings among potentially related word-pairs.

Obviously, these findings represent only a minuscule step towards a full understanding of rule learning in general, much less of language learning in all of its aspects. But the kinds of data considered here may well be representative of those which will eventually have to be identified and examined in future research in these areas, if opinions concerning the nature of language and its acquisition are to be based on firm experimental evidence rather than upon empty "armchair" speculation and purely formal arguments. It is clear, at least, that the identification and collection of new data crucial to the evaluation of alternative linguistic hypotheses is a task of sufficient difficulty to challenge the best efforts of all of us.

REFERENCES

Anderson, S. R. On the interaction of phonological rules of various types. *Journal of Linguistics*, 1975, *11*, 39–62.
Berko, J. The child's learning of English morphology. *Word*, 1958, *14*, 150–177.
Bloomfield, L. A set of postulates for the science of language. *Language*, 1926, *2*, 153–164.
Bloomfield, L. *Language*. New York: Holt, 1933.
Braine, M. D. S. On what might constitute learnable phonology. *Language*, 1974, *50*, 270–299.
Brown, R. Discussion of the conference. In A. K. Romney and R. G. D'Andrade (Eds.), *Transcultural studies in cognition*. *American Anthropologist*, 1964, *66* (3, Pt. 2), 243–253.

Cearley, A. The only phonological rule ordering principle. In A. Bruck, R. A. Fox, and M. W. LaGaly (Eds.), *Papers from the Parasession on Natural Phonology.* Chicago: Chicago Linguistic Society, 1974.

Chafe, W. L. *Meaning and the structure of language.* Chicago: University of Chicago Press, 1970.

Chomsky, N. Current issues in linguistic theory. In J. A. Fodor and J. J. Katz (Eds.), *The structure of language: Readings in the philosophy of language.* Englewood Cliffs, N. J.: Prentice-Hall, 1964.

Chomsky, N. *Aspects of the theory of syntax.* Cambridge, Mass.: M.I.T. Press, 1965.

Chomsky, N. *Topics in the theory of generative grammar.* The Hague: Mouton, 1966.

Chomsky, N., & Halle, M. *The sound pattern of English.* New York: Harper & Row, 1968.

Derwing, B. L. *Transformational grammar as a theory of language acquisition.* London: Cambridge University Press, 1973.

Derwing, B. L. English pluralization: A testing ground for rule evaluation. Paper read at the Annual Meeting of the Canadian Linguistic Association, Toronto, 1974. To appear in G. D. Prideaux, B. L. Derwing, and W. J. Baker (Eds.), *Experimental linguistics.*

Derwing, B. L. Linguistic rules and language acquisition. *Cahiers Linguistiques d' Ottawa,* 1975, No. 4, 13–41.

Derwing, B. L. Morpheme recognition and the learning of rules for derivational morphology. *The Canadian Journal of Linguistics,* 1976, *21,* 38–66.

Derwing, B. L., & Baker, W. J. Rule learning and the English inflections. Final report to the Canada Council, File No. S72-0332, 1974.

Derwing, B. L., & Baker, W. J. On the learning of English morphological rules. Final report to the Canada Council, File No. S73-0387, 1976.

Horn, E. The commonest words in the spoken vocabulary of children up to and including six years of age. In *National Society for the Study of Education, Twenty-fourth yearbook.* Bloomington, Ill.: Public School Publishing Company, 1925.

Innes, S. J. Developmental aspects of plural formation in English. Unpublished Masters thesis, University of Alberta, 1974.

International Kindergarten Union [IKU], Child Study Committee. *A study of the vocabulary of children before entering the first grade.* Washington, D.C.: The International Kindergarten Union, 1928.

Kiparsky, P. Linguistic universals and language change. In E. Bach and R. T. Harms (Eds.), *Universals in linguistic theory.* New York: Holt, 1968.

Koziol, S. M. The development of noun plural rules during the primary grades. *Papers and reports on child language development.* Committee on Linguistics, Stanford University, 1970 (No. 2, December), 76–96.

Lakoff, G. *Irregularity in syntax.* New York: Holt, 1970.

Lightner, T. M. On the use of minor rules in Russian phonology. *Journal of Linguistics,* 1968, *4,* 69–72.

Linell, P. *Problems of psychological reality in generative phonology: A critical assessment. Reports from Uppsala University Department of Linguistics,* 1974, No. 4.

Macnamara, J. Cognitive basis of language learning in infants. *Psychological Review,* 1972, *79,* 1–13.

Marchand, H. *The categories and types of present-day English word-formation.* Munich: C. H. Beck'sche, 1969.

McCawley, J. D. Can you count pluses and minuses before you can count? *Chicago Journal of Linguistics,* 1968, *2,* 51–56.

Miner, K. L. English inflectional endings and unordered rules. *Foundations of Language,* 1975, *12,* 339–365.

Moskowitz, B. A. On the status of vowel shift in English. In T. E. Moore (Ed.), *Cognitive development and the acquisition of language.* New York: Academic Press, 1973.

Nida, E. A. *Morphology: The descriptive analysis of words.* Ann Arbor: University of Michigan Press, 1949.

Segal, E., & Stacy, E. Rule-governed behavior as a psychological process. *American Psychologist,* 1975, *30,* 541–552.

Skousen, R. On capturing regularities. In P. M. Peranteau, J. N. Levi, and G. C. Phares (Eds.), *Papers from the Eighth Regional Meeting of the Chicago Linguistic Society.* Chicago: Chicago Linguistic Society, 1972.

Skousen, R. An explanatory theory of morphology. In A. Bruck, R. A. Fox, and M. W. LaGaly (Eds.), *Papers from the Parasession on Natural Phonology.* Chicago: Chicago Linguistic Society, 1974.

Whitaker, H. A. *On the representation of language in the human brain.* Edmonton and Champaign: Linguistic Research, Inc., 1971.

7

The Formalization of
Linguistic Rules

DAVID R. OLSON

Ontario Institute for Studies in Education

In their paper, Derwing and Baker raise and discuss the interesting question as to whether the regularities that are detectable in language are in fact evidence for the hypothesis that these rules are employed by speakers of that language. The possibility is that these regularities may exist only in what may be called "interpreters' knowledge," structures devised by the scholar for the description of language, rather than in the speaker's knowledge, structures employed by speakers in the generation of sentences. Regularities that are found may be produced by remembering specific forms in a listlike structure rather than through detecting these regularities or generating them by a common rule. Derwing and Baker present considerable evidence that this is not the case, at least for the set of inflectional rules of English. Their findings are congruent with those of Berko (1958), that even the youngest speakers do indeed generate inflections on the basis of some rule that can be applied even to novel lexical items. For other morphological rules, however, such as those relating a common morpheme to different syntactic constructions, it is not clear that the rules of the language are in fact those being used by the speaker/comprehender. The English words *decisive* and *decision* are presumed to contain in their underlying or lexical representations the common morpheme *decide* (Chomsky, 1964, p. 90; Derwing & Baker, this volume, p.101). But how can we be sure that this regularity reflects the rule structures of the native speaker? In Derwing and Baker's words: "To what extent is the linguist's penchant for detailed morphemic analysis realized psychologically by the ordinary language user?" (p. 101).

I shall discuss this issue in some detail because it seems to me that the relation between the rules of the language and the rules of the language user cannot be accounted for simply as the difference between interpreters' knowledge and speakers' knowledge or even as the difference between competence and performance. Rather, I shall argue, it is an issue of the specialization of language in particular cultural contexts and the progressive mastery of these more specialized forms. For those speakers whose language has been specialized for such literate activities as philosophical argument and reading and writing prose text, the rules under discussion become part of the speaker's system for generating sentences. For those speakers whose language serves the more ordinary conversational functions of the mother tongue, those rules are not part of the speaker's linguistic system. The event mediating the acquisition of such structures, then, would be the acquisition of literacy rather than the acquisition of a mother tongue.

Derwing and Baker attempt to determine speakers' knowledge of the rules relating morphemes by obtaining adult subjects' judgments of the morphemic relatedness of word pairs on the basis of their rated semantic similarity and their rated phonological similarity. Literate adults do quite well on such tasks. My expectation is that if the technique is applied developmentally, it would yield conclusions similar to those obtained with other tests of semantic development such as the occurrence of a syntagmatic–paradigmatic shift and the increasing use of superordinate terms as a means for relating concrete nouns. Interestingly, both of these effects are in large part related to schooling and the acquisition of literacy rather than to the acquisition of the mother tongue (Goodnow, 1976; Brown, in press). What is there about literate language that could make the language system more formal, explicit and rule governed?

Written language, I would like to suggest, is not speech transcribed. It is a specialized form of ordinary language. As several writers, particularly Austin (1962) and Halliday (1970), have shown, ordinary language is an instrument that simultaneously serves a number of functions. The two primary functions are those of preserving the social and authority relations between the speaker and hearer—what has been called the interpersonal or rhetorical or illocutionary function of language—and that of specifying the semantic and logical relations between the subject and predicate of a sentence—what has been called the logical or ideational or locutionary functions of language. Halliday describes development in terms of the confluence or integration of these functions in the production of any sentence and in terms of the elaboration and formalization of linguistic structures to give more precise expression to these functions. As a consequence, any adult utterance simultaneously has a logical or ideational component—a component that can be judged as true or false—and a rhetorical or interpersonal component—a component that relates the logical component to the requirements of the listener. While they are progressively integrated in the course of acquisition of the mother tongue, it is these functions that are subsequently differentiated and specialized in the acquisition of literate forms of language. Gellner (1973) describes the differences between the savage and the modern mind in precisely these terms. Adult literate language differentiates and specializes these functions—the logical and the rhetorical—while the savage mind, like the preliterate child, leaves these functions largely undifferentiated. "The enchanted vision [the Savage mind] works through the systematic conflation of descriptive, evaluative, identificatory, status-conferring, etc. roles of language" (Gellner, 1973, p. 174).

Literate language, especially that of prose text, the language of schooling, is responsible, I suggest, for differentiating the logical from the interpersonal functions of language and for specializing the language to better serve the logical functions at the expense of the interpersonal functions. By supressing the interpersonal or rhetorical functions of language, statements can become the specialized instruments of description and explanation. To better serve this specialized logical function, language has to be brought up to a much higher level of formal and explicit conventionalization; meanings must be formalized in a set of explicit definitions and grammatical structures shaped to give a precise expression to logical structures, and the like. The result is not an ordinary language, a "mother tongue." Rather, it is the specialized language of literate prose. More importantly, it is the language that the child learns not at his mother's knee but in the process of schooling.

One consequence of literacy is that the meaning of statements can be differentiated from meaning intention (Grice, 1975). As well as having an interpersonal bias, speech is closely tied to the expectancies of both the speaker and the listener. As a result, what was meant and what was in fact said cannot be readily disentangled on the part of the speaker; similarly what was said and the interpretation assigned to what was said cannot be disentangled on the part of the listener.

This relation between statements and their meanings is quite different for written text. What was meant may be differentiated from what was in fact said. A written text says what it says regardless of any denials, expectancies, or purposes of the writer or reader. The same intention is, ideally, attributed to the statement on every reading; the meaning lies in the text (Olson, in press). If Chomsky's claim is interpreted as a claim about the autonomous meaning of text, of what was said as opposed to what was meant, then it becomes quite reasonable:

> If I use my language to express or clarify my thoughts, with the intent to deceive, to avoid an embarrassing silence, or in a dozen other ways, *my words have a strict meaning* . . . . but the fullest understanding of what I intend my audience (if any) to believe or to do might give little or no indication of the meaning of my discourse. [1972, p. 24]

A nice illustration of the difference between intended meaning and conventionalized meaning comes from a footnote to an otherwise unremarkable book by Hockett (1968) in which he relates how in 1954 he had written a paper that several linguists, including Teeter, had misinterpreted as a theory of "item and arrangement." He continues: "Late in 1965 I explained orally to Teeter what had been my actual intention in the 1954 paper and in the clause he had quoted from it. He insisted that his interpretation was right anyway." My point is that written text is independent of or permits the differentiation of what was said from what was intended: It said what it said regardless of the author's intentions. For text, then, at least in the ideal case, the meaning depends upon the meanings that are formally conventionalized in the text; and since, unlike in conversation, you cannot be asked what you meant, you have to make the explicit statement say exactly what you intended. The sentence has to become an autonomous representation of what was meant. Once text is invented and formalized, we can talk about autonomous meaning and the rules that must hold to sustain the conventionalization. But these rules apply to the structure of the linguistic system specialized for the uses of written literal prose, not to the more informal utterances of the native speaker.

What rules do we then attribute to the native speaker? It depends, presumably, on the degree of conventionalization of his language. If he negotiates his meanings in the contexts of action and in terms of the social relations between the speakers, the logical aspects of his language are going to be somewhat less conventionalized. If, however, he is highly literate and has mastered the more formally conventionalized system for the purpose of generating autonomous statements, then his behavior will be more grammatically rule determined. This latter development, at least to some degree, is an unintended consequence of literacy.

Writing, then, it may be suggested, is an important occasion for the organization and formalization of one's meanings. To make the language independent of situational context, it is necessary to provide definitions for words in terms of the other words in the lexicon. And since in text, one cannot be queried as to the meaning of a sentence, one must attempt to make it an independent, autonomous representation of what was meant. And in many cases, it is only in learning to read and write the language that one may come to see how some of the lexical items, such as the pair *decide* and *decision* or *text* and *context*, are related.

Chomsky (1970) makes the point that the spelling patterns of English are better reflections of an underlying phonology than of the actual pronunciation of the words. As examples, he offers such words as *photographs, photographic, photography*. In the first, the stress falls on the first syllable; in the second, stress falls on the third syllable; while in the third, it falls on the second syllable. Correspondingly, vowel reduction operates by reducing the second vowel in the first two forms and by reducing the first and third vowels in the third form. Hence, the common morpheme is pronounced very differently in the three cases. But the very orderliness of the lexical spellings may be the consequence of the invention of writing; the attempt at economical transcription may make more orderly the relations between meaning-related words. This interpretation is sustained if we look closely over the words to which Chomsky's analysis applies. They tend to be the set of words that are borrowed or "learned," often containing Latin roots: *photograph, telegraph, illustrate, medicate*, and the like (cf. Whitaker, 1971). The orderliness holds much less well for the more common and less regular words from Old English, the vernacular: *tough, bough, cough, dough*, and so on. Only the more common, frequently used words seem to resist the ordering effects of the written language. Chomsky (1970, p. 17) notes that, "the sound system that corresponds to the orthography may itself be a late intellectual product" and may occur only in a literate culture. Here again, then, literacy appears to contribute to the formalization and regularization of language and to give language rules which are, as Derwing and Baker suggest, unknown to many speakers of the language. But for language users who have acquired those more sophisticated rules, I have no doubt that they are as generative and productive as the pluralization rules are for children.

REFERENCES

Austin, J. L. *How to do things with words.* Edited by J. O. Urmson. New York: Oxford University Press, 1962.

Berko, J. The child's learning of English morphology. *Word*, 1958, *14*, 150–177.

Brown, A. L. Development, schooling and the acquisition of knowledge about knowledge. In R. Anderson, W. Montague, and R. Spiro (Eds.), *Schooling and the acquisition of knowledge.* Hillsdale, N. J.: Erlbaum, in press.

Chomsky, N. 1964, cited by Derwing (this volume).

Chomsky, N. *Problems of knowledge and freedom.* London: Fontana/Collins, 1972.

Chomsky, N. Phonology and reading. In H. Levin and J. Williams (Eds.), *Basic studies on reading.* New York: Basic Books, 1970.

Gellner, E. The savage and modern mind. In R. Horton and R. Finnegan (Eds.), *Modes of thought.* London: Faber and Faber, 1973.

Goodnow, J. The nature of intelligent behavior: Questions raised by cross-cultural studies. In L. Resnick (Ed.), *New approaches to intelligence.* Potomac, Md.: Erlbaum, 1976.

Grice, H. P. Logic and conversation. In P. Cole and J. L. Morgan (Eds.), *Syntax and semantics: Speech acts.* Vol. 3. New York: Academic Press, 1975.

Halliday, M. A. K. Language structure and language function. In J. Lyons (Ed.), *New horizons in linguistics.* Toronto: Penguin Books, 1970.

Hockett, C. *The state of the art.* The Hague: Mouton, 1968.

Olson, D. R. From utterance to text: The bias of language in speech and writing. *Harvard Educational Review,* in press.

Whitaker, H. Neurolinguistics. In W. D. Dingwell (Ed.), *A survey of linguistic science.* College Park: Linguistics Program, University of Maryland, 1971.

8

The Conceptual Basis for Naming

KATHERINE NELSON

Yale University

How are the concepts of the child related to the words of the language? This is the central question to be addressed in this paper, and it involves defining the relation of the conceptualizing process to the learning of language as a continuously interactive and organized system. It will be seen that many mistaken conclusions about the cognitive and linguistic sources of meaning and of errors of meaning in the child's use of language derive from a misspecification of this problem. Although it is understood that the linguistic side of the problem (that is, the semantic or lexical systems) can be described in terms of rules, the present problem is *not* one of describing such rules nor of describing the course taken by the child in learning such rules. Rather it is an exploration of *the development of the child's conceptual system* which is assumed to underly the linguistic system and to determine in large part the limits on understanding that system at any given point.

To approach this problem therefore we need to go beyond the child's words to the conceptual layer underneath. In a previous paper (Nelson, 1974a), I suggested that we could describe the child's concepts in terms of

Preparation of this paper was generously supported by a grant from the Carnegie Corporation of New York.

three parts: a functional core which expresses all of the essential, specific definitional relations of the thing or event in time and space; optional or possible—but not necessary—general, spatio-temporal relations of the thing as the child has previously experienced them; and a set of identificational features which describe how one recognizes that a newly encountered thing or event falls under a previously formed concept. The functional core of the concept in these terms organizes what is centrally important or useful to the individual about that thing based on his/her experience with it. It is for this reason that it is a *functional* core; that is, what relates the object to the individual is not its perceptual features but its place in his/her life experience. It is for this reason also that the functional core varies from individual to individual, and may particularly vary from adult to child and from child to child. For example, the concept of clock may be quite different for the young child— involving principally noises, people, and locations—and the adult, for whom the essential core function of clock is time-keeping. Yet both adult and child may identify the same instances of clock as *clock*. That is to say, both adult and child may have the same set of *identificational features* for the concept of clock, although the functional core of the concept is not the same.

In suggesting this concept structure, I have tried to suggest that the *process* of forming concepts normally begins with a functional core to which identificational features are added as soon as it becomes necessary to identify new members, and that this process is as true of adults as of young children. The primary developmental difference to be expected is that children must habitually generate and test more concepts than adults do because they have fewer available from prior experience. I will return to this point later. Here the point is simply that, although there is much to be discovered about the *concept-generating process* in infancy and early childhood—as well as in adulthood—evidence shows that the infant does in fact operate on the basis of concepts before s/he begins to apply names to them.

I want to develop two points based on this evidence that will provide the structure for the discussion to follow. First, we only get into trouble when we try to explain development in terms of the child learning the correct (standard, adult) way to do things: to say things, to conceive of things, or to categorize things. This kind of view unduly rigidifies adult modes at the same time that it denigrates more open and less developed systems. But more than that, it actually prevents us from seeing the child's system. If we take care to look at the child's system, however, we can see that the child does not make mistakes. The child's system may not match the adult system in various ways, but it is our job to determine what the nature of the system is, and how it develops, not to identify its "errors," which are errors only from a different systematic point of view. The first part of this paper is devoted to an exploration of this proposition in terms of the kinds of concepts the child operates with and their relations to the language s/he uses.

The second and more central point I want to consider is that the young child's efforts to make sense of the world through forming concepts and learning words are a first manifestation of a continuing process of stabilizing an inherently unstable experience in order to operate on it and make predictions about it.[1] The child—like the adult—cannot help trying to make sense of his experience; and learning and using language is but one manifestation of this process. So also are our ways of characterizing what the child is doing, as well as our ways of analyzing language and thought into components. However, in this endeavor, because the tools of a closed and stable system are used to deal with an unstable and open system, we often find that the tools are inappropriate to the task. The second part of this paper will explore the implications of this view.

CONCEPTUAL TYPES: FORMATION, GENERALIZATION, AND REPRESENTATION

The basic *developmental* task is to elaborate the cognitive structure and to learn how to match it to the encountered linguistic structure. In other words the child's task is to *develop conceptions and acquire semantics to match*. Solving this problem involves the utilization of some quite general developmental principles, the most important of which involve stability and predictability, which in turn are related to the central role of context in both conceptualizing and using the language.

Consider first some typical concepts referring to objects named by young children who are first learning to talk; specifically, concepts of particulars, reduplicates, similars, and categories of similars. Most single terms referring to objects learned by young children can be assigned to one of these types. The typology describes a continuum from the individual case to identical things to unlike things which enter into hierarchical relations with higher-order concepts. Thus, each poses a somewhat different problem for the concept-generating child as well as for the theorist. In the course of this discussion, we will focus on two provocative problems in regard to conceptualizing: the basis for generalization, and the function of prototypes in concept structure. It will also become clear that many of the problems pre-

[1] This point has been made on a general level by both Cassirer (see Bolton, 1972) and Arnheim (1969). It is developed here for the important light it sheds on the function of concepts in the life of the child.

viously identified as conceptual errors of the child are in fact linguistic confusions or problems of the cognitive-linguistic matching process.

Particulars

The child's concepts of particularly valued individuals are obviously
related to the learning of proper names for them. It is interesting that Katz,
Baker, and Macnamara (1974) have recently demonstrated that even at 17
months many children distinguish linguistically between particular things
(dolls) that take proper names and classes of things (also dolls) that take
general names, when the only cue to this distinction is in the use or nonuse
of the indefinite article. Fodor (1971) pointed out that although both proper
names and general terms are rule-bound, proper names are not extendible
while general names are. By definition, therefore, proper names cannot be
only a special case of general names and the referent relation between word
and object cannot be explained on this basis.

It is important to recognize this point, but it does not bear on the notion
that a general *concept* can be extended from experience with a particular
object or event. Children do refer to particular objects by special names; for
example, *Fido* or *Mrs. Brown*, or even *blankie* for the child's favorite blanket.
Proper names are invented by adults (and are used by young children) to
designate especially valued particular exemplars of more general concepts[2]—
objects, people, animals, and so on for which recognizing individuality is
especially important. While proper names are understood to refer to only one
object and to be unextendible, a valued particular is at the same time a
member of a larger set that takes a general name. The general name is extendible to all the exemplars of the concept, but the particular name is not.
This linguistic convention is apparently easily understood by most young
children who appear readily to comprehend that some objects (people and
pets, for example) are so important in their individual selves that they take
special identifying names.

According to previous accounts, however, it would seem that not all
children are as discriminating in this respect as Katz *et al.*'s (1974) subjects.
For example, the common extension of the proper name *Daddy* to other men
is frequently referred to in the literature. In this connection, Piaget (1962,
p. 255) cites Lucienne at 3 years, 2 months, as follows (L's part of the dialog
in italics): "We passed a man: *Is that man a daddy?—*What is a daddy?—*It's

---

[2] The terms *Fido* or *Mrs. Brown* actually are also specified by an internal representation as is
evident in the fact that they can be named when either no longer exists in actuality (cf. Searle,
1970). This is a somewhat different case from those that we want to call concepts, however,
simply because it does lack generality.

a man. He has lots of Luciennes and lots of Jacquelines.—What are Luciennes?—
They're little girls and Jacquelines are big girls." Piaget cites this passage as
evidence for his theory that young children are incapable of achieving either
true generality or true individuality in their concepts. In the same connection,
he cites the following interchange with Jacqueline, also at 3 years, 2 months,
when she "could not understand that Lausanne was all the houses together
because for her it was her grandmother's house 'Le Cret' that was 'the
Lausanne house!'" After giving her this explanation, Piaget asks her: "What
is Lausanne?—*It's all these houses* (pointing to all the houses round). *All these
houses are Le Cret.*—What's Le Cret?—*It's granny's house, it's Lausanne*" (pp.
225–226). Piaget argues that this illustrates that for the young child a single
object becomes the representative or prototype for the whole concept, whereas
in a true concept all members are equivalent through their common abstract
characteristics. Let us set aside the conceptual problems posed by Piaget's
faulty definition of *Lausanne* as "all these houses" or the linguistic problems
posed by detaching the modifier *Lausanne* from house and giving it an independent status, and examine these examples for what they can tell us about
the relation of particulars to general concepts.

It is obvious in the first example that Lucienne has a concept of daddy, of
Jacqueline, and of Lucienne (herself) that can be extended—at least in
part—to other examples. Actually, it would be more accurate to say that she
has a concept of "big girl" that includes as one of its names (probably the
most important one) the name *Jacqueline*, while *Jacqueline* has its own representation, an individual one, which is in turn one instance of "big girl."
Probably the concept of "big girl" was formed around episodes involving
Jacqueline the person (as the concepts of man and little girls involved Lucienne
and Daddy). Once the concept was formed on the basis of experience with a
particular, it could be extended easily to include other instances that met its
defining rules. Thus the example tells us that a general concept may be
centered on (and perhaps derived from) a single exemplar. Lucienne's problem, however, was not confusing Jacqueline as an individual with the general
concept (note that she was able to state the conceptual relation adequately),
but only substituting the proper name for the general term. It was a linguistic
error, not a conceptual one, and one that Katz *et al.'s* much younger children
did not apparently make, or at least not frequently, and not in comprehension.

What about the Lausanne example? Behind the truly massive linguistic
confusion here (J. has two names for her grandmother's house, one of which
uses the town name as a modifier, but she has no independent name for the
town itself), there seems to be a question as to whether J. has a concept of
town at all. If she believes that Piaget is truly referring to "all these houses"
as Lausanne, then she is not incorrect in believing that he is defining some
new subclass of houses of which Le Cret is a prime example or prototype, one

that can be referred to as either *Lausanne* or *Le Cret*, or even *granny's house*. In this case, we have another example of the formation of a concept on the basis of a particular example, and its extension to others of its kind, that is, to those houses located in Lausanne. This seems a more plausible explanation than Piaget's, which claims that "all these houses . . . thus constituted a complex object depending upon one of its elements which was seen as representing the whole." The example is unfortunately too confused and complex to disentangle with certainty, however.

What I am suggesting here is that particulars have no special status in the child's conceptual system equivalent to their special status in the linguistic system. On the contrary, a concept can be formed and probably usually is (Rescorla, 1976) on the basis of one exemplar; but the child does not assume thereby that it is unique. Rather, his usual practice seems to be to form a potential category that can include new but like instances. In fact, on the conceptual level, there is some question whether the infant either knows or cares whether he is interacting with the same individual thing from one time to another during the period when he first begins to name things. I have several times had the experience of asking a 15-month-old child to find a ball that we had been playing with, which had rolled out of sight temporarily, only to have him go to his own toy box and get a completely different ball. This indicated that the particular individual object had no special status with respect either to its name (*ball*) or its conceptual definition (playing, rolling, etc.).

This is not to say that some particulars (such as mother and daddy) are not important to the child; in fact, their clear existence for the child demonstrates the establishment of concepts of permanent objects much earlier than claimed by Piaget. Nevertheless, they are not different in kind from members of general categories of objects—either reduplicates or similars as described below. One type of concept usually derives from the other and both can serve as the impetus for concept formation and for naming. The child does not need to know therefore that a particular object is going to reappear tomorrow or that it will continue to exist, because the child does not name particular objects but exemplars of concepts. On the other hand, to give a proper, individual name to something does imply belief in both its individual importance and its continued existence. Thus the relation of naming to the establishment of the permanent object concept in Piaget's terms becomes clear: Individual names do require this concept; general object terms do not.

We must not confuse the conceptual issue with the linguistic one, however; proper names are not generalizable, while general terms are. But the existence of a proper name does *not* mean that its referent is the only instance of a concept, only that as an individual it is important enough to have a name of its own.

REDUPLICATES

The suggestion that the infant may not have a firm sense of the individual identity of many things leads to a consideration of the place of what I call "reduplicates" in the infant's first concepts. Some collections of things, or serially experienced instances of categories are less individually identifiable than others. A salient example is sheets of typing paper, but of course snowflakes, acorns, paper clips, yellow lead pencils, and spoons, all fall into this category. When we consider the natural ecology of the child's world, it is striking how many of the things he must contact are of this kind; diapers and bottles, for prime examples, and of course many foods, including apples, bananas, toast, endless jars of applesauce and chopped liver. One is as good (or as bad) as the next. Another one of Piaget's favorite examples of the confusion of individuality and generality is relevant to this point. In this example, Jacqueline at 2 years, 6 months, "used the term '*the slug*' for the slugs we went to see every morning along a certain road. At 2:7 (2) she cried: '*There it is!*' on seeing one, and when we saw another ten yards further on she said: '*There's the slug again.*' I answered: 'But isn't it another one?' J. then went back to see the first one. 'Is it the same one?—*Yes*—Another slug?—*Yes*—Another or the same?—. . .' The question obviously had no meaning for J." (Piaget, 1962, p. 225)

Here again we see some real linguistic confusions, including the use of the definite *it* and *the* for a newly encountered example of the class. And Piaget obviously was confusing several issues when he insisted on knowing whether it was the same or another one, issues about the child's understanding of the terms *same* or *different* which are only now being disentangled by experimental investigators (e.g., Webb, Oliveri, & O'Keefe, 1974). But the individuality of slugs, like pieces of paper, acorns, and diapers, is not of interest. One slug is as good as the next. It seems unlikely that Jacqueline is genuinely confused as to whether there is one or more than one slug, or whether one keeps reappearing in different places; rather it is a question of indifference to her since she is not concerned about the identity of any particular slug. She has something to learn about appropriate linguistic usage, but it does not seem proper to view this as a case of conceptual insufficiency—but rather as an example of one special kind of concept, one that does not recognize differences among its individual instances. In these cases—and they are common in the child's concepts, as in his world, no doubt—extension of the name to new exemplars may take place on the basis of perceptual generalization or confusability. The frequency of such cases may predispose the child to expect that things come in many copies, that events will be repeated, and to extend his concepts—and names—to new instances without special training or tuition.

The discussion thus far has shown the basis for the establishment of prototypes in the child's concepts of valued particulars, and for generalization in
the child's concepts of confusable reduplicates.

Similars

At the next level, that of similars, we come up against those classically
messy cases of dogs, dolls, cars, and cookies named by the child early in the
game (Nelson, 1973). In these cases the correct meaning for the word takes
in a whole category of objects that do have identifiably different characteristics. In some cases the physical resemblances between members of a class
seem less obvious than their differences. For example, the Chihuahua and
the Doberman pinscher seem unlikely to fall into the same category from the
looks of them. Or take the VW microbus—is it a car? a bus? a truck? (Actually
of course it is all three, but then that just forecasts the conclusion that our
natural language categories are not hard and fast logical classes but classes
with fuzzy boundaries; cf. Labov, 1972.) A great deal has been written about
the way children first form and extend word categories of this kind, but we
still lack good systematic studies.[3]

This brings us strongly up against the question that has puzzled so many
people: How does the child form a concept of such diverse classes and how
does he extend it to new members? It is at this point that we need to invoke
a *grouping principle*, and the principle that I have suggested (one that is consonant with Piagetian theory of sensorimotor development) is that of function:
what things do or what can be done with them. This is a very general use of
the term function (culturally defined function is a special case of it), but it is
needed to cover both action and all other spontaneous reactive changes in
state, which are so salient to the young child, as well as the known relations
of things to self and others. Use of this grouping principle can be expressed in
the following aphorism: "Categories are formed on the basis of function and
generalized on the basis of form." Obviously, generalization principles are
needed to identify new members of the category; but they are different from
the grouping principles themselves. They are the source of many of the
"errors" in the young child's early naming. When the process is viewed in
this way, it is obvious that some naming errors may be errors from the child's
point of view as well as the adult's (that is, what he called a ball turns out
not to be one), while others may reflect a true difference in concept definition.

---

[3] I am indebted in the discussion that follows to Leslie Rescorla for sharing her data and some
of her conclusions from her dissertation research, Rescorla, 1976 which is an attempt to fill this gap.

In concentrating on so-called errors of generalization, however, some important points have been underemphasized. First, children do very readily extend words learned on the basis of a particular object to new instances of identifiably different but functionally similar objects as well as to perceptually similar objects. This is a strong indication that the child is not operating on the hypothesis that words apply basically to particulars or to things that are indistinguishable from one another, but on a more general principle that words apply to categories of things that, though discriminably different, have something centrally important in common. What I am suggesting here is that children do not make mistakes of generalization but mistakes, when they are made, of category recognition. What these "mistakes" can tell us, then, is not usually what the nature of the child's underlying concepts is, but what his identification rules are, because they occur when the child says, in effect, "Oh, there's another X." In looking at instances of conceptual inclusion, therefore, we need to distinguish carefully between those based on recognition and those based on classification. The child may think he has recognized something but change his mind when he finds that it does not behave as that class of things should (Nelson, 1973, 1974a). When the child's concept is formed on the basis of functional relationships then an error of recognition may occur even when his functional concept is equivalent to the adult's for that word; and many "errors" of word use may occur before the child has had a chance to build up an adequate set of identifiers.

A related point that tends to be overlooked is that young children are often surprisingly adept at differentiating closely related categories, when they are interested in doing so. A number of children at 2 years have a differentiated category of vehicles, for example, that rivals that of people many years their senior, being able to distinguish steamshovels from earth-movers and derricks, for example, whether as real, toy, or pictorial instances. The rudiments of this facility can be seen often at the very beginning of naming. It is a common pattern for a child to learn several closely related words in a general category within a short period of time, for example, car, truck, and bus; or cake, cookie, and candy; or dog, cat, and puppy (all examples taken from my own data; Nelson, 1973). Furthermore, Rescorla (1976) has pointed out that in many cases the child learns to comprehend a large number of differentiated terms while he is still using a single term in production. For example, one child in her study used car for a wide range of vehicles, including motorcycle, bike, truck, plane, and helicopter. She was, however, able to pick out each of these correctly in response to their appropriate names. Relying on her productive use of the words, one would conclude that she lacked conceptual differentiation, while testing her comprehension reveals that such differentiation is available.

There are other cases where as adults we use a word analogically or extend it to types not previously included in the category, or to instances of which we are unsure. Often, language as an open creative system not only allows but encourages this. Undoubtedly, the young child learning language, who knows few terms, does more of this. For example, one child in Rescorla's sample extended his term for clock to include a medallion on the dishwasher, while another used the same term for dripping water which sounded like "tick-tock." We can imagine a fuller specification of what the child was saying as "It looks like clock" or "It sounds like clock." These analogical extensions were an addition to the more common categorical extension of the word to include watches, meters, and timers. This kind of intentional generalization often seems to follow a period when the word is used more narrowly and categorically (cf. Bloom, 1973). This is an early linguistic example of a quite general developmental sequence involving flexibility of application following a period of rigid rule-boundedness (cf. Nelson & Nelson, in press).

In addition to analogical and categorical generalization, there are other generalization "errors," for example, those based on affective principles (Lewis, 1951), where the child seems to extend a term on the basis of his emotional reactions rather than on any objective quality of the object or experience. These have been documented by many observers and some children seem to be more disposed to them than others. Such reports are often difficult to interpret with assurance, but that is not important. After all, adults do extend words metaphorically and on the basis of affective and aesthetic considerations; these uses cannot simply be expunged from the language and they are surely important to the young child. Many of the idiosyncratic expressions of children seem to be related particularly to emotional states. This area is wide open to further investigation, despite the difficulties of interpretation.

Another kind of "error" more likely to lie in the interpretation than in the child is evidenced in cases where the child did not mean to name an object at all, but for some reason used a word in a situation that made its use look like an instance of inappropriate generalization. When a child, just beginning to talk, speaks only in single words and often practices speaking without the intention to communicate, such instances are probably not infrequent. Rescorla found many of these cases which she termed predicate overextensions in her study; for example, a child who pointed to Daddy's shoe in the closet and said *Daddy*. While the possessive relation seems clear in this case, many other cases are ambiguous and may be termed overgeneralizations inappropriately. I know of no way to guard against such cases, but we should be wary of calling them generalization errors.

Thus we can conclude that while children do make what adults view as mistakes of overgeneralization, these mistakes are probably based on valid underlying general principles of conceptualization, and it is the conceptualization skills themselves that are the most important thing to recognize, if we are to understand the general process of naming.

Superordinates

Having considered some of the problems of generalization that emerge from the process of learning names for first object concepts, let us turn to the complexities of combining such concepts into natural language categories, such as food, animals, vehicles, clothes, or furniture. The process involved is to be distinguished from that of extending a single concept term to new exemplars of the type just discussed. It is rather the process of combining two or more concepts into a superordinate category *without sacrificing the identity of the original concepts.* I have already noted that many of the early vocabularies of young children exhibit several representatives from one of these adult categories. Does that indicate that there is any categorical cohesiveness of hierarchical structure as far as the child is concerned? The early productive use of a single term such as *car* for several classes that are differentiated in comprehension, as discussed above, appears to indicate an early awareness of what we would call a vehicle category. However, few children learn or use superordinate terms at the outset. While Roger Brown (1958) pointed out long ago that parents tend not to use superordinates in talking to children, there are exceptions as in the use of *toys*; and one child in Rescorla's study learned *fruit* as a general term for nectarines, applesauce, and pears.

There is also a good bit of fragmented evidence that even quite young children know and utilize some of the relationships among words, things, and categories. For example, when called upon to remember two objects, 2- and 3-year-olds will remember them better if they are from the same category (animals, utensils, or vehicles) than if they are from different categories (Goldberg, Perlmutter, & Myers, 1974). Similarly, Faulkender, Wright, and Waldron (1974) found that, for 2-year-olds, habituation was faster for category members than for novel items. Moreover, Nancy Katz (preliminary report) reports on the basis of a series of experiments that children of 30 months understand some superordinate terms (e.g., *toy* and *animal*) and are able to categorize objects correctly into these classes, but (consistent with Piaget's observations) they appear to have difficulty coordinating subordinate and superordinate terms.

Unfortunately, most of our present knowledge of hierarchical categorization and its utilization comes from much older children. Both Piaget (Inhelder & Piaget, 1964) and Vygotsky (1962), for example, have emphasized the classification errors of the preoperational or preschool child, and there is, as a result, relatively little work with preschoolers that is concerned with finding what their underlying principles of categorization might be if they are shown to exist. Like the other problems we have considered, however, it seems probable that here the noted deficiencies are more linguistic than conceptual and that even very young children do form rudimentary superordinate categories but do not ordinarily apply special names to them. Certainly by the age of 5, children are able to enumerate many appropriate instances of natural language categories (Nelson, 1974b), and attribute class properties to new members (Harris, 1975).

CONCEPTS AND THEIR REPRESENTATION

One of the things revealed by this consideration of the child's concepts of objects and their associated names is that, although s/he is not particularly sensitive to the distinction between one and many, s/he attempts to impose a stable representation on experience, in effect creating "oneness" out of "manyness." Applying names to things is only one manifestation of this disposition to stabilize and make unitary the variability and continuity of experience. As we have seen, however, the infant's attempt to deal with both individual concepts and linguistic terms at the same time often leads to cognitive–linguistic confusions. In turn, our analytical attempts to describe the two systems may also lead to related confusions, because the ever-continuing effort to stabilize experience that is reflected in the infant's disposition to establish "oneness," is also reflected in the theorist's disposition to establish analytical entities. Let us consider some manifestations of this more sophisticated effort to deal with conceptual variability by applying stabilizing representations to it. As a prime example, consider the persistent notion that the concept can be identified with the object or event from which it derives, that is, the still vivid "Helen Keller insight" that "everthing has a name." Few people now hold this view in its simple form, but it has an extraordinary attraction that cannot be brushed aside. It is the prime example of the reification of words.

Currently more attractive and widespread is the notion that a concept is a set of features or attributes. The notion of semantic features, like the notion of conceptual attributes, has some useful validity. By breaking meaning down into dimensions and components we can reveal something about relations *between* concepts or word meanings. However, we are misled if we believe that the components that we use to stabilize our understanding of certain distinctions actually describe the concept that underlies the word. The child's conceptual problem is to put together the important parts of the ongoing experience into a single representation or concept and only then to find the identifying features that will serve to differentiate among instances of related concepts. It is the analyst who imposes the stabilizing notion of components onto the child's stabilizing concepts; both moves are efforts in the same functional direction.

The notion that a concept may be an image reflects a different approach, but one that again confuses representation with what is represented. The conviction is widespread and growing that children depend more on images than on words in storing their concepts. However, the relation of images to concepts is far from certain, and again, the most probable function of the image is to serve as a stable representation in connection with a concept, functioning at the level of the word, but not equivalent to the concept itself.

The fact is that each of these proposals regarding what a concept *is*—objects, images, sets of features, words—imposes the notion of a static and discrete representation upon a variable continuum of experience with vague boundaries. It is worth considering the proposition that concepts lie somewhere in the middle: less continuous than experience, less discrete than objects. A recent proposal more consonant with this view is that concepts are derived from episodes. It is obvious that much of what is remembered about things is specific to how they were experienced in the past. For example, Schank (1974) has presented a number of examples of conceptual meaning based on the child's first and most salient experiences with the event, as revealed by the spontaneous word associations of a child of about $1\frac{1}{2}$ years. One of his examples, including his gloss of her meaning, goes as follows (Schank, 1974, p. 11):

Situation . . .:   Question: Hana, what do you do if your hands are cold?
Response: Glove
            boots (When she wears gloves she usually wears boots)
            snow (the first time she wore her boots, she went to the snow)
            crunch (the snow went crunch under her feet)
            whee (she went on a sled and I said "whee")

Schank concludes from his material that the "episodes made up of sequences of actions seem to be the crucial organizing factor in Hana's memory" (p. 12). Further, children's concepts are strongly identified with their first occurrence in memory and such memory is "grouped contextually."

This and other examples clearly indicate that the child remembers previously related episodes and has stored the information extracted from these with the word so that it is available when the word is used again or when she experiences glove or boot again. It must be noted, however, that because she talks about these things does not tell us that this particular episodic stuff *is* the concept. She does not, for example, talk about what boots look like, although she is able to recognize them when she sees them. Personal episodic experience is important to the formation of concepts, but without some further conceptual organization, it will remain simply a disconnected particular episode without general meaning. It is, however, important to note that episodic information is extracted, and while such information does not constitute the whole concept, it is included in it.

CONCEPTUALIZATION AS A PROCESS

Thus far it has been suggested that the child succeeds in selecting and stabilizing experiences of different types, using several different mechanisms, and also that we impose another layer of selection and stabilization in describing the resulting concepts. Let us abandon—at least temporarily—the quest for a specification of the form of concepts and consider them as an outcome of the conceptualizing *process*. It can be observed then that conceptualization itself has two outcomes. First, as already stressed, it stabilizes transiently experienced events and, as a result, thought about objects and events becomes possible. What does learning linguistic terms for one's conceptualization add to this? It increases conceptual stability (because of the relatively stable cross-situational use of words) and it also makes communications about one's concepts possible. It increases the *predictability* of experience associated with these events only indirectly, however; for example, the child can react to the word *dog* by activating his expectations about dogs just as he might if he saw a dog. (The child has to learn, of course, which expectations are relevant to words rather than actual events. For example, at the outset, the child reacts to *daddy* or *dog* in a way that indicates he expects daddy or dog to appear. He has to learn that the word does not always implicate an immediate instantiation of the concept.)

Conceptualizing is work and takes time, and the greater the number of situations that can be predicted on the basis of past conceptualizations and their expectations, the less current conceptualizing becomes necessary. Both stability and predictability are assets in dealing with the world. Stable and established expectations are in fact general characteristics of cognition and increase with cognitive development. The child gradually builds up an experiential base of knowledge that increasingly frees him from the necessity of constantly processing new information about novel encounters and from the necessity of forming new concepts. He can increasingly predict what is likely to happen on the basis of his present concepts and he becomes thereby freer to act and to think in a given situation rather than to engage in costly information processing.

For the adult, events are highly predictable in most situations. We look for the deviant event, not to form a new concept or category, but as a cognitive challenge in fitting it into our present conceptual structures. In contrast, the young child, faced with a world where nearly everything is unfamiliar, must concentrate on those aspects that seem most important, and must try to order them in some way so that the next time they are encountered they will be familiar and therefore predictable.

But there is another side to this process: Concepts must remain open and changeable as new experiences with novel instances are encountered. It is not enough to categorize an animal as a dog, because each new dog is different. Each new experience that is not fully predicted must be able to modify one's concept to some extent: It adds a variation to the set of possible identifying features, or it adds a new relation to the set of probable relationships. Thus, to stability must be added flexibility and modifiability. Not only that, but we must be able to differentiate and recombine old concepts in order to form new concepts on the basis of old ones, as well as on the basis of new experience. Conceptualizing is a process that never stops, and although it may result in structures that are stable enough to be manipulated, the process itself is a fluid one.

Development of Word–Concept Relations

Previously, we saw that, although they did not always match, the child's concepts were similar to the meaning of linguistic terms. Now, however, it is clear that the conceptual characteristics just sketched—that is, flexibility and modifiability—are unlike those of linguistic concepts, that is, word meanings. Although words can be combined to form new conceptualizations and new terms invented, word meanings themselves change only slowly over generations compared to the rapid and continually shifting changes that are possible for the individual's concepts, and indeed are necessary throughout childhood. How then can the two systems of concepts and words be coordinated?

In order to deal with these questions, it is helpful to introduce a distinction made by Katz (1972) between narrow and broad semantic concepts. Broad concepts, according to Katz, include not only definitive information but incidental information, while narrow concepts include only the definitional. He gives as an example the concept of Martian, which as a narrow concept means a sentient creature inhabiting the planet Mars. As a broad concept, however, it may include information such as green with long antennae, travels in flying saucers.

Now it is obvious that in talking about how to characterize *cognitive* concepts we have throughout been considering broad concepts, that is, concepts that have organized *all* of the information that one has experienced and filed away in regard to people, things, events, or properties. Some of this information is more crucial in the sense of predicting new cases than others. We noted that some perceptual features, for example, help to identify new instances of the concept (if Martians really *were* green with long antennae, these would rightly be included as identifying features; instead they are simply incidental information). But at the core of any individual concept is an essential functional meaning which can be used to test concept membership; for example, "If it's a ball it will roll and bounce." If the test is violated, we know that, however much the thing *looks* like our prototype of the concept, it is not one of them.[4] Like the child naming dogs, however, we can also make mistakes in recognition. If we think we have an anteater, but it eats grass instead of ants, we may conclude that we were mistaken and inquire as to its true identity. We will not conclude that we actually have a different kind of anteater, because the conceptual test of an anteater is that it eats ants. We may of course imagine that since it looks so much like an anteater it must be a close relative of the anteater, but we do not insist that its outward appearance is defining. That is, we rarely rely on the maxim "clothes make the man" but rather on "handsome is as handsome does."

When a word is attached to a concept, the core meaning is presumably what ultimately defines the word for the individual, and it is therefore the individual equivalent of the narrow linguistic concept, that is, the stable linguistic or socially agreed upon definition. However, the core meaning of the concept to which the word is attached for any given individual may or may not match in any or all respects the narrow linguistic concept or word definition. Moreover, as we have noted, the individual's concept—in contrast to the word meaning or narrow linguistic concept—is less stable in the sense that it may change over time and in different contexts. An individual's concept can be reorganized at the core, can be differentiated, merged into a higher-order concept, and so on. These changes may take place both in the direction of the linguistically accepted definition and away from it.

To recapitulate, we have two levels of conceptual organization, one social and linguistic, the other personal and cognitive. There are, in addition, two layers of concepts at each level—one stable and defining, the other flexible and inclusive. To learn the meaning of a word, the child must eventually match his own core concept meaning to the narrow linguistic concept. If these do not match, the word may be used inappropriately. Obviously, there are many opportunities for partial matching as well as overspecification, and these misspecifications are likely to derive from what the child has considered important and defining in his prior experiences with concept instances.

However, there is some evidence that for the young child the word implies the whole concept, not only its central core. This means that the child attaches

----

[4] This is not to deny the interdependence of form and function characteristics (Labov, 1972). Rather, it is to assert that function takes precedence both ontogenetically (we remember what things look like *because* of what they do) and definitionally (the crucial test tends to be the functional one).

a lot of excess baggage to the meaning of words, even when his core concept and his identificational features match those of the adult's. Saltz (1971) provides an example from his work with considerably older children—during the early school years—who appear to have a broad concept of daddy attached to the term *daddy*, such that daddies must be good. A daddy cannot therefore be a robber, and children will vociferously deny the possibility that daddies can be robbers. Very early, the child must be able to detach the core concept from its prior relations in order to consider it in new relations and thus to understand and produce novel sentences, for example (see Nelson, 1974a). However, it appears that for the young child these relations must not contradict previously established ones. Thus, the child may be able to conceptualize and talk about daddy building a house or climbing a mountain or flying to Mars, although he has not previously experienced any of these, but he will not admit to daddy robbing a bank because that is in conflict with the prior established relation that daddy is good. That is, although the core concept may enter into new relations, it cannot enter into relations that conflict with any prior information already included in the inclusive concept, which is, roughly, everything I know about X.

For quite a long time the child may attach the word to all of the expectancies in the inclusive concept (that is the concept that organizes all of the information the child has about that object or event). This is apparent in the kinds of definitions young children give as well as in their word associations. For example, the following definitions (from Krauss, 1972) appear not to refer to what the essential meaning of the term is for the child, but to something about its associated expectations.

> "Dogs are to kiss people."
> "A party is to say how-do-you-do and shake hands."
> "Buttons are to keep people warm."
> "Dishes are to do."
> "A watch is to hear it tick."

In a similar way, the word associations of young children, unlike those of older children, reflect the functions and perceptual attributes of the stimulus word as well as idiosyncratic contextual association. Thus the word seems to activate intraconceptual relations of a wide-ranging (noncore) variety. Later, the word appears to activate interconceptual relations such as coordinates and contrasts (Hall & Halperin, 1972; Nelson, 1977; Riegel, 1970).

In order to conceptualize freely and use the language appropriately and creatively, however, the core concept must become identified with the narrow linguistic concept and the inclusive concept must retain its predictive function while at the same time giving up its validating function. The child must become able to think about bad daddies as well as good daddies. But if bad daddies are possible, does it follow that everything is? How can the child avoid the conceptual chaos implicit in the realization that any relation can be posited even if it conflicts with what is known? To deal with this problem the child must come to use words only in their narrow socially agreed-upon definition while at the same time he retains all of the experiential material in the broad concept. The broad concept, therefore, serves as a source of predictions about future experiences but not as a restrictor of acceptable relations. This is a move that takes place much later than the initial word–learning period examined here, however, and its dimensions remain to be explored. These very sketchy suggestions are only indications that there is a great deal yet to be learned about the relation between conceptualizing and naming by the young child long after the period of first word learning.

CONCLUSION

This paper has attempted to show that the young child engages in a general conceptualizing process forming different kinds of concepts (such as particulars, reduplicates, similars) all of which involve similar operations designed to stabilize transient experience and to provide a basis for prediction about future events. To understand the acquisition of linguistic terms and their meanings we must understand the conceptual development process and how it interacts with language learning. Prototypes, images, and words can all be viewed functionally as part of the individual's attempt to make stable and discrete an inherently transient and continuous experience. It is suggested that while conceptualizing serves to order experience, the conceptual product is inherently less stable and discrete than language itself or the representations and systematic descriptions we apply to it. The young child's conceptualizations, because they are less differentiated by context, and because they must be more open to new experience, are in turn less stable than the adult's. New analytic tools—less rigid than those currently used for semantic analysis—are needed if we are to understand the continuously interacting systems involved in this development and to ultimately answer the question asked at the outset of this paper.

ACKNOWLEDGMENTS

I would like to thank William Kessen for insightful comments on previous drafts; and for their helpful comments and reactions, I would like to thank the participants of the Conference on Language Learning and Thought in Infants (McGill University, May 1975).

REFERENCES

Arnheim, R. *Visual thinking*. London: Faber & Faber, 1969.

Bloom, L. *One word at a time*. The Hague: Mouton, 1973.

Bolton, N. *The psychology of thinking*. London: Methuen, 1972.

Brown, R. How shall a thing be called? *Psychological Review*, 1958, *65*, 14–21.

Faulkender, P. J., Wright, J. C., & Waldron, A. Generalized habituation of concept stimuli in toddlers. *Child Development*, 1974, *45*, 1002–1010.

Fodor, J. A. The ontogenesis of the problem of reference: A review of some theories of linguistic symbols. In C. E. Reed (Ed.), *The learning of language*. New York: Appleton, 1971.

Goldberg, S., Perlmutter, M., & Myers, N. A. Recall of categorically related and unrelated lists by two-year-olds. *Journal of Experimental Psychology*, 1974, *18*, 1–8.

Hall, J. W., & Halperin, M. S. The development of memory-encoding processes in young children. *Developmental Psychology*, 1972, *6*, 181.

Harris, P. L. Inferences and semantic development. *Journal of Child Language*, 1975, *2*, 143–152.

Inhelder, B., & Piaget, J. *The early growth of logic in the child*. London: Routledge & Kegan Paul, 1964.

Katz, J. J. *Semantic theory*. New York: Harper & Row, 1972.

Katz, N. Superordinate naming and hierarchical classification of young children. Preliminary report, 1975.

Katz, N., Baker, E., & Macnamara, J. What's in a name? A study of how children learn common and proper names. *Child Development*, 1974, *45*, 469–473.

Krauss, R. *A hole is to dig*. New York: Harper & Row, 1952.

Labov, W. The boundaries of words and their meanings. Paper presented at the Conference on New Ways of Analyzing Variation in English, Washington, D.C., October, 1972.

Lewis, M. M. *Infant speech* (2nd ed.). London: Kegan Paul, 1951.

Nelson, K. Structure and strategy in learning to talk. *Monographs of the Society for Research in Child Development*, 1973, *38* (1–2, Serial No. 149).

Nelson, K. Concept, word and sentence: Interrelations in acquisition and development. *Psychological Review*, 1974, *81* (4), 267–285. (a)

Nelson, K. Variations in children's concepts by age and category. *Child Development*, 1974, *45*, 577–584. (b)

Nelson, K. The syntagmatic–paradigmatic shift revisited. *Psychological Bulletin*, 1977, *84*, 93–116.

Nelson, K., & Nelson, K. Cognitive pendulums and their linguistic realization. In K. E. Nelson (Ed.), *Children's language*. New York: Gardner Press, in press.

Piaget, J. *Play, dreams and imitation* (Translated by C. Gattegno and F. M. Hodgson). New York: Norton, 1962.

Riegel, K. F. The language acquisition process: A reinterpretation of related research findings. In L. R. Goulet and P. B. Baltes (Eds.), *Theory and research in life-span developmental psychology*. New York: Academic Press, 1970.

Rescorla, L. Concept formation in early word learning. Ph.D. dissertation, Yale University, 1976.

Saltz, E. *The cognitive basis of human learning*. Homewood, Ill.: Dorsey Press, 1971.

Schank, R. C. Is there a semantic memory? Unpublished manuscript. Instituto per gli Studi Semantici Cognitivi, Castognola, Suitz., 1974.

Searle, J. *Speech acts*. Cambridge: Cambridge University Press, 1969.

Vygotsky, L. *Thought and language* (Translated by E. Haufman and G. Vakar). Cambridge: M.I.T. Press, 1962.

Webb, R. A., Oliveri, M. E., & O'Keefe, L. Investigations of the meaning of "different" in the language of young children. *Child Development*, 1974, *45*, 984–991.

9

Concepts and Artificial Intelligence

SEYMOUR PAPERT

Massachusetts Institute of Technology

There are lots of things I would like to say about Katherine Nelson's paper, particularly about the fine detail of the observations, but I shall have to pass over them in favor of the central topic of the paper, concepts and their formation. Here it strikes me as curious and disappointing that Nelson does not advert to the whole enterprise that goes under the name of artificial intelligence, because it has been so involved with concepts. So perhaps I shall spend some time pointing out the links with artificial intelligence.

First I think that Nelson has placed her finger on the important issue in understanding linguistics and certainly the most important in the acquisition of language. Paradoxically, the tremendous development in technical and formal devices for representing language has not been accompanied by a corresponding growth in the devices for representing meanings. So there is a problem relating language to meaning. I would like to confine myself to the meaning end of that comparison and say something about what a concept is. In doing so, I find myself somewhat hesitant lest I should find myself committed to the "concept of concept." Nevertheless, I hope I can say something without having to deal with that issue.

What is a concept, then, and what can it be made of? Our attempts to answer this question will resemble discussions of what genes were 50 years ago. People could say a lot about genes, but they had very little idea of what they actually were. Today we know pretty well what genes are and we can define them in terms of DNA, which is probably very different from Mendel's idea of a gene. Our knowledge of concepts is like the earlier knowledge of genes. But I can enhance my knowledge by attempting to build a model of concepts and see what sort of formal entities we will require. In this context one of the questions that can be raised is: Do they have parts? Nelson tells us they do, and in particular that the parts form two major subdivisions. One of these defines the essence of the concept, the other corresponds to the features that we use to recognize an object that exemplifies the concept. Our experience is such that the distinction is impossible to maintain. One might be able to manage it with a concept like ball, but when one tries to carry it through to more complicated concepts, it does not work. Moreover, I think it gratuitous to identify the core concept with a set of functions. How in this account could a child form a concept of the moon?

I would like to illustrate a somewhat different approach with an example from an early program which was drawn up by Patrick Winston of M.I.T. One of the interesting aspects of his program was that it could learn to a limited extent, and in particular it could learn what an *arch* is. Because Winston was dealing with a computer, he could not be satisfied merely to list all the properties of an arch. As an aside, I get the impression that the features in Nelson's concepts are joined together by some sort of association. That would never do for a computer program. Let us see what Winston's program had.

Winston's machine lives in a world of blocks which will be familiar to those who have read Winograd's thesis. The machine would like to learn what an arch is, and it is being taught by being told that this is an arch and this is not. I will not go into detail, but it somehow recognizes that there are three parts or blocks in an arch, and for each it creates a node in its own internal representation system. In itself this is a very important primitive operation; it is very different, for example, from anything one finds in traditional logic. What the machine does not do is to take some data and combine them to make a new object. Instead it models the objects in the environment. In addition, the machine can say things about the objects that the nodes represent. It does this by attaching a pointer from the node to one of its concepts. In the example, it attached a pointer from each node to the concept block, and the pointer itself was labeled "is-a." This is a special relation which can be equated with class inclusion. In drawing these pointers, the machine was saying to itself, each of the objects is a block. But there is more to say, because it also recognizes relations among blocks and it sees that one of the blocks is supported by the other two. So it draws a line between the appropriate blocks and labels it "supports." Now it has a first approximation to a concept of an arch.

Winston then shows it a structure made from three blocks; in it, one block rests on the other two, but the other two are touching each other. He asks the machine, and it compares the design of this structure with its concept of arch and answers "yes." Then Winston says, "No, it's not an arch." The machine then thinks, and it thinks by comparing its design for the new structure with its design for the structure that was an arch. It notices that in the arch the support blocks do not touch, and so it enters another annotational link between the two supporting blocks which can be paraphrased by "must not touch." It can continue to modify the concept with annotational links to say certain things must be so, certain things may be so, certain things must not be so, and so on.

I think you will agree that all this is different from the inert list that Nelson is proposing as a concept. The machine is fitted with a set of procedures for building nodes which are then interrelated in the appropriate manner. It does not simply make a list of facts and leave it at that. Indeed, the concept of arch will be related to a number of other concepts in such a manner that the machine's entire conceptual system may come into play in constructing a new concept. This is an important point for which I do not see room in Nelson's account. For example, if a child sees an apple rolling, whether he calls it a ball or not is likely to depend on whether he already has a concept of an apple. So concepts interact in the use we make of them. If Nelson were woodenly to provide for this in her system, she would probably enter with each concept, say of an apple, "is not a ball," "is not an orange," etc., etc. This would, of course, be a rather bizarre way of doing it.

What has work like Winston's done for us, and how is it an advance on what has gone before? To answer this, I would like to draw an analogy with the history of linguistics, though I fear I do not know that history well. However, the way I see it is that the older grammarians, with a good deal of success, knew how to parse a sentence, how to divide it into its constituent noun phrases and verb phrases; and they knew about nouns and verbs and the other parts of speech. In more recent times, there has been a vast growth of additional machinery which increases the analytic and processing power of grammar. Today we have deep structures and surface structures and transformations and markers, and we can describe syntax in a manner that seems beyond the scope of traditional grammar.

What in "conceptology" corresponds to traditional grammar and what has been added? To my mind, what corresponds to the older grammar is logic, the predicate calculus, and such systems. The key addition to that is the idea of a general data structure which together with an "interpretor" program brings into play an enormous power of computation. The point is subtle, because there is a formal sense in which the information represented in Nelson's concept and Winston's is equivalent. They are equivalent from the point of view of the essential complexity of computation. This is a metric that compares difficulty of computation independent of the mechanisms with which one has to compute with. So functions computed on the basis of Nelson's and Winston's representations of concept may be equivalent from the standpoint of essential computability. This does not mean that they are equivalent for psychology. It seems to me that programs, working with other data structures represent information in a form which is much more flexible, and better organized for psychological purposes than Nelson does. I might add in passing that we in AI do not attempt nearly so clear a distinction between a recognitional part and a functional part of a concept.

A computational representation is not a definition as Nelson's is but an instrument to be employed in manipulating blocks. It carries none of the overtones of logical definitions. It does not replace the external object, it is not an abbreviation of the information in that object, it does not seek to eliminate inessential information. Quite literally, it is to be employed in manipulating objects in all their complexity in their complex environment. I think this a qualitative difference which advances our understanding of concepts. It is almost impossible to represent concepts, their development, and functioning by algebraic or logical formulas. One needs a more dynamic representation along the lines suggested by Artificial Intelligence.

10

Problems about Concepts

JOHN MACNAMARA

McGill University

There are a number of problems that a theory of concepts like that of Katherine Nelson must confront if it is not to founder. In this note I will draw attention to some of them. My mentioning a problem does not necessarily imply that I believe it fatal for Nelson's theory. It does mean that I think it is serious and has not been solved in Nelson's paper.

Psychology until very recently knew no approach to concepts which differs radically from Nelson's. All psychological theories assumed that concepts decompose into a set of attributes whose conjunction equals the concept. It is informative to note that modern logic affords a different model. When Tarski (1944) set about defining truth, he was obliged to distinguish between an object language, *for* which truth would be defined, and a metalanguage *in* which it would be defined. The problem of truth need not delay us here. Tarski's attempt is interesting in that the metalanguage subsumed all the terms of the object language. He did not find it necessary to replace each with a definition in the metalanguage. Let us consider English, for the present

These remarks are inspired by the discussion of Dr. Nelson's paper, particularly by Professor Fodor's formal discussion. However the form in which they are expressed is mine and I must accept responsibility for them.

purpose, as the object language, and the conceptual system of meaning as the metalanguage; the moral is, or might be, that the conceptual system need not replace each term with a definition or even description in terms of attributes. It might simply replace each term in English with a single conceptual symbol. This is broadly the position proposed in Fodor (1975) and Fodor, Fodor, and Garrett (1975).

In support of the analogy, there is the observation that few, if any, English terms can be eliminated by means of definitions. That is, if we attempt to define any English word, such as *bachelor*, in terms of a different set of English words, there is usually some uneliminated residual. Thus *bachelor* is not exactly equal to *unmarried, adult, man*. Such a definition comes close, but it does not take account of the fact that a widower is not a bachelor; or that it would be odd to refer to an adult male who was severely mentally handicapped as a bachelor. The set of such snags is not insignificant; and yet *bachelor* is one of the most likely candidates for definitional elimination in English.

What is the difficulty? Is it that there is at least one other attribute in the meaning of bachelor which cannot be captured by any definition? If that were the case, we could posit a meaning primitive which must be added to any definition of bachelor to make the combined primitive and definition equal in meaning to *bachelor*. The trouble is that the primitive would have to change with changes in the definition; and primitives seem contrary to the notion of such change. Another alternative is that the English words of the definition do not map accurately onto the terms of the underlying conceptual system. But that is merely the problem we are attempting to deal with, in a new guise. Presumably, the words of the definition do not map onto the terms of the conceptual system for precisely the reason that the one set cannot be defined in terms of the other without residuum.

If we could manage to get around those difficulties, we are likely to encounter another. Are definitions what we need? Traditionally, a definition is the minimum amount of information necessary to classify all and only the objects that fall under the particular concept. Elsewhere (Macnamara, 1971) I have argued that this is an example of misplaced parsimony; we need access from our words to all that we know about the world. Here we can content ourselves with noting that definitions are attempts to characterize at least those attributes that are necessary and sufficient for class membership. The notion of necessary attributes bristles with difficulties. For example, one would surely be inclined to claim four-leggedness as a necessary attribute of a horse. Yet we would not cease to classify an animal as a horse if one of its legs were amputated.

Moreover, some would say that we can have necessary attributes without definitions. In modal logic, necessary attributes are those which are true of members of a set in all possible worlds. Possible worlds are not without their problems; the point of mentioning them here is that they afford a different perspective on one problem implicit in Nelson's theory.

One of the attractive sides of a theory that decomposes concepts into sets of attributes is that it yields a straightforward explanation of similarity, or relatedness, in meaning. We can explain the overlap in meaning between *church* and *chapel* if we allow that they share many, but not all, attributes. Behind this account lurks a pitfall that is better illustrated than defined. Let us suppose that *bounce* is an element in the meaning of *ball*. But *ball* (in the sense of ballbearing) is an element in the meaning of *axle bearing*. Does it follow that *bounce* is an element in the meaning of *axle bearing*? In other words, is meaning transitive? This is a puzzle that has received little attention, and yet it seems implicit in the theory we are examining. Incidentally, it is just as much a puzzle for Winston's program, of which Professor Papert spoke, as it is for Nelson's theory.

Usually, the set of attributes into which a concept decomposes is an unstructured list. Nelson introduced some divisions but really no structure. A case can be made, however, that one important aspect of cognitive development is the building of structure among what might have begun as isolated observations. We can say more of a ball than that it bounces *and* it is for playing with, *and* it is round, and so on. We learn that it rolls *because* it is round; we can play certain games with a ball *because* it bounces. In other words, there are intelligible relations among attributes. So if attributes of real objects enter as elements in the corresponding meanings, there ought to be room for structure of quite a deep cognitive sort.

Implicit in Nelson's account of concepts (and in Papert's account of Winston) is the notion that, in cognition, reality is represented; and it is represented in a language that is abstract, or different in form from the sensory signal. That a ball is *for playing with* is not something given, as such, in the visual array. The theory of abstract representation leads inevitably to the position that in order to learn about the world and to grasp the meaning of one of the languages one encounters (English, for example), one needs to know another language already. To the extent that the abstract language of cognition is not given in experience but rather used to express experience, it must be available in order to make sense of experience. This is in principle what St. Augustine maintained in the opening pages of his *Confessions*. And this is what in principle Wittgenstein rejects in the opening pages of his *Philosophical Investigations*, for the reason that, to him, the claim seemed patently absurd (see Fodor, 1975.) In a nutshell, those who propose a theory of abstract representations are with Augustine; whether they know it or not, they have swallowed the notion of an innate language of thought. Note that the theory does not commit one to innate ideas, simply to an innate language in which ideas can be expressed.

It is sometimes thought that the language of concepts uses a small number of primitive terms, say a dozen or two. However, if we accept the view that few English terms can be eliminated by definitions, or even by lengthy discussions, it follows that nearly all English terms have in their meaning at least one primitive which is not expressed by any other English word or combination of words. At any rate, the number of primitives is unlikely to be small.

Nelson attempts to keep distinct a set of features that expresses function and a set that contains the perceptual characteristics for identifying members of the set. In note 5, she modifies her claim to: "function takes precedence both ontogenetically . . . and definitionally." She abandons the claim that the two types of features are independent. It would perhaps be wiser to abandon the distinction altogether and merely retain the fact that much of our knowledge of objects is not in the form of sensorially based stable characteristics but includes functions. Functions may just as easily play a part in identifying class members as stable perceptual characteristics.

There is, however, a deep-rooted problem associated with all theories that explain perception, and thus the identification of class members, by means of a set of attributes. As Nelson observes: How does the child know which similarities among objects are important, and which dissimilarities are? This is the problem with which Plato left us. Plato's own answer, innate concepts, is not a solution. Even if the child was born with a large set of concepts, he would still have the task of matching them with objects in the world. The problem has not lessened; its form has merely changed. By way of illustration, suppose an innate concept for dog did not include any element for color and that for *grey squirrel* contained the element *grey* with suitable descriptors. Then the child can know whether or not the greyness of a particular creature is a criterion only if he knows that it is a squirrel and not a dog. But how does he know that?

Presumably an answer with or, more conveniently, without innate ideas must be sought in the salience of attributes for children. All attributes are not equally attended to. This is precisely what computer simulators build into their programs. Winston's computer is given only tunnel vision so that it does not become "distracted" with objects in general but confines itself to the block world. Moreover, it is equipped with the programmer's guesses about perception in the form of an order of matters to attend to. Winston's computer did not attempt to explain why one structure was an arch and another was not by measuring the distances between the ceiling and the blocks or even between the walls and the blocks, but between the two supporting blocks. It did not seek a solution in the precise position of the structure or the precise surface of each block that was on the table. Winston wisely did not program it to do these and innumerable other things. And presumably nature does the same for us.

Any computer model of perception, and Nelson's model is not formally different from one, is a mechanistically determined one. The perceptual device is determined to "seek" for some set of sensorially given attributes and to decide whether or not they are present. One of the troubles with this is that when such a device is let loose in the real world, it seems to involve an infinite (or at any rate embarrassing) regress. We know cats from squirrels often by the ease with which the latter climb trees. But that presupposes a knowledge of trees and of climbing. We know trees because they stand on the ground and grow trunk, branches, and leaves; but that presupposes knowledge of ground, trunk, branches, and leaves. And so on. It is unlikely that we will ever find an adequate description of leaf in terms of line segments and angles which will suffice to determine whether an object is a leaf. There might always be a type of leaf which we had not encountered which did not meet the description and if evolution continues, we know that our description may have to be revised, unless the description in terms of line segments and angles is so general that it will not distinguish between leaves and many other things. The real trouble is that a leaf is a leaf as much by the function it serves and the place it grows as by any measurements. But the secret to such matters as functions is that they involve intelligible relations. There is no guarantee that these will turn out to be computable by any mechanism. The real source of our difficulty may be that we have neglected the warnings of those philosophers, notably Husserl, who claim that perception and all other functions of consciousness are not causally related to events in the external world. Again the topic is one that cannot be explored here, but we ought to be aware that some of the great minds of our time dispute the most basic assumptions implict in our models.

REFERENCES

Fodor, J. A. *The language of thought*. New York: Crowell, 1975.
Fodor, J. A., Fodor, J. D., & Garrett, M. The psychological un-reality of semantic representations. *Linguistic inquiry*, 1975, *6*, 515–531.
Macnamara, J. Parsimony and the lexicon. *Language*, 1971, *47*, 359–374.
Tarski, A. The semantic conception of truth. *Philosophy and Phenomenological Research*, 1944, *4*, 341–375.

11

Strategies and the
Mapping Problem in
First Language Acquisition

EVE V. CLARK

Stanford University

When the child starts to learn his first language, one of his main tasks is to find out how words and utterances should be mapped on to what he already knows. Slobin (1973) argued that the child has to master the necessary concepts before he can look for ways to express them with whatever language he has acquired. It is the child's cognitive, nonlinguistic, knowledge that provides him with his first hypotheses about what words might mean—what the mapping is between what he knows and the words that others use. In fact, by the end of his first year or so, the child has already amassed a great deal of knowledge about his surroundings. He can identify different objects, their properties, their usual orientation, and so on. He gathers his information through his perceptual system, taking in what he can see, hear, smell, taste, and manipulate as he matures (Clark, 1974a).

The child's knowledge about his surroundings appears to be organized in terms of general categories and relations, and what he knows about each.

The preparation of this paper, and the author's research reported herein, was supported in part by the National Science Foundation, Grant No. GS-30040. I would like to thank C. B. Farwell, P. L. Friedman, and D. B. Rosenblatt, for their assistance in carrying out some of the studies reported here.

The cognitive principles that the child applies in organizing his knowledge appear to provide the basis for his strategies of "interpretation" when his mapping of different words is still far from complete. Previous investigators have focused on the child's strategies for dealing with certain syntactic constructions. Bever (1970), for example, described several strategies for assigning the grammatical roles of Subject–Verb–Object to Noun–Verb–Noun sequences. Slobin (1973) looked at the typical "errors" children produce in a variety of different languages, and proposed a set of general strategies for the segmentation of utterances and for the identification of the semantic relations within utterances. Slobin, like Bever, focused mainly on the acquisition of syntactic structure. In the present paper, I would like to go one step further back, and examine some of the strategies applied in the initial mapping between words and the child's world. In doing this, I shall focus on the child's strategies for assigning meanings to words in the course of acquisition.

I will begin by considering how the child names category members in the early stages of the mapping process, both in terms of what he knows about particular objects and in terms of the communicative situation. Then I will look in turn at the mapping of dimensionality into language, the mapping of spatial relations into language, and lastly the mapping of deictic relations into language. In each case, I will outline what the child appears to know a priori, and then show how certain aspects of this knowledge are central to the strategies the child relies on as he works out the mapping for each new word.

WORDS AND CATEGORIES

Children begin to use their first words sometime between 12 and 18 months. Before this, they have spent a year actively taking in information about their surroundings. From early infancy on, children look at things: from toys and blankets in their cribs to people's faces outside. From 3 or 4 months on, their caretakers begin to show them things, letting them look and touch and mouth. Before long, they can reach for things themselves and gradually learn how to grasp whatever catches their attention. They attend to movement as well as shape from early on, and pay particular attention to things that move: people, animals, and vehicles. Soon children can recognize particular faces (and voices), as well as objects they are familiar with. They know their everyday routines of dressing, eating, and sleeping, and as they become more mobile, they steadily enlarge their horizons with crawling and then walking. By the age of 1 year, most children not only recognize many of the things around them, they also know how to manipulate them and sometimes how to use them.

This sketch of the child's knowledge at the point where he begins to use words to pick out different objects suggests that the child has both specific knowledge about certain objects (their shape, size, or texture; how they move, the noise they make, their function, etc.) and general knowledge about larger classes. For example, the child knows by now that there is an important class or group of entities that might be regarded as *movers* or *agents*. These things can move on their own and they also move other objects to new places. The typical members of this class are people, animals, and vehicles. Another class consists of *movable* entities: things that can be moved and manipulated, but which have to be acted on by a mover for anything to happen (e.g., toys, cookies, bottles). *Places* for things form another class: the places where things are usually kept, or which are associated with particular activities such as sleeping (crib), eating (table, high chair, kitchen), and playing (toy box, playpen). *Recipients* might form yet another class, but this one partially overlaps with the class of movers: Recipients are generally people the child can give or show things to. Lastly, the child may have identified some objects as *instruments*, things used to achieve particular goals: a chair to climb on so as to reach the tabletop, a spoon for eating cereal, and so on.

Each of these classes consists of objects clustered on the basis of similarity in shape, size, texture, or some combination of such properties. The child acquires specific knowledge about an object as well as the general knowledge that it is a *mover* or a *movable* in his world. Rosch (1975) suggested that there is a natural basis for setting up categories within such classes in the correlations of attributes that one finds. For example, creatures with feathers are more likely to have wings as well than are creatures with fur. For the same reason, it is more likely that one can sit on objects with the visual appearance of chairs than on objects with the visual appearance of cats. It seems only reasonable to suppose that such factors play an important role in the child's prelinguistic categorization of the world. In summary, the child has already organized his knowledge about his surroundings in quite a complicated way when he begins to work on the mapping between his conception of the world and his emerging language.

Diary studies of the acquisition of many different languages contain numerous observations of word use by very young children, and in particular, of their overextensions of words. For example, many children overextend a word like *ball* when they apply it to oranges and doorknobs as well as balls, or a word like *ticktock* when they apply it to all sorts of things besides clocks as long as the objects have a dial of some kind. Overextensions like these are extremely common in the speech of children between the ages of 1;0 and 2;6 (see Clark, 1973a, 1974a, 1975).

The commonest basis for an overextension appears to be some shared property of *shape*. Some typical examples of this are given in Table 11.1. Interestingly, shape also appears to be the primary basis for organization

TABLE 11.1

Some Overextensions Based Primarily on Shape

Lexical item	First referent	Domain of application[a]
mooi	moon	cakes, round marks on windows, writing on windows and in books, round shapes in books, tooling on leather book covers, round postmarks, letter *O*
nénin	breast, food	button on garment, point of bare elbow, eye in portrait, face in portrait, face in photo
buti	ball	toy, radish, stone spheres at park entrance
ticktock	watch	clocks, all clocks and watches, gasmeter, fire hose wound on spool, bath scale with round dial
gumene	coat button	collar stud, door handle, light switch, anything small and round
baw	ball	apples, grapes, eggs, squash, bell clapper, anything round
kotibaiz	bars of cot	large toy abacus, toast rack with parallel bars, picture of building with columned facade
tee	stick	cane, umbrella, ruler, (old fashioned) razor, board of wood, all sticklike objects
kutija	cardboard box	matchbox, drawer, bedside table
mum	horse	cow, calf, pig, moose, all four-legged animals

Source: From Clark (1975) [reproduced by permission of Georgetown University Press].
[a] Words were overextended to other objects in the order listed.

in classifier languages. These languages contain classifiers for objects in the form of particles that have to be used whenever one talks about a number of objects. For example, a phrase like *three oranges* would be rendered by something like *three round-shape-objects oranges*. The commonest classifiers pick out three major features of shape—round, long, and flat—and then optionally combine these with other properties, such as verticality, rigidity, and so on (Clark, 1974b).

Other overextensions seem to be based more on properties of *movement*, *size*, *sound*, *texture*, and *taste*. Some examples of these are shown in Table 11.2. In addition to these, a few overextensions appear to be based on specific actions. For example, one child reported in the diary literature used a word based on *open* in reference to opening and shutting doors, peeling fruit, opening a box, and getting his shoes unlaced (Clark, 1973a). Bowerman (1975) reported a rather similar situation for the word *kick*: It was used to refer to the child herself kicking a fan, to cartoon turtles doing the cancan on television, to a moth fluttering its wings, to bumping a ball so it moved with the front wheel of her bicycle, and to pushing her teddy bear's stomach up against someone else's stomach. These overextensions typically involve

TABLE 11.2

Some Overextensions Based Primarily on Movement, Size, Sound, and Texture

Lexical item	First referent	Domain of application[a]
sch	sound of train	all moving machines
ass	toy goat on wheels, with rough hide	animals, sister, wagon, all things that move, all things with a rough surface
fly	fly	specks of dirt, dust, all small insects, child's own toes, crumbs of bread, a toad
em	worm	flies, ants, all small insects, heads of timothy grass
bébé	baby (self)	other babies, all small statues, figures in small pictures and prints
fafer	sound of trains	steaming coffee pot, anything that hissed or made a noise
sizo	scissors	all metal objects
va	white plush dog	muffler, cat, father's fur coat
wau-wau	dog	all animals, toy dog, soft house-slippers, picture of old man dressed in furs

Source: From Clark (1975) [reproduced by permission of Georgetown University Press].
[a] Words were overextended to other objects in the order listed.

actions associated with particular situations, and might therefore be regarded as more functional in nature (see Clark, 1975, for further discussion).

When the child uses a word and overextends it to some object that would not be picked out by that word in adult speech, it looks as though the child has not yet identified all the conditions of application relevant to that word. As a result, we can use the data from overextensions to make inferences about those conditions that the child has identified, and argue that, for him, those constitute the entire sense of the word in question. But there is one additional factor that has to be taken into account: From the communicative point of view, the child's resources are very limited. His vocabulary is still very small and, in fact, his overextensions clearly reflect his reliance on a strategy that will maximize what he has acquired so far. He seems to apply the word that *fits best* in context. For example, the child is clearly calling attention to a horse when he points at it even though he actually says *Doggie!* The child's strategy can be characterized as a general rule for word use:

> Identify whatever seems to be the most salient characteristic perceptually, and assume (until given counter-evidence) that the word picks out objects with that characteristic. Act on this assumption whenever you want to name, request, or call attention to something.

Reliance on such a strategy would explain why the child sometimes fluctuates in the criterial features he uses in his overextensions. For example, some overextensions begin with objects that have the same shape, and then shift to others with similar texture but a different shape (Clark, 1973a; Bowerman, 1975). These data suggest that the child's overextensions are really *partial overextensions*. In other words, the child applies a word whenever there is a certain degree of overlap between what he has picked out as the conditions of application and the properties of the object he wants to call attention to (see also Labov & Labov, 1974).

The inferences we can make from the child's spontaneous uses of words, then, are that the words contain *at least* those conditions of application that appear to be operating in the overextensions (Clark, 1975). The child's communicative strategy has a further consequence: There may well be an asymmetry between overextensions in production—where the strategy is being applied—and those in comprehension—where a different strategy may operate (see also Huttenlocher, 1974). Thomson and Chapman (1975) examined the status of some spontaneous overextensions made by five 2-year-olds, and found that several of the words were not overextended in comprehension. These data provide further support for the proposal that the child is using a communicative strategy in his spontaneous uses of words.

To summarize, the child starts off with a good deal of knowledge about the objects in his world and how they are related to one another. He uses this knowledge as the basis for the first meanings he attaches to words. This is discernible in the overextensions that he makes in trying to communicate at a stage when his resources are very limited.

DIMENSIONALITY

Objects in the world have size, height, length, width, and thickness. They exist in three-dimensional space. In addition to their size, they often have a usual or normal orientation. For example, a bed has its most extended dimension in the nonvertical plane, while a door hung in a doorway has its most extended dimension in the vertical plane. In tackling the mapping problem for dimensional words, the child may have to take into account all these things and more.

The words used for dimensionality in English tend to come in pairs: *big–small, tall–short, long–short*, and so on. Of these pairs, one term is usually positive and one negative. (The positive term is usually unmarked as well, and the negative marked, according to Greenberg's, 1966, criteria.) Terms like *big* and *small* can apply freely to one, two, or three dimensions. Other words, though, pick out only one dimension; thus, *tall* and *high* pick out vertical extension and position, respectively, while *long*, *thick*, and *deep* pick out nonvertical extension (Bierwisch, 1967; H. Clark, 1973). The conditions of application for dimensional adjectives vary with the adjective. For *big–small* they are relatively simple because these words can apply to any number of dimensions. *High* and *tall* are more restricted because they can apply to only one dimension, the vertical one. *Long* also applies to only one dimension, but this time the dimension is nonvertical. *High*, *tall*, and *long* are all commonly used to refer to the most extended dimension of an object, in contrast to *wide*, *thick*, and *deep* that normally refer to secondary dimensions, the less extended ones (Bierwisch, 1967). The more constraints on using a dimensional word, therefore, the more complicated it should be for the child to work out the mapping relations that obtain for the adult speaker.

What do children know a priori that might help them (or hinder them) in mapping dimensional words? They clearly attend to the relative size of objects they play with and manipulate, and they may use size as a criterion in naming things (Clark, 1973a). Size, though, takes a secondary role beside shape. There is one dimension, however, that appears to be particularly prominent for young children, and that is the vertical dimension. Ghent (1961) found that young children showed distinct preferences for certain orientations of nonsense forms: When asked to choose from a pair of pictures of realistic figures or nonsense forms the one that was upside-down or wrong, 4- and 5-year-olds treated both kinds of material in the same way, picking one figure as wrong in either case. Older children showed more hesitation with the nonsense objects. The results, overall, showed that children preferred objects to have their most extended axis in the vertical plane, and any asymmetric feature such as a circle or bar attached to one end of a vertical line was always treated as the top of the figure (see also Braine, 1972).

The salience of vertical extension shows up in other studies too. Lumsden and Poteat (1968) asked 5- and 6-year-olds to pick out the *bigger* of two rectangular displays. They found that vertical extension was disproportionately weighted, even by 6-year-olds, who would choose a rectangle with greater height in preference to one with four times the surface area and less vertical extension. This preference, of course, makes it virtually impossible to distinguish between the child's meanings for *big* and *tall* (e.g., Maratsos, 1973).

Normal orientation is usually given in terms of the relation an object bears to the vertical dimension: This is what defines the upright since the reference point or starting point is usually the ground (see H. Clark, 1973, for further discussion). Ghent (1960) found that children below the age of 5 in fact have considerable difficulty in recognizing pictures of realistic objects when these are rotated out of their normal orientation. She found that 3-year-olds, for instance, recognized twice as many objects the right-way-up as they did objects rotated 90° left or right, or 180° to an upside-down position. From age 5 on, though, children appear to have very little difficulty with this task. This suggests that the younger the child, the more dependent he will be on the normal or usual orientation for recognition of such familiar objects as a horse, a wagon, or a sailboat.

One of the first recent studies of dimensionality was one by Donaldson and Balfour (1968). They were concerned with how 3- and 4-year-olds understood the words *more* and *less*. Their results showed that children this age appeared not to distinguish between the two words although these words are opposites for the adult speaker of English. *Less* was actually treated as if it meant *more*: When the children were asked to choose which of two trees had *less* apples on it, they consistently chose the one with more (see also Palermo, 1973).

Several investigators proposed that children at this stage therefore know the meaning of *more*—know, that is, that *more* refers to a positive quantity. They also seem to know that *less* refers to amount or quantity, so it seemed reasonable to assume that the children simply inferred that *less* must mean the same thing as *more* (Donaldson & Balfour, 1968; Donaldson & Wales, 1970; Clark, 1973a). This analysis assumes that the children have already acquired the full (adult) meaning of *more* (they gave correct responses to it) and they have only a little further to go with *less*.

An alternative is to assume that both meanings, for *more* and for *less*, are still incomplete at this point, and that what we see is the outcome of some a priori nonlinguistic preference (Clark, 1973b, 1975). Suppose that both words simply mean something like "Amount(x)." This is supported to some extent by the children's spontaneous uses of these words: For example, when asked which tree had *more* on it, some children said *Both of them* or *That one does an' that one*, and so on. They rarely used *less* spontaneously, but one child when asked to make the amount less on one tree objected *But it is less on that tree* (Donaldson & Wales, 1970). The incomplete meanings for each of these words could be combined with a preference in many contexts for the greater of two amounts, or for greater extension along particular dimensions such as height or length (see H. Clark, 1970).

Klatzky, Clark, and Macken (1973) examined this position by giving children in this age range a concept-attainment task with nonsense syllables used for the positive and negative ends of several dimensions. The children consistently learned the positive nonsense words more quickly and with fewer errors than the negative ones. Since translation could be ruled out, these data support the existence of a general conceptual preference for greater extension. Thus, the apparent interpretation of *less* as "more" is probably just that to begin with. The children are probably combining partial semantic knowledge (*more* and *less* both mean *Amount (x)*) with a nonlinguistic strategy of picking the object with greater extension or amount. And this response happens to coincide with the meaning of the positive term *more* (Clark, 1973b).

The mapping problem that faces the child in the domain of dimensionality, then, is that of working out which words fit with his a priori preferences for greater extension, and with his preference, among dimensions, for vertical extension. These preferences combined would clearly favor the acquisition of positive dimensional terms over their negative counterparts because the mapping there is a more direct one. In addition, the child has to work out the precise conditions that govern the uses of words for primary and secondary dimensions of objects. A door, for instance, is normally described as *high, wide,* and *thick,* going from the most extended dimension to the least extended, with the primary dimension picked out first. Tabletops are usually *long* and *wide* (in that order), while desks are *wide* and *deep* when someone sits behind them, but *long* and *wide* for the furniture movers (see Bierwisch, 1967).

Donaldson and Wales (1970) found that children used positive terms much more often than negative ones, both in their spontaneous speech and in an elicitation task. The term they used most frequently of all was *big,* the one with fewest constraints on its use (see also Wales & Campbell, 1970). They also looked at children's comprehension of different dimensional terms in a task where the child had to pick out the extreme on some dimension (e.g., the *biggest* block) and then pick out a second object compared to a standard (e.g., a block *bigger than* X). Children did better on positive terms than on negative ones, and did far better on the pair *big–wee* (small) than on any other. It was not clear, though, whether there was any particular order of acquisition among the other adjective pairs.

Clark (1972) gave children aged between 4;0 and 5;5 a word game with pairs of dimensional adjectives in which the children had to give back the opposite of each word the experimenter said. The pairs the children knew best posed no problem. Less well-known pairs produced a number of substitutions (usually better-known terms), and the least-known terms elicited "Don't know" responses. Overall, the pairs of dimensional terms appeared to have a very stable order of acquisition. This was shown by the increase in semantically appropriate responses as well as the steady increase in adultlike responses with age. The pair with the fewest conditions of application, *big–small,* is acquired first, and this pair is used most often to provide substitutes whenever the child is unsure of another term. Next come the pairs *tall–short* and *long–short,* then *high–low,* and in a group at the tail end are *thick–thin, deep–shallow,* and *wide–narrow.* The oldest children were still producing a very high percentage of "Don't know" answers to the last two pairs. The order of acquisition depends heavily, it seems, on the complexity of the conditions of application for each pair of adjectives. Pairs with the fewest conditions are acquired earlier. The substitutions given for terms that referred to verticality suggest that these children were well aware that terms like *tall* and *high* picked out the vertical extension: *High* and *tall* were substituted for each other; *up* was substituted for *high, above,* and *over.* The same pattern emerged for negative term substitutions, with *short* [tall] and *low* being interchanged, and *down* being substituted for both *low* and *below* (see Clark, 1972, p. 757). These substitutions strongly suggest that the 4-year-old child has already carried out much of the mapping for terms specific to verticality as well as for the more general dimension of size, *big–small.*

In summary, the child's a priori preferences for picking out greater extent will usually make it easier for him to map positive terms than negative ones. He will generally be right in his responses where positive terms are involved, so he will have less adjustment to make in his preliminary hypotheses about what these terms mean. He has to change drastically, though, when it comes to the negative terms. The child's preferences for vertical extension over other dimensions should also help in the mapping of vertical terms like *tall–short* and *high–low.* The child's strategies, derived from his conceptual preferences, will lead him to assign a correct mapping (from the adult point of view) first to those terms with the simplest conditions of application, namely *big–small.* This is because the use of these words will never be wrong as long as the child uses them to refer to dimensionality of some sort. It is only later on that the child will come to realize that other terms, with a more complex mapping, pick out details of particular dimensions and can be used in lieu of *big* or *small* when the conditions of application are met.

SPATIAL RELATIONS

What does the child know a priori about the spatial relations between the objects around him? He knows, for example, that some objects have flat supporting surfaces while others act as containers. Containers, in fact, appear to exercise a special fascination over the very young child (Bower, 1974). The child also knows something about normal orientation—which way up a chair or glass goes, and so on. He also knows, or is rapidly finding out at about 12 months, that one can place small objects on top of larger ones, but not the reverse. Size, in fact, plays a role for containers too: For instance, small things can fit inside larger ones, whether they are nesting cups or wastepaper baskets or buckets, but large objects will not fit inside small containers. We might expect, then, that surfaces and containers should play some part in the child's acquisition of words for different spatial relations. And the salience of verticality could also be important in focusing the child's attention on the tops of objects.

The first prepositions that children use spontaneously to denote relations in space are *in* and *on*. These appear in children's speech between age 2;0 and 2;6, and generally seem to be used correctly. Clark (1973b) looked at how soon children appeared to understand these two prepositions, together with *under*, in a series of comprehension tasks. Each child got instructions like "Put A in/on/under B." Children over 3;0 made very few errors, but from 1;6 to 2;11, the results looked rather curious. First of all, even the youngest children appeared to get *in* right. *On*, though, was often treated as if it meant "in," and *under* was sometimes treated as if it meant "in" and sometimes as if it meant "on." The critical factor in accounting for these patterns of errors was whether B was a container or whether it simply had a flat supporting surface on it and no containerlike space. Whenever B was a container, the child placed the other object, A, inside (and thus always got *in* "right" automatically); when B was not a container, the child placed A on top of the supporting surface. These strategies can be characterized as two ordered rules:

1. If B is a container, A is inside it.
2. If B has a horizontal surface, A is on it.

The two rules accounted for 92% of the errors made by the youngest children (1;6–1;11) and for 91% of the errors in the next age group up (2;0–2;5). The next oldest group (2;6–2;11) made fewer than 10% errors overall, but the rules still accounted for 71% of them. Instead of considering only responses that were initially scored as errors, however, it could be argued that Rule 1 ought to account for all the *in* instructions and for half the *on* and *under* instructions (that is, wherever B was a container) among the younger children. Rule 2 should account for the other half of the *on* and *under* instructions (that is, wherever B has a flat surface). Overall, the two rules accounted for 89% of the data from the youngest children, while "correct" responses accounted for only 53% of these data (see Clark, 1973b, Tables 1 and 3).

Further evidence that the children were really using general rules much like 1 and 2 came from a second experiment with the two youngest groups of children where each child was given a copying task. The experimenter first placed one object in a spatial relation to another, either inside, on top, or about an inch away. The child was given an identical pair of objects and simply told "Do what I did." As predicted, wherever the experimenter's configuration conformed to the rules identified in the first experiment, the child managed it, and wherever the configuration did not conform, the child simply applied the rules and came up with predictable errors. Since there was no mention of the words *in*, *on*, and *under* in this task, it is clear that the "correct" responses from the earlier comprehension task do not necessarily reflect any semantic knowledge. Instead, they reflect the nonlinguistic or conceptual preferences the young child has for putting objects inside containers, or, failing that option, putting them on a supporting surface.

The child also uses some of the general knowledge he has about orientation and the normal spatial relations between particular objects in these tasks. For example, some of the youngest children in the first experiment persistently turned a box lying on its side so that its opening faced upward. In the copying task, several children who were supposed to copy the experimenter's placing an object on top of an upside-down glass consistently righted the glass and then put the object inside. A couple of these children also changed the experimenter's glass too. A child of 1;6 or 2;0 clearly knows that glasses have their openings up. And once the glass is righted, the child can simply apply Rule 1 as before. A few 2½-year-olds provided further evidence of knowing the normal spatial relations when they objected to putting something *under* a crib: The reason was that one sleeps *in* a crib. However, they knew by that age what *under* meant and would carry out the instructions appropriately.

Wilcox and Palermo (1974/5) collected some additional data on *in*, *on*, and *under*, and found exactly the same pattern of errors among the youngest children as Clark (1973b), namely a preference for putting objects inside containers whenever possible, and otherwise putting them on some surface. Wilcox and Palermo, though, deliberately chose pairs of objects that might be expected to have conventional relations to each other in space: a truck and a piece of road for it to go on (Wilcox and Palermo, for some reason, always asked the child to manipulate the road, not the truck), a boat and a bridge over a piece of river for it to go under, and a teapot with a table for it to go on. Despite this potential bias in favor of *under* instructions with the road–truck and boat–bridge pairs, the youngest children usually responded by putting the road inside the truck for both *in* and *under*, and by putting the boat on the bridge for both *on* and *under*. By about 2;6 though, the children's knowledge of the conventional relations seemed to take over, and they began to do better with *under* than with *in* or *on* with these two pairs. These data therefore provide additional support for the argument that the child's a priori conceptual preferences play a critical role in his learning to map words onto specific spatial relations (Clark, 1973b).

Do the same rules crop up when it comes to the acquisition of words for other spatial relations? If these rules reflect general conceptual preferences, then it seems only reasonable to expect that they should. As part of a more extensive study of children's acquisition of prepositions, I also looked at the pairs *up–down*, *at the top–at the bottom*, *over–under*, and *above–below*. In this task, both *up–down* and *over–under* were used to indicate direction rather than position in space. *Over–under*, as a pair, was further complicated by the fact that *on* is more like the opposite of *under* than *over* is for very young children. *Under*, of course, can be used for either direction or position.

The same children who took part in the experiments just described (Clark, 1973b) served as the subjects in this study too. Each of the 70 children received four instructions with each preposition in one of two formats, for a total of 32. The actual instructions were of the forms shown in (i) and (ii), according to the prepositions used:

(i) Put A at the top/bottom of/above/below B.
(ii) Make A go up/down/over/under B.

As in Clark (1973b), A was a small furry animal of some kind, and B was one of a slide, a staircase, a ladder with shelflike rungs, a bridge, and a barred fence.

TABLE 11.3

Percentage of Correct Responses by Age to Each Preposition-Pair

Group[a]	Mean age	Up–down	Top–bottom	Over–under	Above–below
1	1; 9	55	33	26	20
2	2; 3	82	48	48	11
3	2; 9	80	69	64	16
4	3; 3	79	81	70	20
5	3; 9	99	94	81	51
6	4; 2	100	92	87	66
7	4; 8	88	100	87	94
Mean		83	74	66	40

Note: Each percentage point is based on 80 data points.
[a] Each group contained 10 children.

The percentage of correct responses to each preposition-pair is shown in Table 11.3. There was a steady increase in the number of correct responses with age ($F(6, 63) = 16.82$, $p < .001$).[1] The easiest of the pairs, overall, was up–down, and the relative order of acquisition was up–down, then top–bottom, then over–under, and lastly above–below.[2] This mirrors the order found in Clark (1972).

[1] As the children got older, there was a steady increase in the number of correct responses to each pair of prepositions taken separately: up–down, $F(6, 63) = 4.89$; top–bottom, $F(6, 63) = 15.43$; over–under, $F(6, 63) = 10.49$; and above–below, $F(6, 63) = 12.56$, all $p < .001$.

[2] The pair up–down elicited fewer errors than top–bottom ($t(189) = 2.9$, $p < .01$), the next easiest pair. Top–bottom, in turn, produced fewer errors than over–under ($t(189) = 2.45$, $p < .02$); and over–under produced fewer errors than the most difficult pair, above–below ($t(189) = 8.47$, $p < .001$).

The majority of the errors for *up* consisted of the child's making the movable object, A, go down the slide (61%). The remaining responses counted as errors consisted of the child's placing A on the topmost or next-to-topmost step of the staircase (39%). *Down* produced some "up" errors, with motion plus placement on top (43% of the errors), as well as some errors from placing A on the next-to-top surface (29%). In other words, a Rule 2-type strategy accounted for 72% of all the errors made with *down*.

Top and *bottom* produced error rates of 12% and 40% respectively. For *top*, correct responses could simply be the outcome of applying Rule 2. In addition, 4% of the responses involved motion plus top surface placement, and another 6% involved choice of the next-to-top surfaces on the stairs and the ladder. Rule 2, then, would account for all the correct responses as well as for 83% of the errors made. The errors for *bottom* consisted of choices of the top surface 75% of the time, and of the next-to-top surface the rest of the time. The surface strategy, therefore, accounted for all the errors on *bottom*.

Over had a high error rate, 53%, and was acquired quite a bit later than *under*. Of the total responses, 25% consisted of the child trying to balance A on top of the fence (position rather than motion). Another 18% consisted of treating *over* as "under," and 9% of treating *over* as "through" (e.g., by squeezing A between the bars of the fence). For *under*, there were virtually no errors after age 3;0 (replicating the data in Clark, 1973b), and the overall rate was fairly low at 25%. Of these, 72% consisted of placing A on top of the fence or the bridge.

Lastly, *above* and *below* elicited the highest percentages of errors with 60% and 61%, respectively. For *above*, 47% of the responses involved placing A on the same surface as the block in the three-part relation. (The instructions were actually "Put A above/below the block on B.") A surface–based strategy would also account for the correct responses where children placed A on the top step or on the top rung. A rule like Rule 2, therefore, would account for 87% of the responses to *above*. The error pattern for *below* was very similar, with 38% of the responses consisting of putting A on the top surface, and 22% on the same surface as the block. In other words, a surface strategy would account for all the errors on *below*.

The strategy of placing objects on the topmost or next-to-top surface accounted on average for 76% of all the responses made in this task. What is important here is that the children appeared to use the same strategy across a variety of different situations and in response to very different instructions. In each instance, the children appeared to assume that the prepositions had something to do with a spatial relation, defined by contact between A and B. They never made errors by setting A down next to or even far away from B. There were no containers used in this task, so the obvious strategy to apply would be to place A on a flat, supporting surface (Rule 2), and this seems to be exactly what most young children do much of the time. This strategy maps fairly well into the positive prepositions studied here, but it clearly does not work for the negative ones or for the more complex three-place relations like *above* and *below*. Eventually, this strategy will have to be relinquished for those cases (Clark, 1973b, 1975).

To summarize, the child's nonlinguistic organizational preferences appear to play an important role in predetermining which words the child is likely to acquire more easily, and which terms he may appear to understand before he has actually mastered their meanings. In general, the child juxtaposes objects by putting one inside the other or one on top of the other, following what look like earlier preferences still (Bower, 1974). These preferences appear to operate across a wide domain—the domain of spatial relations—and are most compelling for the child under 2;6 or 3;0. The child's strategies provide him with a way to cope with a situation even when he does not understand what was actually said. The strategies identified so far all turn on properties of the objects that are related to each other in space. I want to turn next to a different kind of relationship in space, the relation between the speaker and his addressee, and look at how the child deals with various deictic terms.

DEICTIC RELATIONS

Deictic terms are terms used in utterances to "point out" a particular object, position, or direction in relation to the speaker of the utterance. Consider the following sentences:

(1)   *I've read **that** book but not **this** one.*
(2)   *Won't **you come** in for a minute?*
(3)   ***He**'s been waiting **here** for two hours.*

In (1), the speaker, *I*, contrasts two books. If the speaker uses no gestures, we can infer in context that *that book* was the book further from the speaker, and that *this one* was the nearer of the two. The sentence in (2) might be said by someone inside the place in question to someone outside, or by one person to another when both were outside. The addressee, in either case, would have to be outside for it to be appropriate to use the verb *come*. In (3), the speaker must be at the same place as *he*, otherwise it would be inappropriate to use *here*. Each of the words in boldface in (1)–(3) provides deictic information interpretable only in the actual context of each utterance. When does the child work out the mapping for the deictic contrasts between *here* and *there*, or *this* and *that*, or *come* and *go*?

Many of the diary studies report that deictic words based on *here*, *there* or *that* appear very early in the child's speech, often among the first words.

Leopold (1949), for example, found that one of the earliest and most frequent words used by his daughter was *da*. It seemed to have no stable referent and was always accompanied by her pointing at something to draw attention to it. In a more recent study of children's early vocabulary, most of the children Nelson (1973) followed used at least one deictic term by the time they had acquired 30 words, and many of them included a deictic word among the first 10. In general, such deictic words always appear to be accompanied by a gesture, usually a pointing gesture.

The use of an accompanying gesture seems to continue well into and beyond the stage where the child starts to use two-word utterances. Bloom (1970), for instance, noted that Kathryn always pointed when she used sentences like *That + noun*. Children at this stage do not yet contrast pairs like *here* and *there* to indicate relative proximity to the speaker. Each term used is accompanied by pointing, and the gesture itself *cancels* any implicit contrast, just as it would for the adult speaker.

In a recent study, therefore, we looked at how children could deal with instructions that contained contrasting *here* and *there* or *this* and *that* (Clark & Sengul, 1974). We gave 2- to 5-year-olds a comprehension task in which we varied the position of the speaker vis-à-vis the child—she sat either beside or opposite the child. Our results showed that children seem to go through three stages in the course of working out such deictic contrasts. At the first stage, there is no contrast at all between, say, *here* and *there*. At Stage 2, the child has acquired a partial contrast and gives adultlike responses, for example, only when the speaker is seated beside him or only when the speaker is opposite, but not in both situations. Finally, at Stage 3, the child displays the same knowledge of the contrast, across situations, as the adult does. The context of such a task seems to impose very few constraints on what the child can do, unlike the materials in the locative experiments, and we found that children used a variety of different strategies, although each child was internally consistent. They started from one of four possible points at Stage 1 and then moved on to Stages 2 and 3 in different ways, depending on how they started out originally.

Where do children begin? First of all, they appear to choose a Point of Reference and then decide which of the two objects to move with respect to that Point of Reference. Some children consistently picked themselves, while others, just as consistently, picked the speaker. Having chosen a Point of Reference, the majority of the *no contrast* children chose the object at the side of the table nearest that Reference Point after hearing every instruction. A very small number of children, instead, chose the object away from their Point of Reference.

The typical pattern of "correct" and "wrong" choices for the children who used themselves as the Point of Reference is shown in Table 11.4. Since the

TABLE 11.4

Error Patterns Where Child Chooses Himself as Point of Reference

	Speaker beside child		Speaker opposite child	
Child's choice	here	there	here	there
NEAR	correct	wrong	wrong	correct
FAR	wrong	correct	correct	wrong

Source: Based on Clark and Sengul (1974).
Note: NEAR = side of table where child is seated.
FAR = side opposite where child is seated.

child at this stage does not contrast *here* and *there*, he always chooses the object at the side of the table where he himself is seated, and ignores the speaker's position completely. This means that he will only get *here* "right" when the speaker is beside him, and only get *there* "right" when the speaker is opposite.

Table 11.5 shows the analogous pattern of "correct" and "wrong" responses for the children who chose the speaker as their Point of Reference. In this case their choices shift with the speaker's position, but they make no contrast between the words *here* and *there* within each situation. The strategies we have described accounted for the majority of the errors we found at Stage I (see Clark & Sengul, 1974). At Stage 2, the picture became much more complex: The children had a partial contrast, but only in one of the two situations—either when the speaker sat beside them, or when the speaker was opposite. Finally, at around age 5, they mastered the contrast fully.

Terms like *here* and *there* impose minimal constraints on what the child can do in context. His choice of a Point of Reference is limited to the participants, and his choice of object is likewise limited, but within these constraints, children could and did opt for all the logical possibilities. The choices of object *near* the Point of Reference were much more frequent than the choice of object

TABLE 11.5

Error Patterns Where Child Chooses Speaker as Point of Reference

	Speaker beside child		Speaker opposite child	
Child's choice	here	there	here	there
NEAR	correct	wrong	correct	wrong
FAR	wrong	correct	wrong	correct

Source: Based on Clark and Sengul (1974).
Note: NEAR = side of table where speaker is seated.
FAR = side opposite where speaker is seated.

further away. (Both were actually equidistant from the child.) This preference for proximity over distance seems compatible with the child's general preferences among spatial relations where proximity, if possible with contact, dominates.

In another set of studies, we looked at how children dealt with the deictic contrasts between the verb pairs *come* and *go*, and *bring* and *take* (Clark, unpublished data). In one study, we placed two circles on the floor, with a pile of animals between them, stationed the child beside one circle and the speaker/experimenter beside the other. The latter then gave the child instructions like "Make the horse come/go to the circle" and watched to see which circle the child would choose.

The younger children (age 3;0 up to age 5;0) showed no consistent preferences for one direction over another when they moved an animal. Later on, though, some children settled on more consistent ways of responding, and again some chose themselves as the constant Point of Reference and others chose the speaker. Most of the younger children, when asked, usually claimed that *come* and *go* were "the same," as were *bring* and *take*. When pressed on this, some of them came up with stock collocations like "Come here," "Go there," or "Go away" as definitions. By age 5, several children seemed to have grasped the idea that some directionality was involved, and began giving definitions like "Come is here and go is away" or "Come is go to a person and go is go away from a person." (These children, however, showed no such insight in the comprehension task itself!) Other 5-year-olds would simply point out that the two words—*come* and *go*—were "not spelled the same" or that "one begins with a C and one with a G." Another child proposed that *come* involved directionality "to me," and quite reasonably insisted that *go* meant no more than "just walking." Overall, these data suggested that these verbs are treated at first as if they are simple verbs of motion. It is only later that the child comes to realize that they also tell you something about directionality in relation to where the speaker is.

In another study with slightly older children (Clark & Garnica, 1974), we asked children to identify the speaker or the addressee of various utterances containing the verbs *come, go, bring,* or *take*. Each child was presented with a group of three animals, one inside a fenced garden, say, and two outside, and the experimenter would then say, for instance, "The dog says *Can I come into the garden?* Which animal is he talking to?" The child then picked an animal and, after that, was allowed to move the speaker (the dog) to the appropriate place. The task was a fairly complex one, but even the youngest children in our pilot studies (under 5) were very confident they understood it completely. We eventually did the study with children between 5;6 and 9;5.

Even the youngest children (6-year-olds) appeared to understand *come* and *bring* perfectly, but none of them got *go* or *take* right. Instead, the children treated *go* as if it meant "come" and *take* as if it meant "bring." Somewhat

TABLE 11.6

Rules Used to Identify Speaker and Addressee

Stage	Speaker	Addressee
1	Choose goal	Choose goal
2	Choose nongoal	Choose goal
3	a. If *come*, choose goal	Choose goal
	b. If *go*, choose nongoal	
4	a. If *come*, choose goal	a. If *come*, choose goal
	b. If *go*, choose nongoal	b. If *go*, choose nongoal

Source: Based on Clark and Garnica (1974).

older children, though, got *come* right only half the time, and they also got *go* right half the time. The same applied to *bring* and *take*. It therefore seemed very unlikely that the younger children really knew what *come* and *bring* meant (see Clark, 1973b). Rather, they seemed to have lighted upon a strategy that happened to coincide with adultlike interpretations of *come* and *bring*, but that produced the wrong outcomes for both *go* and *take*.

The strategies the children appeared to use at different stages in the course of acquisition were characterized as rules for identifying the location of the speaker and the addressee in context. The rules that the children seemed to rely on are those shown in Table 11.6. These rules accounted for the specific error patterns found in different groups, and also for almost all of the responses that were given.

Overall, these studies of deixis suggest that children tackle different deictic systems at different stages of their language development. At about age 3 or 4, they start working on speaker-based contrasts like that between *here* and *there*, and it is probably not until about age 8 or 9 that they master the more complicated deictic distinctions found in verbs like *come* and *go*.

The domain of deictic relations is yet another area where the child's strategies play an important role during acquisition. Some strategies map fairly directly onto adult procedures, and others do not. Because some do, though, we have to be wary on occasion of attributing too much knowledge to the child. He often seems to understand more than he really does, and even his own words may mislead us at times.

CONCLUSION

Some of the child's a priori conceptual preferences happen to "match" the meanings attached to particular words by the adult, and, as a result, the child's strategies for dealing with different situations play an important role in acquisition. The child may approach particular situations with certain preferences and then notice that certain words seem to "go with" those situations. He may then make his first hypothesis about the meaning of that word contingent on his conceptual preference. Later, he comes to notice other things about the situation that may explain why he fails to make himself understood or why he might be misunderstanding others. This is presumably what leads the child to alter his strategies until eventually he narrows or changes them to fit the conditions of application used by adult speakers (Clark, 1975). The conceptual organization of what he knows appears to be virtually inseparable from his semantic development, at least during the early stages of language acquisition. He builds up his language on a cognitive foundation (Slobin, 1973).

By identifying the child's strategies in dealing with different conceptual domains, and by tracing the changes that take place as the child learns more about how the language maps onto each domain, we can find a way in to the maze that faces us when we wish to study the acquisition of meaning. Moreover, the child's preferences or biases tell us a good deal about his a priori conceptual organization too, by pinpointing the relations and properties that he appears to find salient in his first attempts at tackling language.

REFERENCES

Bever, T. G. The cognitive basis for linguistic structures. In J. R. Hayes (Ed.), *Cognition and the development of language*. New York: Wiley, 1970. Pp. 279–352.
Bierwisch, M. Some universals of German adjectivals. *Foundations of Language*, 1967, *3*, 1–36.
Bower, T. G. R. *Development in infancy*. San Francisco: Freeman, 1974.
Bowerman, M. The acquisition of word meaning: An investigation of some current conflicts. Paper presented at the Third International Child Language Symposium, London, 1975.
Bloom, L. M. *Language development: Form and function in emerging grammars*. Cambridge, Mass.: M.I.T. Press, 1970.
Braine, L. G. The apparent upright—Implications for copying and perceptual development. Paper presented at the XXth International Congress of Psychology, Tokyo, Japan, 1972.
Clark, E. V. On the child's acquisition of antonyms in two semantic fields. *Journal of Verbal Learning and Verbal Behavior*, 1972, *11*, 750–758.
Clark, E. V. What's in a word? On the child's acquisition of semantics in his first language. In T. E. Moore (Ed.), *Cognitive development and the acquisition of language*. New York: Academic Press, 1973. Pp. 65–110. (a)
Clark, E. V. Non-linguistic strategies and the acquisition of word meanings. *Cognition*, 1973, *2*, 161–182. (b)

Clark, E. V. Some aspects of the conceptual basis for first language acquisition. In R. L. Schiefelbusch and L. L. Lloyd (Eds.), *Language perspectives—Acquisition, retardation, and intervention.* Baltimore, Md.: University Park Press, 1974, Pp. 105–128. (a)

Clark, E. V. Classifiers and semantic acquisition: Universal categories? Paper presented at the 73rd Annual Meeting of the American Anthropological Association, Mexico City, Mexico, 1974. (b)

Clark, E. V. Knowledge, context, and strategy in the acquisition of meaning. In D. P. Dato (Ed.), *Georgetown University Round Table on Languages and Linguistics 1975.* Washington, D. C.: Georgetown University Press, 1975. Pp. 77–98.

Clark, E. V., & Garnica, O. K. Is he coming or going? On the acquisition of deictic verbs. *Journal of Verbal Learning and Verbal Behavior,* 1974, *13,* 559–572.

Clark, E. V., & Sengul, C. J. Deictic contrasts in language acquisition. Paper presented at the Annual Meeting of the Linguistic Society of America, New York, 1974.

Clark, H. H. The primitive nature of children's relational concepts. In J. R. Hayes (Ed.), *Cognition and the development of language.* New York: Wiley, 1970. Pp. 269–278.

Clark, H. H. Space, time, semantics, and the child. In T. E. Moore (Ed.), *Cognitive development and the acquisition of language.* New York: Academic Press, 1973. Pp. 28–63.

Donaldson, M., & Balfour, G. Less is more: A study of language comprehension in children. *British Journal of Psychology,* 1968, *59,* 461–472.

Donaldson, M., & Wales, R. J. On the acquisition of some relational terms. In J. R. Hayes (Ed.), *Cognition and the development of language.* New York: Wiley, 1970. Pp. 235–268.

Ghent, L. Recognition by children of realistic figures in various orientations. *Canadian Journal of Psychology,* 1960, *14,* 249–256.

Ghent, L. Form and its orientation: The child's eye view. *American Journal of Psychology,* 1961, *74,* 177–190.

Greenberg, J. H. *Language universals.* The Hague: Mouton, 1966.

Huttenlocher, J. The origins of language comprehension. In R. L. Solso (Ed.), *Theories of cognitive psychology: The Loyola Symposium.* Potomac, Md.: Erlbaum Associates, 1974. Pp. 331–368.

Klatzky, R. L., Clark, E. V., & Macken, M. Asymmetries in the acquisition of polar adjectives: Linguistic or conceptual? *Journal of Experimental Child Psychology,* 1973, *16,* 32–46.

Labov, W., & Labov, T. The grammar of "Cat" and "Mama." Paper presented at the Annual Meeting of the Linguistic Society of America, New York, 1974.

Leopold, W. F. *Speech development of a bilingual child* (4 vols.). Evanston, Ill.: Northwestern University Press, 1949.

Lumsden, E. A., & Poteat, B. W. S. The salience of the vertical dimension in the concept of "Bigger" in five- and six-year-olds. *Journal of Verbal Learning & Verbal Behavior,* 1968, *7,* 404–408.

Maratsos, M. P. Decrease in the understanding of the word "Big" in preschool children. *Child Development,* 1973, *44,* 747–752.

Nelson, K. Structure and strategy in learning to talk. *Monographs of the Society for Research in Child Development*, 1973, *38* (serial No. 149).

Palermo, D. S. More about *less:* A study of language comprehension. *Journal of Verbal Learning and Verbal Behavior*, 1973, *12*, 211–221.

Rosch, E. Cognitive representations of semantic categories. *Journal of Experimental Psychology: General*, 1975, *104*, 192–233.

Slobin, D. I. Cognitive pre-requisites for the development of grammar. In C. A. Ferguson and D. I. Slobin (Eds.), *Studies of child language development*. New York: Holt, Rinehart & Winston, 1973. Pp. 175–208.

Thomson, J. R., & Chapman, R. S. Who is "Daddy"? The status of two-year-olds' over-extended words in use and comprehension. *Papers and Reports on Child Language Development* (Stanford University), 1975, *10*, 59–68.

Wales, R. J., & Campbell, R. On the development of comparison and the comparison of development. In G. B. Flores d'Arcais and W. J. M. Levelt (Eds.), *Advances in psycholinguistics*. Amsterdam: North-Holland Publishing, 1970. Pp. 373–396.

Wilcox, S., & Palermo, D. S. "In," "On," and "Under" revisited. *Cognition*, 1974/5, *3*, 245–254.

12

Children's Internal Descriptions

ZENON W. PYLYSHYN

University of Western Ontario.

When a person (child or adult) interacts with his environment, events are assimilated (to use Piaget's term) through an act of conceptualization. They are not recorded, continuously transformed, degraded, nor filtered in any of the usual senses of these terms which imply operating on spatially or temporally local features. This act of cognizing is one in which objects and aspects of the environment are *individuated*, some attributes and relations are *noticed*, while others are inferred, and in general perceptual structure is imparted to the environment. By structure, here I mean that a representation of the environment is constructed which exhibits the paradigmatic relationship among different perceptual events and the syntagmatic relationships within parts of an otherwise unitary event. Such structures are quite different from those we would be led to infer from an examination of a description of the scene given in the language of physics—for example, a description of the scene before me now and the one this morning given in terms of point illumination intensities and wavelengths would not lead in any natural way to the inference that both described the same room with the same occupants. This is why, in part, machine perception is difficult (for more on this issue see Pylyshyn, 1974).

What I wish to claim, and I can only try to argue this in a very sketchy manner at this time (see, however, Pylyshyn, 1973, in press), is that what is occurring in perception can best be characterized as the construction of an internal description of an event using an internal vocabulary of available concepts. The internal vocabulary arises from a number of sources and is being continually refined and reorganized. It arises from inherent properties of our biological equipment (these might perhaps be called innate concepts), from our culture, from our linguistic environment, and from interactions among these. The second part of my claim is one I have made before (Chapter 3): Although experiences affect our conceptual vocabulary, there is a measure of decoupling in the way in which they develop which makes it possible to tune our descriptive system relatively slowly in response to changing environments (this brings about the assimilation–accommodation opposition central to Piagetian theory). A corollary suggested by this view of decoupling, however, is that young infants share a reasonable amount of common conceptual categories. There are two extreme ways to think of the initial set of concepts (or starting vocabulary). We can think of it as comprising only a very small set of distinctions which become refined with experience, or as an overly rich and highly specific vocabulary which must then be aggregated with experience.

The first of these alternatives, which assumes a small initial vocabulary, seems, on the face of it, most consistent with the type of "overgeneralization" errors cited by Clark. It is also most in harmony with the perceptual development views of Gibson (1969). There are difficulties with it, however, as Fodor (1975) has cogently pointed out. If we are to hold any variant of one of the familiar views of concept learning, we will be forced to accept that the initial vocabulary cannot be a small subset of the final vocabulary. It must, as Fodor has shown, be nearly as rich as the ultimate vocabulary. This presents psychology with an extreme dilemma which, however, I will deliberately sidestep in this discussion. I shall take as a working hypothesis the view that while the set of initial concepts is large indeed, access to them as well as to the knowledge of how they can be grouped, interrelated, and used in acting and speaking requires experience for its development.

There are a number of advantages to thinking of perception as a process involving the analysis of experience in terms of available conceptual categories and the synthesis of an internal description. I have written on this elsewhere so I will not belabor the point here. But I do want to add a few comments, in light of Clark's paper, on why I believe it is appropriate to think of the child as possessing an initial vocabulary of concepts even before it has any recognizable overt linguistic expression.

1. In the first place, something like a concept is necessary in order to learn the names of objects. Sometimes we loosely speak of naming as a relation

between words and objects (in fact, Clark does so in her paper). But since the connection is a mental one—not one embodied outside our brains—it can only be between two perceptual events. De Saussure (1959, p. 66) clearly recognized this when he said, "the linguistic sign unites, not a thing and a name, but a concept and a sound-image. The latter is not the material sound, a purely physical thing, but the psychological imprint of the sound."

In learning the name of an object, a child presumably constructs a link labeled "designates" between the cognized vocal expression and either the most appropriate available concept or, in more complex cases, a structure of available object, attribute, and relation concepts—in other words, an internal description.

2. I believe this formulation also provides a simple way of accounting for certain systematic errors which children make. In particular, it explains why the same kinds of "overgeneralization" (a term I think is misleading) occur whether the task is a linguistic one (such as following the instruction to place one object on another or a nonverbal one (such as imitating an action). Both require that an internal description be constructed.

For example, if a child has mastered a concept such as "quantity-in-appearance" and a primitive equivalence relation applicable to a range of concepts, he will be able to discriminate two objects by size. Without additionally having the concept of order (or the operation of seriation), the child is not in a position to learn the comparative concept "bigger" or "smaller." For adults, it is often difficult to appreciate that such apparently unitary concepts as designated by a word like *more* may psychologically be composed of more elementary concepts and that correct usage may depend on being able to abstract these separate conceptual components.

An example of when a more complex internal description is needed is in the representation of visual form. According to the view I am proposing, a form such as the uppercase letter *R* is represented as an internal nonverbal and nondiscursive description in which concepts such as circular, vertical, adjoining, collinear, slanted, and so on, are used. This kind of articulation of the form accounts for why we readily see that an *R* is like a *P* except for the tail and like a *K* except for . . ., etc. In each of the pairs, the structural descriptions partially overlap, and their differences are already cognized in terms of available concepts.

Now suppose the child has not yet mastered the concept for a certain relation which we might paraphrase as "to the right of" or "to the left of." (Perhaps the child can indirectly derive something like this concept by referencing a more complex description such as "nearest to the hand on which I have a scratch" or some such subterfuge. But in any case, let us suppose that the concept I have tried to indicate is either unavilable or difficult for him to access.) What then is his representation of a figure such as the letter *R*? He may simply use the simpler concept "adjacent" in place of the more refined "left of." This results in a perfectly accurate representation of the figure, with one exception: Both the figure and its mirror image reduce to identical descriptions and therefore are cognitively indiscernible from memory (they are distinguishable when present side by side since a description of $R Я$ is distinguishable from a description of RR even without the concept "left of").

The opposite problem arises when a child constructs a description using concepts that are either too specific or not quite appropriate for some task. For example, Clark cites evidence for the salience of verticality for the child. If above–below or up–down relational concepts are employed routinely in the internal description of patterns, then recognizing the same pattern in different orientations would be a problem for the child, since such patterns have different descriptions. It is possible to describe forms using concepts which give them a canonical description independent of orientation. According to this view, people who did this would have little trouble recognizing the same form in different orientations. Some cultures (e.g., Eskimo) are said to be adept at this. However, it is not clear that people in general do it, since the orientation of a form is usually important. But as Rock (1973) has shown, it is not the orientation relative to the observer so much as the orientation relative to some appropriate frame of reference which is the important factor. This fits in well with the notion of describing, since it removes it from some structural property of the perceptual apparatus. In fact, even Rock now speaks of percepts as more akin to conceptual descriptions.

If we take this view (or in fact any of a constellation of approaches that share the assumption that the environment is conceptualized into something like an internal vocabulary of concepts), then it is natural to ask questions about the initial vocabulary and about the nature of the interlingua and how it develops. Unfortunately, there is very little that can be said about these important issues. The search for a plausible, initially accessible vocabulary is one which students of early infancy are now pursuing with the aid of some rather recent methodological tools (e.g., the work of T. G. R. Bower, 1972). But if the initial vocabulary is universal and if the range of environments and of types of human interactions with our environment can be seen as relatively small, then we can also get clues about the initial vocabulary from studies of cognitive universals—particularly as embodied in linguistic universals. I will have a few points to make about this later.

On the question of the nature of the interlingua and its modification, I have only prejudices based on current achievements in artificial intelligence. Although the use of symbol structures or semantic nets as internal descriptions goes back at least 15 years and covers a wide range of applications, very little is known about their formal properties and limitations (e.g., see Woods, 1975). Other interlingua are now being investigated as candidates for representing knowledge—including predicate calculus formulations and various pure procedure formulations (e.g., actors, productions, demons, etc.), but so far the whole problem area can best be described as uncharted though highly promising.

Let us return for a moment to see what clues about the initial conceptual vocabulary we may obtain from studies of semantic universals. One place where very general conceptual categories are found is in various semantic classificatory morphemes. Some languages demand that each noun or verb or numeral be accompanied by a classificatory morpheme which assigns the named entity to a general semantic category. In many languages, the use of these classificatory morphemes is optional in some cases and is also loosened, somewhat, by a marked–unmarked distinction and by the presence of neutral morphemes. But even in these cases, one can get some idea of what perceptual or functional characteristics are cognized as most important and inquire whether there are universal categories.

My colleague Peter Denny has been studying these classificatory morpheme systems for the last few years and finds a remarkable degree of convergence in the categories singled out by diverse languages. Let me illustrate with a few examples (for further discussion, see Denny, in press). Athapaskan languages all contain classificatory verb stems whose selection is governed by non-linguistic considerations. Although part of the verb, the morpheme actually classifies the noun to which that verb refers. In his formal analysis of this verb system, Basso (1968) identifies some 13 distinct stems and describes them. He then subjects these to a componential analysis to reveal seven semantic dimension: animal/nonanimal, enclosed/nonenclosed; solid/plastic/liquid; one/two/more than two; rigid/nonrigid; horizontal length greater than three times the width or height/horizontal length less than three times the width or height; portable/nonportable. Of the 13 categories distinguished by the seven dimensions, several are of particular interest because they recur rather commonly in other cultures. They are:

Category 1 (pencil, knife, crowbar, file, cigarette): "rigid and extended in one dimension"

Category 2 (pail, glass, lightbulb, egg, package of cigars, coin, egg, book): "rigid and nonextended (i.e., equidimensional)"

Category 3 (paper, blanket, shirt, paper money, sack): "flexible and extended in two dimensions"

Category 4 (rope, thread, belt, chain): "flexible and extended in one dimension"

These categories reappear in Algonquian numeral classifiers, in Taraskan (where they are optional in a large number of cases), and in Bantu noun classifiers (where the extendedness variable has only two values and is orthogonal to another spatial variable—solid or outlined shape). Many of the categories that Clark found in her studies have clear parallels in the classifier systems of many cultures—for example, ones based on the prominence and relative size of the vertical extension, the importance of the containment relation (e.g., in Bantu, there is a nominal morpheme associated with objects that can be thought to contain or potentially contain something (see Denny & Creider, 1975).

Evidence from sources such as these, taken together with the kind of over-extension data Clark finds, helps to afford a more reliable picture of the kinds of (in this case spatial) aspects of the environment that are conceptualized in an initial internal vocabulary. At the same time, such convergent research provides a base from which one can study the influence of culture and of physical environment on the development of the internal vocabulary.

The question of where the initial vocabulary comes from presents us with some deep puzzles. Most people find it difficult to accept the notion of innate concepts—although clearly much of what happens to an infant is predicated on its initial (i.e., innate) condition. Again the principal of partial decom-posability or of limited interaction at the interface between systems suggests that there must be some measure of autonomy in the development of percep-tion and language. There have been attempts (e.g., by Kant) to provide the developing human cognitive system with an initial structure by positing that certain concepts (e.g., those related to our intuitions of space and time) are simply immutable and given to the mind. But others have tried to account for our conception of space on functional grounds. For example, in one of his last essays, Henri Poincaré (1963) mounted a somewhat sketchy argument for the tridimensionality of conceptual space on the basis of its survival value. Later Jean Nicod (1970) tried to bridge the gap between sense data and the axioms of Euclidean geometry in a beautiful piece of work entitled "Geometry and the Sensory World." Piaget and Inhelder (1956) tried to trace the develop-ment of the child's conception of space from a biological and genetic per-spective. But both the nature of the initial system for internally describing space and the way in which such a system can be modified by experience—the assimilation–accommodation duality—remains as mysterious as ever. One problem is that the closer one gets to fundamental conceptual universals, the more difficult it is for us to see the problem in perspective, since it is almost impossible to conceive of alternatives against which to contrast what is, for us, the obvious (e.g., conceptual space has three dimensions because that is how it really is!).

But we do need to try and uncover some of the fundamental conceptual building blocks so that we might relate them on the one hand to biological imperatives and on the other to the way our physical, cultural, and linguistic environments shape our conceptual structures. It is not an easy task, but I have some hope for the study of semantics in view of the development of some important intellectual tools in the last two decades. For if we find suitable ways of representing knowledge in adults (and this is a large part of the effort in recent work in artificial intelligence), we will have some notion of what sorts of things to look for in infants.

It is clear that there is a considerable component of speculation in what I have been saying. What Clark has done in her studies is to give an empirical underpinning to some of this kind of speculation. She has done this by showing that, at least within certain limited domains, the errors and overgeneralizations that a child makes in understanding certain words and situations can be explained to a very large degree by two types of hypotheses. One is that the young child appears to have access to less refined internal concepts than does an adult—and Clark has discovered what some of these are. The second is that in relating his concepts or internal descriptions to his environment—and in particular to adult utterances—the child uses certain strategies rather consistently. These strategies have to do with the priorities given to various concepts within the class of available ones, to the question of how to assign words to the most likely available concepts, and to the practical question of how to respond in a given situation even though the linguistic stimulus is not quite understood (i.e., it underdetermines for the child what is required of him). These are important findings. They contribute to our understanding of children's cognition, and they also represent a small contribution toward a rather deep problem raised many years ago by McCarthy and Hayes (1969), namely the relation between epistemology and heuristics or between what we know and how we use this knowledge to act within limited available resources. But they also open up a host of new questions: Why are the initial concepts the way they seem to be, and *why* should there be such response preferences as for putting objects *in* rather than *on* containers or *on* rather than *under* surfaces? As usual, as we scratch the surface of one problem, a host of deeper issues arises.

REFERENCES

Basso, K. H. The Western Apache classificatory verb system: A formal analysis. *Southwestern Journal of Anthropology*, 1968, *24*, 252–266.

Bower, T. G. R. Object perception in infants. *Perception*, 1972, *1*, 15–30.

Denny, J. P. The "extendedness" variable in classifier semantics: Universal features and cultural variation. In M. Mathiot (Ed.), *Boas, Sapir and Whorf revisited*. The Hague: Mouton, in press.

Denny, J. P., & Creider, C. The semantics of noun classes in Proto-Bantu. *Studies in African Linguistics*, 1976, *7*, 1–30.

de Saussure, F. *Course in general linguistics*. New York: Philosophical Library, 1959.

Fodor, J. A. *The language of thought.* New York: Crowell, 1975.

Gibson, E. J. *Principles of perception, learning and development.* New York: Appleton, 1969.

McCarthy, J., & Hayes, P. Some philosophical problems from the standpoint of artificial intelligence. *Machine intelligence 4.* Edinburgh: University of Edinburgh Press, 1969.

Nicod, J. *Geometry and induction.* Berkeley: University of California Press, 1970.

Piaget, J., & Inhelder, B. *The child's conception of space.* London: Routledge & Kegan Paul, 1956.

Poincaré, H. Why space has three dimensions. *Mathematics and science: Last essays of Henri Poincaré.* New York: Dover, 1963.

Pylyshyn, Z. W. What the mind's eye tells the mind's brain. *Psychological Bulletin,* 1973, *80,* 1–24.

Pylyshyn, Z. W. Minds, machines and phenomenology. *Cognition,* 1974, *3,* 57–77.

Pylyshyn, Z. W. Imagery and artificial intelligence. In C. W. Savage (Ed.), *Minnesota studies in the philosophy of science.* Vol. 9. In press.

Rock, I. *Orientation and form.* Academic Press, 1973.

Woods, W. A. What's in a link: Foundations for semantic networks. In D. G. Bobrow and A. Collins (Eds.), *Representation and understanding.* New York: Academic Press, 1975.

13

The Contexts of Language Acquisition

DAVID R. OLSON

Ontario Institute for Studies in Education

In her paper, Eve Clark (this volume) presents a general approach to the problem of how the child, in acquiring a language, goes about working out the correspondence between an utterance he hears and the cognized context in which it occurs. This is, of course, a central issue in understanding language development, and Clark's evidence and arguments make a substantial contribution to its solution. In discussing these contributions, I propose to consider first some issues that relate to the way the problem of language acquisition is formulated and then to turn to some more specific relations between words and their meanings/uses.

Clark makes the generally accepted assumption that the problem in language learning is primarily one of mapping language onto a previously established picture of reality. The child's nonlinguistic knowledge provides a systematic basis for perceiving and acting in most of the contexts in which he finds himself. Now suppose that in such a context the child hears an utterance. The assumption, as I understand it, is that the child takes whatever he has in mind at that moment to be the meaning of the sentence. As

I am indebted to the Van Leer Jerusalem Foundation for their support in the preparation of this paper.

Macnamara (1972) formulated it, the child first arrives at the meaning by nonlinguistic means and then uses this meaning to crack the linguistic code. Furthermore, that assumption suggests that the mother in speaking to her baby goes out of her way to see to it that her utterance does indeed correspond to the meaning the infant is presumably entertaining.

That is an important assumption, and it contrasts, I believe, with the assumption that language is an autonomous system in which the meaning of a sentence can be represented independently of the uses to which it is put or the contexts in which it occurs (Chomsky, 1972, p. 24). This latter assumption about meaning is also an important one, at least for some uses of language, such as that of formal, written prose in which the listener/reader may be expected to assign an interpretation exclusively on the basis of the linguistic conventions themselves independent of the nonlinguistic context and his interpretive biases. But the assumption that language is an autonomous system seems quite false as a characterization of the child's comprehension particularly at the early stages of language acquisition. To say this is merely to underline Grace de Laguna's (1970) point about the contextual dependency of children's speech and comprehension and the priority of the child's nonlinguistic cognitions in the assigning of meaning.

However, the assumption that the interpretation a child assigns to utterances is a function of his nonlinguistic prior knowledge and the nonlinguistic environment in which the utterance occurs also creates some problems, and it may be worth indicating some of them.

First it assumes that the meaning of the child's perceptions and actions is prelinguistically represented in a form identical to that for the representation of meaning of sentences. Hence, the nonlinguistic meaning can simply be adopted to form the conventions of the linguistic system. This may be false. The representation of experience in a form suitable for practical action and that suitable for language may be quite different; language may require that experience be coded in a form that is contrastively organized, that represents events at a particular level of abstraction to permit conventionalization across speakers and so on. Practical actions and perceptions need not call upon one's semantic or conceptual representations in quite the same way as does language.

The second difficulty with that assumption is that it may lead us to read too much into the child's nonlinguistic knowledge. If one adopts the view that meanings are first nonlinguistic or cognitive and subsequently adopted into the linguistic system, and if one knows that language can subsequently be characterized in terms of a set of case relations within sentences, or in terms of the entailment relations between sentences, he may be led to conclude that the child had prelinguistic knowledge of such things as case relations and entailment relations. That may even be true but it cannot be assumed.

Clark suggests that through his nonlinguistic experience, the child already knows objects in terms of their shape, size, texture, movement, and so on, and that these features are adopted by the linguistic system. Her systematic findings on children's overgeneralizations tend to bear that out. But she also suggests that, on the basis of their nonlinguistic experience, they also form classes of entities corresponding to agents, locations, recipients, and instruments. It would certainly help to explain the learning of a case grammar if it could be shown that children already had such classes in their prelinguistic representations, but I would doubt that children build classes as abstract as that in their prelinguistic behavior. For one thing, I cannot see any function or economy in such classes except as a means of organizing language (cf. Schlesinger, in press, Chapter 5; Bloom, 1973). Admittedly, much of what a child learns to comprehend and express in language, he already knew cognitively before he learned the appropriate linguistic form. But there must come a time when he can learn linguistic forms around which he subsequently attempts to assemble meanings as in the Original Word Game (Brown, 1958); meaning does not always precede the speech form. The danger here is that word-bound adults may read more linguistic structure into a child's prelinguistic behavior than is warranted.

Let us turn to one of the empirical issues discussed by Clark, primarily the specific relations between the structure of nonlinguistic knowledge and the structure of word meanings. She attacks this issue with a broad range of interesting evidence on the forms of the meanings assigned to nouns, to some dimensional terms—largely adjectives—to some spatial prepositions, and to some deictic pronouns.

The problem, as I see it, is how to represent the meanings of words relative to or in terms of the meanings of concepts—of the child's nonlinguistic knowledge generally. Clark presents her evidence in terms of the gradual build-up of meaning features attached to words: "The word refers to . . . the most salient characteristics perceptually," and again, "The conditions of application that the child has identified . . . constitute the meaning of the word in question." The evidence she presents for partial meanings makes that hypothesis plausible. My concerns are three in number. First, can meanings be represented adequately in terms of a set of discrete features that are primarily perceptual—roughly, can *ball* mean "round"? Second, are features attached to the words directly or are meanings organized not around words but rather around object concepts? And third, is a theory of features or qualities suitable for representing the concepts underlying both nouns and adjectives? I suggest that it is appropriate for adjectives but not for nouns.

Let us first consider the representations of meaning inferred from the overextension data gathered on children's production of concrete nouns.

Overextensions, she reports, tend to be based primarily on the properties of movement, shape, sound, texture, and taste. The feature theory of word meaning claims that the word has for its meaning a limited set of these features or conditions of application. To oversimplify perhaps, if the word *ball* has for its meaning the feature "round," and a doorknob possesses that feature, the child calls it a *ball*. But, it seems to me, the feature "round" is not the meaning of *ball*, or indeed that words have meaning features at all. Rather, as in fact Katherine Nelson (1974) has suggested, words have meanings only by reference to concepts. Concepts are the "nodes" around which meanings are assembled and words are merely attached to those concepts much like another property of their meaning. That is, it is the concepts that have prototypes or sets of properties or features and not words at all; words are merely the linguistic representation of those concepts. This view, that concepts have prototypes, feature lists, and the like, while words do not, would be compatible with both of the interesting facts about the overgeneralization data. Overgeneralization occurs because while the child may have a concept for the object involved, he has not yet a well-learned phonological representation for it. Overgeneralization results from his scanning of concept memory for the most similar object concept for which he has a retrievable name. It would also explain the lack of overgeneralization in comprehension; the phonological representation either is linked to the object concept or is not. Since the word per se does not have partial meaning, we have no reason to expect overgeneralization. In general, then, I fail to see the utility of talking as if words had as meanings a set of discrete features; I would prefer to talk of the structure of children's concepts of objects, events, and so on.

In denying that meaning can be represented in terms of a set of discrete features, I do not want to suggest that features are not used in the perception of objects but rather that object concepts are the "nodes" for the representation of experience. The concept of ball is not just a list of its features; the features are features of something—an object. Both words and features, then, are mediated by object concepts. One way of examining the child's acquisition of words representing object concepts and words representing features independently of those objects would be through a study of the order of acquisition of form classes of classifier languages which Clark mentions in her paper. A feature theory should predict that the child first learns the classifier terms which represent properties of objects and then learns the nouns for representing those objects (because nouns are simply longer and more complexly organized lists of such features); on the other hand, the object concept theory should predict that the classifiers are learned only after the concrete nouns are learned. I do not know if there is evidence on this point, but it seems extremely unlikely that classifiers are learned before the nouns.

When the child does begin to differentiate between members of a particular object class represented by nouns, then, presumably, he begins to extract qualities or features and to formulate classes on the basis of those qualities and that, I would guess, is when he begins to learn adjectives. We have a rough analogy: Nouns are to adjectives as objects are to qualities (Bransford, cited by Nelson, 1973; Bialystok & Olson, mimeo).

In regard to adjectives, *big–small*, *tall–short*, and so on, Clark's feature analysis is much more compelling. The fewer the conditions of application, the earlier the term is learned and the preference for greater extensions results in the positive terms being appropriately responded to before the negative terms. This seems a plausible and economical explanation. I am slightly troubled by the fact that if a word corresponds to a child's preferred action, he may correctly respond without having any knowledge of the word meaning and yet because of the appropriateness of the action, the adult would infer that the child knew the meaning of the word. But I think Clark is aware of that problem, and I have no particular suggestions on it.

I have, however, one comment on the way in which the problem is usually discussed. Is "dimensionality" an appropriate description of what the child is in fact learning early on? Do dimensions have a psychological reality for the child? Do the size adjectives *big* and *small* in fact imply a dimension for size? At some point they must, for they are sometimes confused, as Clark has pointed out. But are qualities abstracted and related from the outset? I do not think so; rather the child comes to see that objects can be represented in terms of absolute qualities, that is, as qualities intrinsic to particular objects. But it is only when he sees that he can represent these qualities in terms of quantities that we have the beginnings of dimensions. That is, I am suggesting that mental representations develop from objects to qualities to quantities, rather than the reverse (cf. Inhelder, 1969).

The gradual development of dimensions underlying adjectives can be seen in several ways. It is well known, and Clark contributed to this finding, that some terms that adults take as comparative terms, such as *more*, may mean a recurrence (Donaldson & Wales, 1970). Sign language, I am told, has signs for *lots* and *little* but not regular signs for the comparative forms *more than* and for *less than*. Perhaps the child's first representations of amount are not ordered on a scale or dimension.

Consider the adjective pair, *big–small*. If you tell a child, *A is bigger than B*, and then, *A is smaller than C*, he has grave difficulty in assigning a meaning to the second statement. Why? If he interprets the first statement to mean "A is big" and "B is small," what is he to do with the new statement that he codes as "A is small"? How can A be both big and small? It cannot; therefore, he fails to understand. And he will fail to understand as long as he assumes that size is an intrinsic property of objects. When we tell a child that a mouse is small and an elephant is big, smallness is an intrinsic quality of the mouse. The implicit standard, presumably, is the child's own size. I would guess that, at this stage, size is as much an intrinsic quality of an object as its shape or color. Such a quality, judged on the basis of possession or nonpossession, may be used to identify an object as a member of a particular object concept. In order to differentiate between instances of a concept (adjectivally), he begins to construct a size dimension along which he can array two objects of the same class, a big mouse and a little mouse. Once having this dimension, he can assemble series of objects along the dimension, such as, A bigger than B, but A smaller than C.

Similarly, consider an adjective pair like *hot* and *cold*. Presumably, the child knows one or both of these as intrinsic qualities of objects long before he constructs a dimension, temperature, on which the variability between instances of a concept can be represented. Thus, early on, the child may treat an adjective *hot* as if it were a noun (Edwards, 1975). Perhaps this account can be simplified by saying that, for the young child, qualities such as those of size and temperature are assigned as intrinsic qualities of objects relative to the child's own size and temperature; he has a scale with himself as the midpoint. Subsequently, he "decenters" to yield a general scale on which different instances of the same object can be represented. And finally, the scale is abstracted sufficiently to permit the comparison of different objects: "Which is larger, a small elephant or a big cat?"

Even when he has a scale for size judgments, there may be no ground for thinking that the child has represented size in terms of specific dimensions such as length or width or depth. The children's early size judgments may be nondimensionalized. Once children begin to dimensionalize their judgments, they tend to overemphasize one of the dimensions, usually height, to yield Piagetian type nonconservation responses. But prior to that, there is a stage during which they may make quite good size and numerosity judgments perhaps because they fail to see the display in dimensionalized terms. That would be my preferred way of explaining the interesting data presented by Maratsos (1973) and Mehler and Bever (1967). One could pursue this problem by studying children's size judgments of irregular shapes, such as blobs, which cannot, at least readily, be assigned dimensionalized values.

My final comment has to do with the problem of children's conception of space and how it relates to spatial terms and deictic terms. The problem of the acquisition of spatial terms and deictic terms is fascinating for a number of reasons, one of which is that these terms provide the ground for the breakdown in the immediate "intersubjectivity" between the adult and child. For all the terms discussed so far, if it is a *cat* for you, it is also a *cat* for me. Words imply the same world and the same linguistic conventionalizations for representing that world. But here, the correspondence breaks down. These words, and the personal pronouns, begin to be differentiated on the basis of who is saying them. In the simplest case, both the child and the parent can call the child *Bill*, but they cannot both, correctly, call him *you*. For this reason, presumably children acquire pet names before they learn *Mommy* (Hutten-locher, 1974) and proper nouns before personal pronouns. Another way to say this is that the invariance between speaker/listener breaks down and that is one fact that makes their acquisition much more difficult. Beyond this, children's learning of spatial terms depends, as Clark has shown, upon the nature of the referent object, the dimension and the pole of the dimension specified, and so on, as well as the child's egocentrism and the lack of invariance between speaker and learner. This is an exciting area in which much work is ongoing (Bryant, 1974; Eliot & Salkind, 1975; Bialystok, 1976; Sinha & Walkerdine, mimeo).

In summary, one way to describe the child's acquisition of language is to say that the meaning of an utterance for a young child is not drawn exclusively from the utterance but rather that the meaning is communicated by an array of environmental and conventionalized features of which the formal structure of the utterance is only one. If you offer a candy to a child and the act is accompanied by a set of conventionalized gestures while saying *Do you want some candy?* the child has little difficulty in recovering the speaker's intentions. The child gets that meaning from the whole array. The development of comprehension is a matter of learning to depend, or at least of developing the ability to depend, if the occasion requires it, on the meaning actually conventionalized in the speech signal. The development of production is a matter of learning to put more and more of that meaning into the speech signal at least if the occasion requires it. This is a process that presumably continues well into adulthood, and Clark has shown us some of the ways in which a child gets on with this task.

ACKNOWLEDGMENTS

I am indebted to I. M. Schlesinger and Ellen Bialystok for their helpful comments and to Vera Jacobs for her clerical assistance.

REFERENCES

Bialystok, E. The development of spatial concepts in language and thought. Ph.D. dissertation, OISE, Toronto, Canada, 1976.
Bialystok, E., & Olson, D. Nouns and objects in children's cognition. Mimeo. Ontario Institute for Studies in Education, Toronto, Canada.

Bloom, L. *One word at a time.* The Hague: Mouton, 1973.

Brown, R. *Words and things.* New York: Free Press of Glencoe, 1958.

Bryant, P. *Perception and understanding in young children: An experimental approach.* London: Methuen, 1974.

Chomsky, N. *Problems of knowledge and freedom.* London: Fontana, 1972.

de Laguna, G. *Speech: Its function and development.* College Park, Md.: McGrath, 1970. (Reprint of 1927 edition.)

Donaldson, M., & Wales, R. On the acquisition of some relational terms. In J. R. Hayes (Ed.), *Cognition and the development of language.* New York: Wiley, 1970.

Edwards, D. Constraints on actions: A source of early meaning in child language. Paper presented at the Symposium on Language and Social Context. University of Stirling, Scotland, 1975.

Eliot, J., & Salkind, N. *Children's spatial development.* Springfield, Ill.: Charles C Thomas, 1975.

Huttenlocher, J. The origins of language comprehension. In R. Solso (Ed.), *Theories in cognitive psychology: The Loyola Symposium.* Potomac, Md.: Lawrence Erlbaum Associates, 1974.

Inhelder, B. Memory and intelligence. In D. Elkind and J. Flavell (Eds.), *Studies in cognitive development.* London: Oxford University Press, 1969.

Macnamara, J. The cognitive basis of language learning in infants. *Psychological Review,* 1972, *79,* 1–13.

Maratsos, M. P. Decrease in the understanding of the word "Big" in preschool children. *Child Development,* 1973, *44,* 747–752.

Mehler, J., & Bever, T. G. Cognitive capacities of very young children. *Science,* 1967, *158,* 141–142.

Nelson, K. Some evidence for the cognitive primacy of categorization and its functional basis. *Merrill-Palmer Quarterly,* 1973, *19,* 21–39.

Nelson, K. Concept, word and sentence: Interrelations in acquisition and development. *Psychological Review,* 1974, *81,* 267–285.

Schlesinger, I. M. *Production and comprehension of utterances.* Potomac, Md.: Lawrence Erlbaum Associates, in press.

Sinha, C., & Walkerdine, V. Functional and perceptual aspects of the acquisition of spatial relational terms. Mimeo. School of Education, Bristol, U.K.

14

Language Change in
Childhood and in History

DAN I. SLOBIN

University of California, Berkeley

The development of language in childhood is but one of several ways of studying how language changes over time. Developmental psycholinguistics, in dealing with diachronic processes in the individual, shares much common ground with historical linguistics, with studies of languages in contact, and with the investigation of the evolution of pidgin and creole languages. In all of these instances, it has become clear that the study of language during its unstable or changing phases is an excellent tool for discovering the essence of language itself. At the same time, the more we know about what language is, the more we know about the mind and its growth. The structure of language is constrained by psycholinguistic processes of perception, memory, and

This paper is a revised version of a paper entitled "The more it changes . . . On understanding Language by watching it move through time," delivered as the Keynote Address to the Stanford Child Language Research Forum (April 4, 1975). Work on the paper was supported, in part, by a grant from The Grant Foundation to the Institute of Human Learning ("Cross-Linguistic Study of Language Acquisition"; Dan I. Slobin, Principal Investigator) and by support from the National Institute of Mental Health to the Language-Behavior Research Laboratory, Department of Anthropology, University of California at Berkeley.

cognition, by sociolinguistic processes, and by the development of these processes in childhood. My focus here is on clarifying the psycholinguistic processes which make language possible. And I propose to carry out this task by studying the way language changes: the way it changes as the speech of the child approaches the speech of his community, or as the speech of one community approaches that of another community, or as a language system becomes established and keeps adjusting to perturbations from within and without. In a remarkable way, language maintains a universal character across all of these continuing changes, so that the more it changes, the more sure we can be of what it is.

One cannot separate a theory of language *change* from a theory of language *structure*. And both change and structure are bound by the same psycholinguistic and sociolinguistic constraints imposed by the processing of speech in real time and in social settings. Both change and structure are constrained by the uses to which language is put. Our investigation, therefore, must begin with a characterization of the cognitive and communicative determinants of the nature of human language.

The speaker of a language wants to express himself clearly, efficiently, effectively, and reasonably quickly; and the listener wants to quickly and efficiently retrieve a clear and informative message. These needs and constraints of speaker and listener determine the structure of language. I conceive of four basic ground rules to which a communicative system must adhere if it is to function as a full-fledged human language. Let me present them as imperatives to this creature we are all studying—imperatives to the semimythical being whom I'll refer to simply as *Language* (with a capital L). The four charges to Language are: (1) Be clear. (2) Be humanly processible in ongoing time. (3) Be quick and easy. (4) Be expressive.

The first charge, *to be clear*, means that the surface structures of Language must not be too different in form and organization from the semantic structures which underlie them. I stated this charge several years ago as an operating principle of child language (Slobin, 1973, Operating Principle E): "Underlying semantic relations should be marked overtly and clearly." The universals of child language which result from that operating principle, as I will show in a while, also appear in other situations of language change. That is, there is a tendency for Language to strive to maintain a one-to-one mapping between underlying semantic structures and surface forms, with the goal of making messages easily retrievable for listeners. To be "clear," in the way I am using the term here, is to strive for semantic transparency.

The second charge, *to be humanly processible in ongoing time*, means that Language must conform to strategies of speech perception and production. Greenberg and others have summarized the sets of linguistic features which typically cohere in languages of given types, such as the positioning of nominal and verbal modifiers on the basis of dominant word order of a language. Recent work by psycholinguists on perceptual strategies (cf. Fodor, Bever, & Garrett, 1974), along with studies of computer processing of language and various process-oriented models of language, suggest that perceptual and productive rules can account for the range of possible manifestations of surface syntax. Much of the work in experimental psycholinguistics—both adult and child research—has been devoted to characterizing mechanisms of language performance, and is directly relevant here.

The third charge to Language, *to be quick and easy*, allows for human weakness and perversity. Somehow it's hard to keep languages from getting blurry. We seem to try to blur and smudge phonology wherever possible, to delete and contract surface forms, to conflate underlying forms in surface expression. Perhaps the old arguments of least effort still play some role here. At any rate, there are communicative needs to get a lot of information in before the listener gets bored or takes over the conversation; and there are short-term memory constraints to get a message across before the speaker or listener loses track of what is going on. And so, contrary to the charges to be clear and processible, there is also a charge to cut corners.

The fourth charge to Language, *to be expressive*, has two important aspects: to be *semantic* and to be *rhetorical*. By "semantic" I mean the expression of propositional and referential content. There is a universal set of basic conceptual categories which must be expressed in every language. These are the categories which are most salient to the child, and which are essential to every communicative act. Beyond the set of most salient concepts, there is a hierarchy of increasingly complex notions. To be minimally expressive semantically, a language must have means of encoding at least the universal core of salient concepts and relations; to be fully expressive, a wider and more complex range of notions must be encodable.

The charge to be rhetorical takes account of the fact that Language is used for more than conveying logical propositions and referential information. Language must provide alternate ways of expressing notions, and must provide means for compacting semantic content on the surface, in order for the speaker to communicate *well*—that is, to communicate effectively, engagingly, appropriately, and so forth. The speaker must be able to direct the listener's attention, to take account of his knowledge and expectations; the speaker must have means for surprising, impressing, playing up to, or putting down his interlocutor; he must have linguistic means of expressing relations of status and affiliation between himself and his conversational partner.

To be fully expressive semantically and rhetorically increases the complexity both of communicative intentions and of surface structure, thus putting strains on the charges to be clear and to be processible.

Language is always under *competing* pressure to conform to all four of these charges. Because the pressures are inherently competitory, languages are constantly changing, and universals, except for those which are principles of change itself, always refer to idealized static language situations.

Child language is at first most influenced by the first two charges—to be clear and to be processible. The child is minimally pressured to transmit a densely structured message in a compact time interval or to adapt his communication to the pragmatics of a wide range of interaction situations. Child speech is close to underlying semantic intent in form and is guided by the most basic processing rules. In this regard it is similar to contact vernaculars or pidgin languages—and indeed, turning the comparison around, David Smith (1973, p. 291) and other students of pidgin and creole languages have pointed out that child language is "pidginized," in that both child language and pidgins are characterized by relatively simple form and restriction of function in comparison with more developed linguistic systems—including creoles, language of older children, and standard languages.

Creoles and standard adult languages must attend more closely to the third and fourth charges as well: to be quick and easy and to be fully expressive. It is these two needs which provide the impetus for language change, while the first two needs—to be clear and processible—constrain the directions of change of a given language system within a small range of possibilities. A gain in compactness or expressiveness of communication is often purchased at the expense of ease of processing or semantic transparency of the message. The tension between these four factors is present in all situations of language change: child development, historical change, language contact, depidginization or creolization. The speech system of an individual or community at any point in time can be characterized in terms of these four factors or goals. A full definition of the possible ways of carrying out these goals simultaneously would be a full exposition of linguistic universals, and would answer the question: What does a linguistic system have to be in order to qualify as a possible native language? Only languages which carry out these four goals will be learnable, usable, and potentially available for all mature communicative functions.

I would like now to discuss these four goals of Language in the context of change. In so doing, I want to avoid the question of the source of change and the complex issue of the degree to which children are responsible for linguistic change. My aim is to make a sketch of the change process itself, trying to find similarities in several different kinds of diachronic stories. By examining how each of these charges is carried out under conditions of change, I believe we will arrive at a clearer notion of the nature of the charges themselves.

I will discuss the four charges separately, though many of the diachronic situations I will present are obviously influenced by the joint action of several of the charges. Let me try to trace out the consequences of each of the charges in four types of linguistic change: the development of language in children, the change of established languages over time, the changes occurring in one language as a result of contact with another in the minds of bilingual speakers, and the changes which occur when a pidgin becomes a native language and expands to fulfill more and more mature communicative functions—that is, the processes of creolization and decreolization.

To remind you of the terminology: pidgin languages are contact vernaculars used between speakers of different native languages for specialized communication. Such a language can be minimally simple or quite elaborated, but it maintains the characteristic that none of the speakers has acquired it as a first language. A pidgin with native speakers is called a creole. Pidgins undergo definable changes in the course of creolization. As a creole expands and differentiates to carry out a full range of linguistic needs of a community, it undergoes further definable changes. This process of decreolization presumably results in the emergence of a new and complete language. The differences between a pidgin and a creole provide important clues as to what Language must do in order to fully carry out the four charges. It has been repeatedly pointed out (e.g., Bickerton, 1975) that a pidgin cannot function as a suitable native language because it is too slow in tempo and fails to make necessary semantic and pragmatic distinctions; I will examine this issue as I go along.

So what we have available for consideration here is a range of linguistic systems—from minimal to maximal—and some information about separate instances of change, both ontogenetic and diachronic. In the space of this paper, I can only sample from these instances, pointing to an eventual unified theory of Language and language change.

BE CLEAR

CHILD LANGUAGE

In my earlier work on "operating principles" of child language (1973), I cited numerous examples of attempts by children to maintain acoustically salient and isolable surface expressions of semantic entities, preferring a one-to-one mapping of content and form wherever possible. For example, when English-speaking children discover that contracted auxiliaries can be analyzed, they often go through a period of exaggerated analysis, using forms like *I will*, *I will not*, and *do not*, where adults would use *I'll*, *I won't*, and *don't*

(Bellugi, 1967). When Italian children discover the role of subject pronouns, they go through a phase in which the normally optional pronoun is always expressed (Bates, 1976). Zero morphemes are avoided in the acquisition of inflectional paradigms: the English-speaking child prefers *hitted* to *hit* for the past tense. The Arabic-speaking child uses the plural in expressions with numeral and noun for all numbers, contrary to the input language (Omar, 1973). Slavic-speaking children express each grammatical case with an inflectional suffix, even though the language leaves some cases unmarked in some genders. Lexical causatives are often replaced by periphrastic expressions, as the English *make dead* for *kill*. So there seems to be a general tendency in child language away from synthesis, contraction, and deletion, and towards more analytic expressions wherever possible. Many more examples could be added.

Furthermore, systems which maintain the principle of semantic clarity are also easier to acquire. In our cross-linguistic research at Berkeley we are comparing the acquisition of English, Italian, Serbo-Croatian, and Turkish as native languages. The Turkish system of agglutinative inflectional morphology is remarkably transparent. There are strings of clearly segmentable suffixed morphemes, each bearing one element of meaning. The system is totally regular—there are almost no exceptions to general rules, and there are no arbitrary subclasses on the basis of features such as grammatical gender or phonological shape of stem. Each inflectional morpheme is syllabic and acoustically salient. For example, consider the following portion of the nominal inflectional paradigm:

Partial Turkish inflectional paradigm
 el 'hand'
 -im first person possessive
 -ler plural
 -de locative

Combinatorial possibilities
elim   'my hand'
eller   'hands'
ellerim   'my hands'
elde   'in hand'
elimde   'in my hand'
ellerimde 'in my hands'

This is an exceptionally neat example of an analytic paradigm, and is a joy to descriptive linguists, who use it as a model in introductory textbooks. It is apparently a joy to the Turkish child as well, and the entire system is mastered well before the age of 2.

The Serbo-Croatian inflectional system contrasts sharply. It is a classic Indo-European synthetic muddle, with the choice of nominal case ending influenced by issues of grammatical gender, animacy, number, and phonological shape of stem. There are many irregularities, a great deal of homonymy, and scattered zero morphemes. For example, whereas the Turkish accusative inflection is a uniform suffix, the Serbo-Croatian accusative—considering the singular noun only (since it will be different for plurals, and different again for adjectives)—is realized as a final -*u* for feminine nouns, -*a* for masculine animate nouns, and zero for other masculine and neuter nouns. Those same endings appear elsewhere in the paradigm as well; for example, -*u* is also a dative or locative ending in some genders; the final -*a* of masculine animate accusative is also the feminine nominative; and so on. Little wonder that the Yugoslav child does not master such a system until about age 5—3 years or so later than the Turkish child. The first stage of Serbo-Croatian, however, like the first stage of Russian and of German and other highly inflected Indo-European languages, adheres to the charge to be clear. The child chooses a single suffix for each grammatical case and uses it in all instances, ignoring gender, irregularities, and so forth. In effect, he has made his Indo-European language as analytic as possible, and then spends several years accepting the morphophonemic complexities of his mother tongue. The principle of marking semantic relations by nominal suffixes is as accessible to the Indo-European child as to the Turkic (or Japanese or Korean or Finnish or Hungarian) child. It is the violation of the charge to be clear which slows up the Indo-European child in his course of acquisition. And the Indo-European languages tend to collapse and simplify their inflectional systems over time or in bilingual contact situations, whereas the Turkic system of agglutinative inflectional morphology has remained stable across a great range of time and contact situations.

The picture is exactly reversed, however, in regard to syntax. Indo-European-speaking children acquire means for inserting one sentence into another at a very early age. Our Yugoslav children were forming relative clauses, for example, when they were 2 years old. Here it is Indo-European which maintains a clear mapping from underlying semantics to surface form. Consider an example from Serbo-Croatian. A 2-year-old girl said the equivalent of "I want doll that daddy bought." The two underlying sentences are well-preserved on the surface, with the minimal adjustment required by a relative pronoun and deletion of a repeated object in the embedded sentence. The comparable form in Turkish syntax is not mastered until age 5. The reason is that, in this case, it is Turkish which is maximally opaque. The details are too complex to summarize, but, basically, the predicate of the embedded sentence must be turned into a participle, preposed, and possessed by its agent, resulting in something which could be roughly paraphrased as "Daddy's boughten doll I want."

Baba-	*nın*	*al-*	*dığ-*	*ı*	*bebeğ-*	*i*	*istiyorum.*
father-	genitive	buy-	object relative particle-	possessive suffix	doll-	definite direct object inflection	I-want

One can expect late-acquired and difficult constructions such as this to be weak points in a language, and I will show later that Turkic relative clauses and verb complement constructions are most vulnerable to change in bilingual contact situations. But first let us look at the charge to be clear in the light of historical linguistics.

HISTORY

Similar tendencies to maintain a one-to-one mapping between semantics and syntax can be seen in the historical evolution of Language, though always in competition with the charge to be quick and easy. Robin Lakoff (1972) has characterized Indo-European drift as a "metacondition on the way the grammar of a language *as a whole* will change" (p. 178). She discusses a number of general developments in Indo-European, such as the obligatory use of anaphoric, non-emphatic subject pronouns, the use of prepositions instead of case endings, the development of periphrastic causatives, inchoatives, auxiliaries, and so forth. All of these developments move away from oversynthesis and toward greater semantic transparency. She characterizes this metacondition as an instruction to the language "to segmentalize where possible." She is not willing to ascribe universal or psychological significance to this principle, because it is not manifested in all instances of language change. But I would argue that whenever a language has gone too far from the principle of one-to-one mapping or semantic transparency in some area of its structure, the tendency to segmentalize will assert itself, just as it does in child language and, as I will point out, in pidgins. The first two charges—clarity and processibility—strive toward segmentalization. The other two charges—temporal compactness and expressiveness—strive toward synthesis, however. As a result, Language constantly fluctuates between the poles of analyticity and syntheticity, since none of the charges can be ignored. I will return to the question of the Linguistic Cycle later, in relation to the third charge. For now I just want to point out that there seems to be a universal tendency away from oversynthesis, and that this tendency is manifested both ontogenetically and diachronically.

CONTACT

When two languages are in contact in the minds of bilingual speakers, the charge to be clear influences what will be borrowed from one language into the other. Weinreich (1953), in his classic survey of languages in contact, suggested that a language will borrow those forms needed to replace a zero morpheme or a morpheme which is acoustically not very salient in its own system prior to contact (p. 33). For example, the comparative in Ukrainian "is expressed by an unstressed bound suffix (involving frequent root modifications)" (p. 34). The Romanian comparative is a simple preposed particle, *mai*, meaning 'more'. In a Ukrainian–Romanian bilingual situation, the Romanian particle entered Ukrainian speech, resulting in forms equivalent to *more older*—a clearer marking of underlying semantics and quite reminiscent of child speech. (One might also note the extension of the analytic comparative and superlative in English, gradually replacing inflectional forms. We no longer can say *elegantest*, as John Milton did, and even *profounder* or *pleasanter*, to my ear, should be replaced by *more profound* and *more pleasant*; cf. Barber, 1966.)

Weinreich clearly states a version of our position in discussing grammatical transfer between languages: "Significantly, in the interference of two grammatical patterns it is ordinarily the one which uses relatively free and invariant morphemes in its paradigm—one might say, the more explicit pattern—which serves as the model for imitation" (p. 41). He cites several unrelated cases in which a language using a bound possessive morpheme has replaced it with a pronominal possessive construction. This has happened to Estonian under German influence, to Amharic in contact with Cushitic, and to Israeli Hebrew in interaction with Yiddish and other Indo-European immigrant languages.

The preference for clear mapping of underlying forms is evident not only on the morphological level, as I pointed out in comparing the acquisition of relative clause constructions in Indo-European and Turkish. You will recall that the Turkic languages have extraordinarily complex means for the surface realization of structures in which one sentence is subordinated to another. (I offered the example of object relative clauses; similar arguments could be made in regard to subject relatives and verb complement constructions.) One would expect that Turkic speakers would prefer more transparent means of expressing such constructions as relative clauses. There are many examples of long-term interaction between Turkic and Indo-European languages, since the two language types are in contact over a long belt, stretching from Central Asia into the Balkans. In every case I have investigated, the Turkic language always borrows or invents a relative particle on the model of the Indo-European contact language, while keeping the Turkic inflectional morphology intact. This has happened to Azerbaijani under the influence of Persian, to Karaite Turkish in the Crimea under Russian influence, to Gagauz Turkish under Romanian influence, and in several other cases. Circumlocutions to avoid relative clause constructions are common in child speech and informal speech in Turkey, resulting in forms closer to the Indo-European model—something like: "Well daddy bought a doll, huh? I want that one." (As I will point out later, such forms are strikingly similar to the new means of relativization currently evolving in Tok Pisin, a New Guinea pidgin which is presently creolizing.)

This phenomenon suggests a general principle of language contact: *Forms which are late to be acquired by children are presumably also relatively difficult for adults to process, and should be especially vulnerable to change.* Such forms will be modified or replaced in a contact situation if the neighboring language has semantically equivalent forms which are acquired at an earlier age. Thus relative age of acquisition can be taken as an index of psycholinguistic complexity, and can be used to predict degree of resistance of a form to change. Kiparsky has phrased a similar rule for historical linguistics: "Basically, we can say that rules are susceptible to loss *if they are hard to learn*" (1971, p. 627).

This generalization is restricted, however, by the other charges to Language: Sometimes (as Ferguson has pointed out to me in regard to Amharic) a complex form can be maintained or even borrowed for expressive purposes—to mark the status or social affiliation of the speaker, or the style of the discourse. And, furthermore, change must be consistent with the general typological features of the language in order to maintain processibility. It would be difficult for an Indo-European language to borrow agglutinative suffixes without altering many other characteristics of its structure, though far-reaching typological changes have occurred historically.

PIDGIN/CREOLE

Paul Kay and Gillian Sankoff characterize pidgin language as "derivationally shallower than natural languages and reflect[ing] universal deep (=semantic) structure in their surface structures more directly than do natural languages" (1974, p. 66). This sounds like maximal adherence to the charge to be clear, and bears a strong similarity to many characterizations of child language. Kay and Sankoff define this goal of Language in terms of surface structures which are "in conformity with universal deep structure." Pidgins and early stages of creoles are maximally analytic, having no inflectional morphology at all and using separate lexical items or particles like adverbs and prepositions, along with word order, to express underlying semantic relations. When relieved of the pressure of the third and fourth charges, then, Language reflects the first charge most clearly.

BE PROCESSIBLE

I have discussed only the first of the four charges to Language so far. The charge to be clear requires a fine intermeshing of semantic and syntactic processes. The second charge, to be processible, raises issues of producing and perceiving speech in real time. Linguists and psycholinguists are speaking more and more about perceptual strategies, and most of what I will have to say here deals with the receptive end of communication. Similar short-term constraints, of course, apply to the speaker as well as the listener, but this area of psycholinguistics has been less well elaborated.

Every change in a language system must conform to the limitations of processing strategies. It is becoming clear that such strategies are of necessity interlocked, so that a change at one point in a system necessitates changes elsewhere in order that the meaning of messages can be encoded or decoded within the capacity of a human language processor.

CHILD LANGUAGE

Much of recent experimental work with child language has been devoted to strategies for speech perception and comprehension. I have formulated "operating principles" which rely on a natural tendency to look for meaning at the ends of words and in the order of morphemes (Slobin, 1973). Bever (1970) and others have proposed developmental sequences of word order strategies. And Fodor, Bever, and Garrett (1974) have elaborated a general psycholinguistic model based on the proposition that languages provide surface cues to underlying structures precisely because such cues are required for perceptual strategies involved in the ongoing parsing of sentences.

Developmentally, we know that some perceptual strategies are more accessible than others. It is apparently easier to attend to postpositions than to prepositions, to continuous rather than discontinuous structures, and so forth (Slobin, 1973). Constructions which can be signaled by special particles, like relative pronouns, are more readily processed by young children if those markers are not deleted. The child's attempts to be clear in his own speaking—such as avoiding contractions, overusing prepositions, and placing abnormal stress on inflectional morphemes—probably serve the function of keeping his ongoing speech more perceptible to himself, that is, to keep him from losing track of where he is in a developing utterance. At the same time, as we have discovered in our cross-linguistic research, some perceptual strategies appear to be *equally* accessible at the beginning of grammatical development—such as attention to either word order or inflections in guiding sentence interpretation.

But such facts cannot account for linguistic *change*, because they do not apply singly, but in interrelation with one another. A VSO language, for example, will not develop postpositions, even if they are more perceptible than prepositions, because other perceptual strategies require that a language of this type be prepositional. The contribution from developmental and experimental psycholinguistics must be to define the limits of perceptibility and learnability of grammatical structures, thus defining the range of possible languages and directions of change.

HISTORY

When a language is in the process of change, however, the perceptual strategies most accessible to children should play a role in determining the direction of change. Charles Li and Sandra Thompson (1974), for example, note that Chinese is in the process of moving from a VO to an OV language. The change is not complete, and for some expressions forms of two types are present. For example, there are co-occurring VO and Preposition-OV forms, such as:

Nǐ qù nǎr? 'You go where?'
Nǐ dào nǎr qù? 'You to where go?'

The latter form provides more surface cues to underlying structure, in that the preposition can help guide sentence interpretation strategies. If the new OV form with preposition is more accessible to basic perceptual strategies, we should expect it to be preferred in acquisition. The direction of linguistic change seems to be one of enhancing processibility.

Bever and Langendoen (1971) have made the most elaborate argument in this regard, in tracing the history of relative clause constructions from Old English to Modern English. They suggest that, with the decline of nominal inflections, perceptual confusions occurred in various relative clause constructions, eventually resulting in new restrictions on the use of relative pronouns in order to avoid such confusions. At each point in its history, the language has apparently been strongly constrained by the charge to conform to perceptual strategies.

In the space I have here I can only hint at the importance of perceptual strategies in accounting for linguistic universals, but the ramifications of this point should be of great interest to students of child language development. A thorough attempt to relate a set of typological universals to perceptual strategies has recently been made by Kuno (1974) in *Linguistic Inquiry*. It is too lengthy to summarize here, but it is important to me in that he has appealed to perceptual constraints on the processing of self-embedded constructions to account for apparently universal relations between basic word order typology and the positioning of relative clauses, nominal modifiers, and conjunctions. For example, SOV languages are characterized by the use of postpositions and prenominal relative clauses. Kuno suggests that these clusters of typological features function to avoid center-embedded constructions as much as possible, thus reducing overall psycholinguistic complexity in the language.

A simpler example to present here is one offered by Lehmann (1973). He argues that the primary concomitant of the verb is the object. Although he does not offer a perceptual argument, one could say that the verb and its object constitute a kind of perceptual Gestalt which resists interruption. In a language which is in a consistent stage of its development, one finds a distribution of elements which guarantee the integrity of this Gestalt: in an OV language, verbal modifiers follow the verb and nominal modifiers precede the noun, keeping O and V together; in a VO language, verbal modifiers precede the verb and nominal modifiers follow the noun, again preserving the Gestalt of verb and object. Languages which are inconsistent in regard to the placement of verbal and nominal modifiers are probably undergoing change. One would expect that children learning such languages would apply natural perceptual strategies, with the eventual effect of removing the inconsistencies. That is, the parts of a linguistic system which are not in accord with universal principles of language processing should pose difficulties to the child, and should show the greatest variation and protraction in individual ontogenetic development.

There are at least two ways in which a language can become unclear perceptually. In the simpler case, phonological change or fusion can make some distinctions less distinct acoustically. In such cases, perceptual clarity is re-established by extending the use of existing forms, such as the English relative pronoun or the Romance prepositions and articles, or by introducing new forms consistent with the overall structure of the language. For example, the Turkic languages are OV and agglutinative, and, accordingly, are suffixing and postpositional in type. Repeatedly in their history, postpositions become reduced to noun suffixes, followed by the introduction of new postpositions. As long as the basic word order type remains stable, and the overall system is consistent, the perceptual and processing strategies produce the same result over time: new particles in the same position and bearing the same meaning as old particles whose acoustic clarity has eroded.

But a language can also become unclear perceptually when it is changing in basic word order type, as in the example of Chinese. In such cases, the perceptual strategies operate to ensure consistency in the overall system. When Proto-Indo-European presumably was in a transition from an OV to a VO language (Lehmann, 1973), there must have been a period in which postpositions were very difficult to process, and speakers had no recourse but to indicate the relevant notions prepositionally in order for their speech to adapt to the inherent real-time constraints on programming and interpreting utterances.

CONTACT

There certainly are cases of bilingual situations in which such attempts to maintain a consistent set of processing rules can be demonstrated. Apparently in a long-term bilingual or multilingual situation, where speakers must constantly use two or more languages, there is a striking tendency for grammatical convergence between the languages. Gumperz and Wilson (1971) have made a remarkable demonstration of this point in a study of Kupwar, a village in India where Urdu, Marathi, and Kannada have been maintained for centuries within a community of interacting speakers. Urdu and Marathi are Indo-European and Kannada is Dravidian. In Kupwar, however, the local variants of these three languages are virtually identical in their surface syntax and phonetics, while maintaining distinct vocabulary and morphophonemics. It seems that it is extremely difficult—if not impossible—to maintain separate systems of psycholinguistic processing rules in situations of daily, continuing bilingualism.

Attempts by bilinguals to reduce two languages to one set of processing rules can be revealed over a very short time span. Donald Larmouth (1974), in a recent paper on four generations of Finnish speakers in Minnesota, has demonstrated such changes. For example, the system of Finnish inflections has been lost, requiring that Minnesota Finnish become a rigid SVO language. Note that this makes Finnish compatible with the sorts of word order perceptual strategies proposed for English by Bever. Weinreich (1953) reported a similar change in Slovenian under the influence of Italian in a bilingual situation. The fate of Finnish postpositions in Minnesota is also of interest: They move in position to become prepositions, on the English model.

Note that such a change is possible because Finnish and English are both SVO languages, and such languages can apparently function with either prepositions or postpositions. Presumably an SOV language could not accept a prepositional system without a concomitant change in basic word order.

What happens when very young children learn two languages of different types? There is some suggestive evidence that such children go through a stage of imposing similar ordering rules on both languages. The preschool bilingual child is not necessarily constrained by the interlocking set of syntactic patterns which characterize a language as to basic type, because these patterns are defined across the whole linguistic system—for example, relating the positions of relative clauses, noun and verb modifiers, conjunctions, and so forth. Knowing only a part of each language, the young child is freer to violate typological constraints than an older speaker would be.[1] For example, Imedadze's (1960) daughter was learning Georgian—an ergative language, along with Russian—an accusative-type language. She went through a period of using the Georgian ergative suffix as if it were an accusative inflection, placing it on the word which would require an accusative inflection in Russian rather than the native ergative position. Malmberg's Finnish-speaking child, learning Swedish, used Swedish prepositions as postpositions, on the Finnish model (Malmberg, 1945; reported by Ervin-Tripp, 1973, p. 271). Note that in both of these cases, as in the Gumperz and Wilson Indian case, each of the two languages maintains its lexical material, but the position of grammatical markers results from application of a single set of production rules for both languages. Presumably such constraints on uniformity of processing strategies across languages account for the kind of widespread and significant grammatical change which has occurred historically in situations of long-term contact between languages differing in basic typological features.

PIDGIN/CREOLE

Pidgin and creole situations can be used in two different ways to define more precisely the manner in which Language must adhere to the charge to

---

[1] This claim should be investigated in developmental studies. My argument here is that typological consistencies within a given language are formed by a complex interplay of processing constraints and efficiency pressures across a large range of linguistic forms. Kuno (1974), for example, shows that prenominal positioning of relative clauses in SOV languages and postnominal positioning of relative clauses in VSO languages acts to minimize (but not abolish) the occurrence of center-embedded structures (which impose a burden on sentence processing). But for this phenomenon to have an effect on the individual, he must be mature enough to produce a variety of complex sentence types. In addition, Kuno shows how similar considerations account for the positioning of conjunctions and question words, the use of pre- or postpositions, and the presence or absence of relative pronouns. It may be that the child must command a range of linguistic forms before the psycholinguistic pressures for typological consistency exert an influence on his language. On the other hand, the child may be sensitive at quite an early age to the interrelations between positional constraints in his language. For example, having acquired SOV order and postpositions, the child may "expect" or at least feel most comfortable with prenominal positioning of relative clauses.

The examples given in the paper are of bilingual children. This issue would be very difficult to investigate in monolingual acquisition of a typologically consistent language, since errors in positioning of grammatical elements tends to be infrequent. However, much could be learned from investigation of the acquisition of typologically inconsistent languages, that is, those languages presently in the process of change from one basic word order type to another. For example, Amharic is apparently in a late stage of change from VSO to SOV, presumably under the influence of Cushitic languages (Bach, 1970; Little, 1974). As a result, there are both pre- and postpositions, and even constructions of preposition–noun–postposition. One would expect children to prefer postpositional structures and to omit prepositions. Generally, the research strategy would be to predict that children will find it easier to learn to place grammatical forms in positions consistent with the basic word order of the language.

be processible. On the one hand, an examination of the most elementary contact vernaculars can reveal the minimal grammatical equipment required to render Language humanly processible. Kay and Sankoff clearly state the goal of this sort of endeavor when they propose (1974, p. 62): "Since the communicative functions fulfilled by contact vernaculars are minimal, these languages may possibly reveal in a more direct way than do most natural languages the universals of cognitive structure and process that underlie all human language ability and language use." On the other hand, the changes brought about in conditions of creolization—when the communicative functions of a language system expand—can reveal the nature of more complex processing rules. I would like to explore each of these paths, first by considering a minimal contact vernacular, Russenorsk, and then by looking at one aspect of a rapidly evolving creole, New Guinea Tok Pisin.

Russenorsk (Broch, 1927) was a trade language used between Russian merchants and Norwegian fishermen in the Arctic Ocean for at least 100 years before 1917. It was used only during the brief summer trading period each year, for the minimal functions of trading fish for agricultural products. It provides a striking example of the basic perceptual cues which a language must provide in order to be processible. The parallels to very early child language are intriguing. There were no nominal inflections and a fixed SVO order. Although the difference between nouns and verbs could probably be identified on semantic grounds, the language had begun to evolve a general verbal suffix which served simply to mark the verb as such. Tense and aspect were indicated periphrastically. Subject and object were thus identified by word order, and verb by word order and verb marker. The only remaining perceptual problem was to differentiate noun–noun constructions as to underlying case relations. Two juxtaposed nouns were interpretable as expressing a genitive relationship, with fixed order of possessor–possessed. All other case relations between nouns were expressed by a generalized preposition, which could be interpreted as locational, directional, dative, and so forth, on the basis of the plausible semantic combinations of the two nouns, as you can see in the following examples. (The generalized preposition, *po*, is a merger of a very frequent and polysemous preposition in Norwegian and Russian. In these examples, content words are translated into English.)

Little money **po** *pocket.* 'Not much money *in* the pocket.'
Master **po** *boat?* 'Is the master *on* the boat?'
What you business **po** *this day?* 'What are you doing *on* this day [= today]?'
Po *you wife?* 'Is there *by* you a wife?' [= Do you have a wife?]
Steer **po** *shore.* 'Steer *to* shore.'
Speak **po** *master.* 'Speak *to* the master.'
How-many day **po** *sea you?* 'How many days were you *at* sea?'

How-much weight flour **po** *one weight halibut?* 'What quantity of flour *in exchange for* what quantity of halibut?'

There were a few basic question words, no conjunctions, no embedded constructions. So a language, to be processible, must at least have means of identifying nouns and verbs, and must provide means of distinguishing various case relations. This can be done with word order rules, one general verbal marker, and one general preposition.

Now consider a pidgin language which is undergoing rapid enrichment as it expands to become a native language and the official language of a speech community. Gillian Sankoff is providing us with more and more fascinating information about New Guinea Tok Pisin, a version of pidgin English which has been acquiring native speakers before her very eyes (Sankoff & Laberge, 1973; Sankoff & Brown, 1976). As the language has become the medium of fluent, urban discourse, it has had to face the problem of making it clear to the listener where the boundaries are between embedded relative clauses and matrix sentences. The version of the language described by Sankoff has introduced a relative particle based on the deictic *ia* (derived from English *here*). The exciting thing about Sankoff's analysis of this innovation is her demonstration that the relative marker functions to keep speaker and listener cued in to the rapid flow of meaning in ongoing discourse. The particle serves as an auditory bracketing of the relative clause, and allows the speaker to check if the listener is aware of the bracketing. Consider the following examples (Sankoff & Brown, 1976):

*Na pik **ia** [ol ikilim bipo **ia**] bai ikamap olsem draipela ston.*
'And this (the) pig they had killed before would turn into a huge stone.'
*Meri **ia** [em i yangpela meri, draipela meri **ia**] em harim istap.*
'The girl, who was a young, big girl, was listening.'
*Em wanpela America **ia** [iputim naim long en].*
'It was an American who gave her her name.'

The particle functions both as a cue to the listener's perceptual strategies and as a device for the speaker to keep track of the listener's attention. The particle *ia* is a deictic element which can also be used simply to focus on the phrase to which it is attached. Once a phrase is brought into focus, however, additional information can be added, as in the above examples. This is a basic form of subordination, and the point of origin of the relative clause. Once the additional information has been given, the end of the interruption or subordination is marked by another occurrence of *ia*, often with rising intonation to allow the listener to indicate assent. The left-hand *ia* and the right-hand *ia* are clear guides to perceptual strategies, letting the listener know that an embedding has interrupted the matrix sentence. In fact, the right-hand *ia* can be omitted in sentence final position, as in the third of the examples above, indicating that its special role as a perceptual marker is to return the listener to processing of the matrix sentence.

We know from psycholinguistic research with children that relative clauses are more easily processed if a relative particle is present, and adult psycholinguistic research has shown that the relative pronoun in English is an important guide to perceptual strategies (Fodor, Bever, & Garrett, 1974). It is indeed striking that an evolving language is constrained in similar fashion to introduce a marker of relative clauses. It is also striking that the device chosen—bracketing of the relative clause with discourse-based particles—is the same means used by Turkish children and Turkish colloquial speech to avoid the complexities of the Turkish relative clause. The Turkish equivalent of the first Tok Pisin example given above would be something like: "Well they killed a pig, huh? That pig would turn into a huge stone." What corresponds to a relative clause is bracketed by an introductory particle (originally a locative interrogative) focusing the listener's attention, and it is terminated by a particle, often with rising intonation to check the listener's attention. (It is pure chance that the right-hand particle in Turkish is *ya*!)

When a language is faced with the communicative need to use one proposition to modify part of another, it is apparently necessary to make sure that the listener knows when he is to be processing the main proposition and when he is to be processing the embedded proposition. In an established language, the cues to relative clauses function below the level of consciousness to guide the perceptual strategies of the listener. In developing languages, however, it seems that it is the speaker who is aware that the listener may have difficulty in keeping track of the course of the utterance. It is significant that relative particles are often derived from deictic or interrogative words, as if the speaker were actively directing the listener's attention, by pointing and questioning, to the flow of information between propositions.

BE QUICK AND EASY

The charges to be clear and to be processible are constantly eroded by an opposing charge—*to be quick and easy*. All of our skilled motor behavior is pulled by opposing tendencies to be precise and to accomplish a task without working too hard. Compare your elementary school handwriting with your present handwriting; or think of the first stages of learning to drive or tie a shoe, or what have you. It has been widely noted that older children speak more quickly and fluently than younger children; that mastery of a foreign language is marked by increased speech rate; and that the speech rate of a creole is much more rapid than that of its ancestral pidgin language.

Why should mature communication be marked by rapid tempo? Not only is there a natural tendency to minimize effort, but there is also a need to compact more information into a surface utterance, relating parts of the utterance to other propositions—implied, presupposed, or expressly communicated. The charge to be expressive, when fully developed, requires the speaker to communicate an elaborated message—a message which takes account of the background knowledge and involvement of the listener. As the surface density of the message increases, Language must provide more perceptual cues, like the relative markers I discussed earlier in relation to the second charge. At the same time, however, there is a conflicting tendency on the part of the speaker to reduce verbal emphasis on those markers in order to stress various aspects of the semantic message itself.

CHILD LANGUAGE

Earlier, I mentioned children's tendencies to decontract, to put abnormal stress on grammatical functors, and so forth. But such acoustically striking reflections of attempts to maintain clarity quickly pass. It is as if a spotlight moves over each grammatical element: when a particular form is focused on in the course of development, the child is struggling to master it—an auxiliary, a negative particle, an inflection. With mastery, the light moves on. The grammatical form is now in the shadow, on the periphery of linguistic consciousness, joining into the rapid flow of un-self-conscious speaking.

HISTORY

From time to time in linguistic history, however, the process is not quite as smooth. The facts of phonological change are well known and have various origins and consequences. Sound change can wreak havoc with grammatical distinctions, producing unacceptable levels of homonymy or ambiguity when grammatical markers lose acoustic salience or sufficient distinctiveness from each other. For example, reduction of final syllables and stress on initial syllables has eroded Germanic inflectional systems, resulting in languages like our own, with their analytic word forms and word order rules. The cycle between analytic and synthetic, with concomitant restrictions on word order, has been well demonstrated. In the case of Egyptian (Hodge, 1970), where we have the incredibly great time depth of over 4000 years of data, the language has apparently completed the full cycle twice. The tension between the first and third charges to Language—clarity and speed—results in very rapid formal changes. For example, in less than two millenia, Spanish has replaced the synthetic future tense of Latin with an analytic construction, as in *amare habeo*, and has reduced that innovation to a synthetic tense inflection, *amaré*.

Such phenomena, of course, make up the heart of introductory courses in historical linguistics. We still have a lot to learn, however, about the roles played in this sort of linguistic change by ontogenetic and pragmatic factors.

PIDGIN/CREOLE

In the study of creole languages, we are in an excellent position to locate the source and trace the development of changes in rate and compactness of expression. The most dramatic example, again, comes from Gillian Sankoff's study of New Guinea Tok Pisin (Sankoff & Laberge, 1973). She and Suzanne Laberge have examined ways in which Tok Pisin as a native language differs from its structure as a fluent second language. Native speakers of Tok Pisin are mainly under the age of 20, learning the language from non-native-speaking parents who use it as the common family language. The characterization of child speech in Tok Pisin offered by Sankoff and Laberge is a cogent summary of adherence to the third charge to Language (pp. 35–36):

> The children speak with much greater speed and fluency, involving a number of morphophonemic reductions as well as reduction in the number of syllables characteristically receiving primary stress. Whereas an adult will say, for the sentence "I am going home,"
>
> (1) Mì gó lòng háus;
>
> a child will often say
>
> (2) Mì gò l:áus;
>
> three syllables rather than four, with one primary stress rather than two.

Note that the parents are also *fluent* speakers. Apparently there is something about child speech, or the nature of a *native* language, which plays a leading role in bringing Language to adhere to the third charge.

As Tok Pisin became the medium for a wide variety of communications—such as parliamentary debates, newspapers, and radio—its grammar began to change. This change is accelerated in the speech of children acquiring Tok Pisin as a native language. For example, the future marker began as a sentence introductory adverb *baimbai* (from the English *by and by*). This marker became reduced to *bai*, moved within the sentence to preverbal position, and acquired obligatory status. At this point, the first and second charges are well adhered to: the preverbal tense marker is in a semantically clear position and is acoustically salient. The fact that it is obligatory probably aids perceptual strategies required for rapid speech processing, but this same fact runs counter to the charge to minimize effort and focus on message content.

This third charge comes into play when *baimbai* is reduced to a single syllable, *bai*. In the speech of native Tok Pisin-speaking children, the particle tends to be reduced to *bə* and receives less stress than in adult speech. It is moving from a particle to an inflectional prefix, with the possible eventual fate of being swallowed up by the verb.

In this case, as in the case of the relative marker *ia*, Tok Pisin shows the evolution of grammatical markers in present-day time. This remarkable situation makes it possible to observe the natural course of construction of a grammar suited to carry out all four of the charges to Language. It seems, given the limited but suggestive evidence at hand, that it is adult speakers who invent new forms, using them with some degree of variability in their speech. Children, exposed to this variability, tend to make these new forms obligatory and regular.

BE EXPRESSIVE

Be Semantically Expressive

I now want to turn to the fourth charge to Language: *Be expressive*. As I pointed out at the beginning, this charge has two aspects—one semantic and one rhetorical. The first aspect, to be semantically expressive, most broadly conceived means simply that utterances must make sense. That truism, of course, is hardly interesting. In the light of language development and change, though, some aspects of making sense seem to be more basic than others. Recent work in linguistics (e.g., Traugott, 1973) and psycholinguistics (e.g., E. Clark, 1974) suggests that some notions may be more *salient* psychologically, whereas others may be more distant from the most natural or obvious manner of conceiving of events. The more salient or basic notions can be defined as those which are earliest to develop in childhood. These should also show the greatest degree of universality and should be best maintained across the various change situations we are considering here. I can only hint at a few of these notions for now.

CHILD LANGUAGE

Eve Clark (1974) has proposed a model for language acquisition according to which the child first attempts to map linguistic forms onto pre-existing perceptual categories. For example, she proposes the following sort of strategy for determining meanings of concrete nouns and prepositions of spatial relations (p. 36):

Pick out whatever seems to be the most salient characteristic(s) perceptually, and assume [until given counter-evidence] that that is what the word refers to. Act on this assumption whenever you want to name, request, or call attention to something.

I think this strategy can be generalized from "perceptually salient characteristics" to "salient cognitive categories" generally. The particular cognitive categories I want to consider here relate to verbal notions of tense, aspect, and modality, because they appear across a number of change situations. My approach, as before, will be to use ontogenetic data to determine a natural sequence, and then examine that sequence in historical, contact, and pidgin–creole situations.

Francesco Antinucci and Ruth Miller (1976), working in our laboratory at Berkeley, suggest that tense markers are first used to express aspectual notions. In Italian child speech, for example, the past participle is first used only to refer to the end state of some process, such as "fall," "close," "break," "burn," and the like. Verbs which describe states and activities with no clear end state, like "walk," "play," and "sleep," are at first not used in the past tense. Similarly, in English data the first productive past tense forms are limited to events resulting in a present end-state, like *falled, spilled,* and *covered,* while state verbs and activity verbs are still not used with a past tense inflection. The past tense seems to be used not to refer to the action of the subject prior to the utterance, but rather to focus on the perceptible end state of the object. Only later can the child shift his attention from the current state of affairs to the antecedent determining event, and extend the inflection to refer to past time generally. Other studies, such as those by Bronckart and Sinclair (1973) and Ferreiro (1971) in French, and Baron (1972) in English, have also revealed the early saliency of aspectual notions such as duration, repetition, inception, and conclusion of events.

To return to Eve Clark's approach, the first meanings to be acquired should be closest to the child's non-linguistic strategies for representing events to himself. She suggests that such meanings "can be regarded as cognitively simpler than others" (1973, p. 180). To extend this very schematic argument, we should observe a saliency of means of expressing aspect over tense in other situations of language change, with the expectation that expressions of aspect should develop before expressions of tense.

HISTORY

In the realm of language change, the evolution of Italian from Latin seems to parallel the present-day ontogenesis of Italian (Antinucci & Miller, 1976, p. 184.) When the Latin past tense inflection was lost, due to phonological change and other factors, a periphrastic perfect tense was introduced, at first serving only the limited function of referring to the end state of a completed process. Only later was this form extended to refer to the location of processes in the past. Within the history of Indo-European generally, there is evidence that the aspectual opposition between perfective and imperfective preceded the development of temporal opposition (Bronckart & Sinclair, 1973, p. 128), suggesting even greater generality of the cognitive saliency of aspect over tense. Apparently when a new form enters a language its range of meaning is likely to be restricted to what Clark calls a "cognitively simpler" core. The extension of meaning from that core must also follow natural cognitive patterns, whether occurring in ontogenesis or in other diachronic linguistic processes.

CONTACT

In language contact situations, grammatical borrowing should be most probable if a language is weak in formal means to express a salient semantic notion, again using ontogenetic order of acquisition as an index of cognitive saliency. For example, a periphrastic means of expressing a salient category may be replaced by an inflectional marking, on the model of a contact language. This is apparently what happened to Bulgarian in contact with Turkish (Galton, 1967). Turkish has an inferential modality to refer to non-witnessed events. This form is easily mastered by 2-year-old Turkish children, suggesting that it is a salient notion. Bulgarian developed a verbal conjugation to refer to non-witnessed events, enriching the adverbial or periphrastic means previously available. Presumably a language gains in expressiveness if a salient notion can be expressed by an obligatory surface marker, and notions of modality are best marked on the verb. Under constraints of the charge to be processible, however, Bulgarian could not borrow the infix used in Turkish, but devised a Slavic verbal suffix, consistent with the typological characteristics of Bulgarian. Apparently, Turkish suggested to Bulgarian that this salient category could be expressed inflectionally on the verb.[2]

There is also some evidence from language contact situations for the saliency of aspect. Yiddish (Baviskar, 1974), a Germanic language spoken on Slavic territory, developed an elaborated non-Germanic aspectual system along the lines of the well-developed Slavic system. (The suggestion of the

[2] The notion that some formal means of expression are "weaker" than others deserves elaboration. The Bulgarian–Turkish situation suggests that inflectional marking is somehow preferable to adverbial or clausal marking, and that obligatory marking is preferable to optional—at least for the more salient notions. A similar argument could be made in regard to the evolution from *baimbai* to *bə-* in Tok Pisin. Just as this approach requires a hierarchy of cognitive notions in terms of saliency or naturalness, it requires a hierarchy of means of formal expression in terms of ease of acquisition and processibility.

accessibility of aspectual notions to children is also supported by the apparent ease with which Slavic-speaking children acquire this portion of their grammar; Radulović, 1975.)

My knowledge of grammatical transfer in contact situations is scanty. But I would expect that factors of cognitive simplicity or saliency, established in ontogenetic studies, would play a leading role in predicting the possibility of interlingual borrowing or modeling.

PIDGIN/CREOLE

Kay and Sankoff have a very clear statement on the role of saliency in accounting for the initial set of grammatical markers in a pidgin and the course of elaboration of grammar with depidginization. I would like to quote their statement, with the psycholinguistic footnote that the sort of ordering they suggest should eventually correspond to a universal ontogenetic ordering (Kay & Sankoff, 1974, p. 69):

> Given the hypothesis that there is a certain basic (and small) set of underlying semantic notions which are always grammatically marked, even in the most reduced contact vernaculars, and that as communicative functions increase, other markers are introduced, it is possible that in the development of contact vernaculars there exists an ordering in the introduction of such additional markers. For example, prepositions may be ordered such that when a pidgin has only two, one marks genitive and the other has a generalized locative function, with specific locatives (e.g., *in, on, under*) coming later; location may be marked earlier than time; pronominal systems may mark person and number before they mark gender or case, and so on. The general point is that certain semantic notions which may be more psychologically salient or functionally necessary or both are grammatically marked earlier than others. Contact vernaculars at various stages of development may provide evidence for verifying such notions of universal saliency or function.

Derek Bickerton (1975), along lines similar to those developed by Elizabeth Traugott (1973), has proposed a "natural semantax" which can be revealed in the development of creoles. He specifically proposes a creole tense–aspect system which has apparently arisen independently in unrelated creolizing situations, hypothesizing that this system is a natural reflection of "specific neural properties of the human brain." It is of interest to me that this tense–aspect system is not concerned with the time line of past–present–future, but, like the child language studies I have mentioned, reflects a concern with such matters as repetition and duration of events and the distinction between states and processes.

Bickerton (1975) proposes several basic cognitive prerequisites for such a tense–aspect system, and they are all well-attested in psychological studies of cognitive development:

In order to operate [the creole tense–aspect system] a speaker needs to be able (a) to know the order in which past events occurred (b) to distinguish between sensory input and the product of his imagination (c) to tell whether something happened once only, or was either repeated or protracted in some way (d) to distinguish states from actions. [p. 19]

This sounds like a description of the cognitive bases for development of temporal notions abstracted from specific event characteristics. And apparently as a creole language becomes more fully developed, aspect markers such as these expand to become tense markers. For example (Labov, 1971), in Hawaiian creole a particle (*wen*) which began as a perfective aspect marker referring to completed past actions has become a general past tense marker.

Where can one go with such intriguing parallels between widely separated instances of linguistic change? The issue is clearly not one of cognitive development alone, since I have argued that the saliency of aspect over tense can be demonstrated in adult language change as well as in ontogenesis. I suspect that we will find a large part of the answer when we have a better understanding of the communicative functions of tense and aspect in different sorts of discourse situations. The important feature of grammatical tense is that it encodes a temporal relation between the referent situation and the moment in which the utterance is spoken. This is inherently a discourse phenomenon, as opposed to distinctions of aspect and modality, which describe features of events independent of the situation of the ongoing discourse. The communication of tense is apparently necessary only when a speech system is used between speakers of a certain level of maturity for a certain range of functions. I am vague here because I have not thought sufficiently about these matters, but the basic distinction I am proposing is one between salient or basic categories of perception and cognition, which will be encoded in all forms of Language—including preschool and pidgin speech systems—and more elaborated distinctions, resting on more complex cognitive processes, and required for mature and stylistically differentiated communication.

Be Rhetorically Expressive

The notion of stylistically differentiated communication brings us to the final charge—the charge to be rhetorically expressive. It is this charge, especially, which requires the complexity of grammar. It is no accident that a developing language like Tok Pisin should have to find means of encoding relative clauses, while a contact vernacular like Russenorsk or a 2-year-old speech system can manage without such means. In order for Language to be rhetorically expressive it must be possible to present information in a variety of ways, focusing on this or that, guiding or checking the listener's attention, distinguishing between what is new or old information, expected or unexpected statement, and so forth. Gillian Sankoff, in discussing the origins of the *ia* particle, provides clear examples of this expressive goal of language. She notes that:

> ... *ia* placed after a noun or pronoun has the function of focusing on that element, often in contrast to some other referent which might also have been referred to by that noun or pronoun. ...
>
> In emphasizing and focusing on the element it qualifies, *ia* provides a slot for further information about the element in question to be included if necessary. This information is basically of two sorts: first, information presumed by the speaker to be in the category of "shared knowledge" between him/herself and the conversational partner(s). Such information may be presumed to be shared either because it has been mentioned or given earlier in the same conversation, or because for other reasons (e.g., common background) it is assumed to be shared. ... [*ia*] bracketing provides a device for the issue of sharedness to be interactionally negotiated, in cases where there may be some doubt about whether or not the information supplied is shared in ways sufficient to adequately (and uniquely) identify the referent. [1974, pp. 13, 14]

Note how much of this description of the use of *ia* assumes that the speaker is taking the role of his listener, actively programming his speech to be effective and intelligible in a given discourse situation. Early child speech and contact vernaculars are used in a limited range of contextually dependent interactions. There is little or no need to talk about what is not apparent; nor, I would expect, is there much motivation to explore and monitor the possible inner states of the listener. This is true, to a certain extent, of conversations between adults and 2- or 3-year-old children; furthermore, the young child's limited ability to "decenter" in the Piagetian sense precludes much of the discourse dynamics summarized by Sankoff.

It is striking to consider the extent to which grammar functions *especially* to fulfill rhetorical needs. Most studies of child language comprehension put the child into a situation where there are no contextual cues to the meanings of utterances, but, in real life, there is little reason for a preschool child to rely heavily on syntactic factors to determine the basic propositional and referential meaning of sentences which he hears. Judith Johnston and I have gone through transcripts of adult speech to children between the ages of 2 and 5, in Turkish and English, looking for sentences which could be open to misinterpretation if the child lacked basic syntactic knowledge, such as the roles of word order and inflections. We found almost no instances of an adult utterance which could possibly be misinterpreted. That is, the overwhelming majority of utterances were clearly interpretable in context, requiring only knowledge of word meanings and the normal relations between actors, actions, and objects in the world. Why, then, should the child learn to cope with the complexities of varying word orders in Turkish, or cleft and passive sentences in English, and the like? Partly, of course, it could be because the child simply cannot help paying attention to and assimilating grammatical detail: That is the nature of the machine. And some knowledge of grammar is necessary in order to be able to segment incoming speech into clauses for deeper analysis. But more of the answer may lie in the importance of grammar for directing and focusing attention in discourse—both for the child as listener and as speaker. His eventual mastery of grammatical complexities may be attributable, to a large extent, to a growing need to comprehend expressive aspects of messages and to communicate expressively—that is, to direct his listener's attention skillfully in a discourse, trying to maintain interest, attention, and understanding. There is some evidence, for example, that the emergence of grammatical devices is directly tied to emerging abilities to topicalize or focus. Brian MacWhinney (1975) and Elizabeth Bates (1976), for example, suggest that the first use of word order in child speech (at least in Hungarian and in Italian) is for pragmatic focus, rather than the expression of underlying grammatical or semantic relations.

It remains to spell out in more detail the role of rhetorical factors in child language, language contact and change, and pidgin and creole situations. For now I want to simply point out that, in general, it is the charge to be expressive which introduces much of grammatical complexity into Language. A pidgin language, as I have pointed out in the extreme case of Russenorsk, like a 2- or 3-year-old language, admirably fulfills the first two charges to Language. But when a language acquires a broad range of communicative functions— either through maturity of its speakers, in the case of an established language, or depidginization and creolization in the case of pidgin languages—it loses this enviable clarity. Why should communicative needs require *grammatical* complexity? Apparently grammar develops, both in creoles and in children, to fulfill more communicative needs than the direct expression of propositional content. Adherence to the first two charges alone would produce a language in which the range of surface expressions for each underlying semantic configuration would be extremely limited. As such, ongoing speech would be as close to a series of underlying propositions as possible, given the time constraints on processing. But speech in the settings of mature and developed communication requires more. As Labov (1971, p. 72) has pointed out, grammar is not just a tool of logical analysis. In his words: "Grammar is busy with emphasis, focus, down-shifting and up-grading; it is a way of organizing information and taking alternative points of view." From the point of view of developmental psycholinguistics, we would do well to study the emergence of such communicative functions of speech in children in order to obtain a fully coherent view of linguistic development.

I began with the goal of defining Language by studying it in its unstable and changing phases. I want to close by emphasizing that this goal cannot be achieved without attending to the complex and contradictory pressures of four different charges to Language. A fully developed human language must be pragmatically flexible, semantically expressive, rapid in tempo, readily decipherable, and semantically clear. Children have the capacity to construct such languages, and the human mind has the capacity to consistently maintain and adjust Language so that it remains in consonance with all of these goals. Watching Language move through time, it becomes clear that the more it changes, the more it remains the same.

ACKNOWLEDGMENT

Many students and colleagues contributed to my development of the ideas presented here. Special thanks go to Paul Kay and Gillian Sankoff, who first involved me in the study of pidgin and creole languages; and to Judith Johnston and Bambi Schieffelin, who helped me understand what I was trying to say.

REFERENCES

Antinucci, F., & Miller, R. How children talk about what happened. *Journal of Child Language*, 1976, *3*, 167–190.

Bach, E. Is Amharic an SOV language? *Journal of Ethiopian Studies*, 1970, *8*, 9–20.

Barber, C. *Linguistic change in present-day English.* University, Ala.: University of Alabama Press, 1966.

Baron, N. S. The evolution of English periphrastic causatives: Contributions to a general theory of linguistic variation and change. Unpublished doctoral dissertation, Stanford University, 1972.

Bates, E. *Language and context: The acquisition of pragmatics.* New York: Academic Press, 1976.

Baviskar, V. L. The position of aspect in the verbal system of Yiddish. *Working Papers in Yiddish and East European Jewish Studies*, No. 1. YIVO Institute for Jewish Research, 1974.

Bellugi, U. The acquisition of negation. Unpublished doctoral dissertation, Harvard University, 1967.

Bever, T. G. The cognitive basis for linguistic structures. In J. R. Hayes (Ed.), *Cognition and the development of language.* New York: Wiley, 1970. Pp. 279–362.

Bever, T. G., & Langendoen, D. T. A dynamic model of the evolution of language. *Linguistic Inquiry*, 1971, *2*, 433–461.

Bickerton, D. Creolization, linguistic universals, natural semantax and the brain. Paper presented at International Conference on Pidgins and Creoles, University of Hawaii, 1975.

Broch, O. Russenorsk. *Archiv für slavische Philologie*, 1927, *41*, 209–262.

Bronckart, J. P., & Sinclair, H. Time, tense and aspect. *Cognition*, 1973, *2*, 107–130.

Clark, E. V. Non-linguistic strategies and the acquisition of word meanings. *Cognition*, 1973, *2*, 161–182.

Clark, E. V. Some aspects of the conceptual basis for first language acquisition. *Papers and Reports on Child Language Development*, No. 7, April 1974. Stanford University, Committee on Linguistics. Pp. 23–52. (In R. L. Schiefelbusch and L. L. Lloyd (Eds.), *Language perspectives: Acquisition, retardation and intervention*. Baltimore: University Park Press, 1974. Pp. 105–128.)

Ervin-Tripp, S. M. Some strategies for the first two years. In T. E. Moore (Ed.), *Cognitive development and the acquisition of language*. New York: Academic Press, 1973. Pp. 261–286.

Ferreiro, E. *Les relations temporelles dans le language de l'enfant*. Geneva: Droz, 1971.

Fodor, J. A., Bever, T. G., & Garrett, M. F. *The psychology of language: An introduction to psycholinguistics and generative grammar*. New York: McGraw-Hill, 1974.

Galton, H. The evolution of Bulgarian syntax: A phenomenological study of "analytism." *Balkansko yezikoznaniye/Linguistique balkanique*, XII. Sofia: Bulgarska Akademiya na Naukite, 1967. Pp. 45–99.

Gumperz, J. J., & Wilson, R. Convergence and creolization: A case from the Indo-Aryan/Dravidian border. In D. Hymes (Ed.), *Pidginization and creolization of languages*. Cambridge: Cambridge University Press, 1971. Pp. 151–168.

Hodge, C. T. The linguistic cycle. *Language Sciences*, No. 13, December 1970, 1–7.

Imedadze, N. V. K psikhologicheskoy prirode rannego dvuyazichiya. *Voprosy psikhologii*, 1960, *6*(1), 60–68.

Kay, P., & Sankoff, G. A language-universals approach to pidgins and creoles. In D. DeCamp and I. F. Hancock (Eds.), *Pidgins and creoles: Current trends and prospects*. Washington, D. C.: Georgetown University Press, 1974. Pp. 61–72.

Kiparsky, P. Historical linguistics. In W. O. Dingwall (Ed.), *A survey of linguistic science*. College Park, Md.: University of Maryland Linguistics Program, 1971. Pp. 576–649.

Kuno, S. The position of relative clauses and conjunctions. *Linguistic Inquiry*, 1974, *5*, 117–136.

Labov, W. On the adequacy of natural languages: I. The development of tense. Unpublished paper, 1971.

Lakoff, R. Another look at drift. In R. P. Stockwell and R. K. S. Macaulay (Eds.), *Linguistic change and generative theory*. Bloomington: University of Indiana Press, 1972. Pp. 172–198.

Larmouth, D. W. Differential interference in American Finnish cases. *Language*, 1974, *50*, 356–366.

Lehmann, W. P. A structural principle of language and its implications. *Language*, 1973, *49*, 47–66.

Li, C. N., & Thompson, S. A. An explanation of word order change SVO→SOV. *Foundations of Language*, 1974, *12*, 201–214.

Little, G. D. Cushitic influence in Amharic. In R. W. Shuy and C-J. N. Bailey (Eds.), *Towards tomorrow's linguistics*. Washington, D.C.: Georgetown University Press, 1974. Pp. 267–275.

MacWhinney, B. A psycholinguistic approach to pragmatic focusing. Paper presented at Stanford Child Language Research Forum, Stanford University, April 1975.

Malmberg, B. Et barn bytar sprak. *Nordisk tidskrift*, 1945, *21*.

Omar, M. K. *The acquisition of Egyptian Arabic as a native language.* The Hague: Mouton, 1973.

Radulović, L. Acquisition of language: Studies of Dubrovnik children. Unpublished doctoral dissertation, University of California, Berkeley, 1975.

Sankoff, G. The origins of syntax in discourse: Some evidence from Tok Pisin. Unpublished paper, Université de Montréal, 1974. [Revised version published as: Sankoff, G., & Brown, P. The origins of syntax in discourse. *Language*, 1976, *52*, 631–666.]

Sankoff, G., & Laberge, S. On the acquisition of native speakers by a language. *Kivung*, 1973, *6*(1), 32–47.

Slobin, D. I. Cognitive prerequisites for the development of grammar. In C. A. Ferguson and D. I. Slobin (Eds.), *Studies of child language development.* New York: Holt, Rinehart & Winston, 1973.

Smith, D. M. Creolization and language ontogeny: A preliminary paradigm for comparing language socialization and language acculturation. In C-J. N. Bailey and R. W. Shuy (Eds.), *New ways of analyzing variation in English.* Washington, D.C.: Georgetown University Press, 1973. Pp. 287–296.

Traugott, E. C. Some thoughts on natural syntactic processes. In C-J. N. Bailey and R. W. Shuy (Eds.), *New ways of analyzing variation in English.* Washington, D.C.: Georgetown University Press, 1973. Pp. 313–322.

Weinreich, U. *Languages in contact: Findings and problems.* The Hague: Mouton, 1963. (Originally published as Number 1 in the series *Publications of the Linguistic Circle of New York*, 1953.)

15

On Universals of
Language Change

I. M. SCHLESINGER

Hebrew University of Jerusalem and
Israel Institute of Applied Social Research

It was only a few years ago that Slobin (1973) presented his major contribution to the theory of language acquisition by formulating a number of universals of language development and a series of operating principles by which the child approaches the task of learning grammar. This was a change of direction in the then current theorizing, which generally was engaged in writing grammars of child language. As I have argued elsewhere (Schlesinger, 1975), there are far too few constraints on writing such grammars for the endeavor to be really fruitful. Slobin's approach to exploring universals brings us face to face with the issue that really matters: how the child's grammar *changes* and develops into the adult grammar.

The problem of change turns up again—but this time within a much vaster panorama—in Slobin's new paper. This time he is not limiting himself to the changes in the language of the child. He studies the tendencies that determine child development as they reveal themselves wherever language changes; for instance, in pidgin languages and creoles, in bilingual contact and in historical change of language.

One cannot fail to be impressed by this ambitious undertaking. The principles he proposes make a wealth of data seem to fall into a coherent pattern, and this makes his present approach so appealing. It would be picayune, therefore, to dwell on the quite obvious methodological dangers attendant on his approach. The problems raised by postulating conflicting tendencies at work, the outcome of which can be either one of two opposites—for example, a synthetic or an analytic language—are too obvious to require expounding here. No doubt, constraints will have to be built into the theory so that it states clearly what outcomes are *not* to be expected. In its due time the theory will thus have to be pruned. Till then we should take advantage of its still being young and in a flexible state and consider how it can be enriched and broadened. The few suggestions that follow are made with this objective in mind.

Slobin proposes that there are parallel lines of development in four areas and shows that these may differ in the extent to which they are subject to the operation of universal determinants of language change. There is an obvious way to order the four areas in respect to the stage of development of the systems in question. Child language is the least developed, a well-established native language the most, and pidgins and creoles are in an intermediate position. The same ordering is obtained when we consider the degree of extraneous influence that impinges on the system, and as a result of this, its rate of change: The child seems to be subject to the most intensive influence and his language changes faster than other systems; pidgins, creoles, and languages in contact follow, in this order. Now, the relative effect of Slobin's four determinants of change may be hypothesized to be dependent on each of these two dimensions of ordering: stage of development and stability of the system (amount of influence and rate of change). The study of the interaction of these determinants would therefore gain by considering a system that follows a different pattern in respect to these two dimensions. I would like to propose therefore such a system, which somehow cuts across the boundaries: In regard to stage of development, it seems to be about on a par with pidgins, whereas as far as extraneous influence and rate of change are concerned, it is much more similar to a native language that is in bilingual contact. I am referring to the sign language of the deaf—not the brand known in North America as American Sign Language, which is a highly developed dialect having a history of two centuries of influence and interference from spoken language, but its poor relatives thriving in countries where sign language has been left alone to go its own course. In particular, I would like to discuss a sign language I have studied, viz., the Israeli Sign Language (ISL).

ISL is of relatively recent origin. A few decades ago, there was no community of deaf persons in Israel. The spontaneous sign languages of isolated deaf individuals, enriched by signs imported from immigrants of various countries, crystallized into the manual system presently in use among deaf adults. As mentioned, the language is rather undeveloped but relatively stable at present. What makes it unique is its short history: The closest approximation to the study of a language in its "primitive" stage is the study of a sign language like the Israeli one. This is a new language that has been relatively little influenced by other sign languages. Unlike child language and pidgin languages, it is not derived from another language.

ISL, then, may shed new light on the universals of language change. I have no time here to examine in detail how it conforms to Slobin's "charges," and a few desultory remarks will have to suffice; for a fuller treatment, I refer you to Cohen *et al.* (1977) and Namir and Schlesinger (in press).

The "charge" of clarity seems to be influential in the case of ISL. It has no inflections and is very much a segmentalized language. In view of ISL being at an early stage of development, this would be expected on the basis of Slobin's reasoning. On the other hand, there is ample evidence that ISL follows the maxim "be quick and easy." There are many blends (i.e., contractions of two signs on the analogy of "cheeseburger" and "smog" in spoken language). Unlike spoken language, where we are constrained to arraying meaningful elements linearly, simultaneity is possible in a sign language, and accordingly we find cases where components of a compound sign are performed simultaneously. In respect to compounds, there is another interesting phenomenon, namely that one of the components may be dropped to avoid reduplication in the utterance. Thus, "café" is signed by the signs for *sit* and *coffee*, but "sit in a café" is signed by the same sequence, *sit coffee*, and not *sit sit coffee*. Relevant to Slobin's remark about semantic expressiveness is the observation that certain aspects of an action are expressed in sign languages. The American Sign Language has been found by Susan Fischer (1973) to use reduplication of the sign for marking stative, iterative, and durative actions, and we have made similar observations for ISL. At the same time, however, there are independent signs to mark past and future, the present being unmarked. Finally, ISL seems to fall short with regard to rhetorical expressiveness: We have been unable to observe any alternative structures of the sign utterance related systematically to rhetorical intention.

One of the most striking characteristics of ISL, however, is that it not only lacks inflections but also, contrary to what one would expect on the basis of the linguist's lore, there is no fixed word order to express the most important grammatical relations. This only shows that what at one time appears to be a universal may turn out, when the facts are all in, to be nothing but a sweeping generalization. It seems therefore that now that sign languages are being closely studied, it would be somewhat parochial to theorize about language in general without taking sign language into account.

It is Slobin's bold new conception that there are a limited number of determinants of linguistic change operating in a variety of areas—child language, pidgin languages, and native languages. The notion of determinants of change itself is not a new one, however. Almost half a century ago, a German linguist,

Havers (1931), discussed various such determinants or "driving forces" ("Triebkräfte"), as he calls them. His list includes, in addition to Slobin's clarity and convenience, the need for plasticity, the need for expression of emotion, esthetic considerations, and sociolinguistic considerations (such as according status, deemphasis, euphemism, etc.). All this is supplemented by a wealth of data, and thus Havers' work is worth consulting and may lead to an expansion of Slobin's framework. Whether even this list will be exhaustive seems to be doubtful. This will be my final point, which I intend to approach by a detour, however.

There is one assumption in Slobin's paper which I think is extremely doubtful. He refers to a universal core of semantic notions which have to be expressed in all languages. At first sight, this appears a very plausible claim to make, and it is, moreover, in line with the Chomskyan thesis of a universal deep structure. Nevertheless, when considering the data, there seems to be nothing to support this notion. As soon as one looks around for this core, it begins to recede indefinitely. Take Slobin's example of aspect, which is more primitive than tense. But for all that, it apparently does not belong to the universal core, because there is no aspect expressed obligatorily in all languages.[1] The inferential ("nonwitnessed events") is easily mastered by 2-year-olds, Slobin tells us, but it does not turn up in many languages. The same holds for the durative and other aspects. Further, such an apparently essential notion as number (i.e., singular versus plural) is not found in a wide variety of languages (Cassirer, 1953, p. 235 ff.). But, you may argue, at least the concepts of actor, action, and patient of action are universally expressed in language. Wrong again, because there is at least one language, which has no grammatical means to express these concepts, namely ISL (Schlesinger, 1971).

At first this seems puzzling: How can one do without such basic notions as these? The answer is that one does not. The puzzle is based on a simple confusion between what is extralinguistic and what is linguistic, or, stated differently, a distinction must be made between cognitive structures on the one hand and the linguistic structure of semantic relations underlying speech on the other (Schlesinger, 1974). Every normal human being (and many subhuman organisms as well) conceives of the world in terms of actors, actions, and patients of actions, but it does not follow that he has to express these in his language. Such a language is nevertheless adequate for communicative purposes, because in everyday give and take, the speaker can depend on

---

[1] Dan Slobin commented on this at the conference that aspect may be universal in the sense that *all* languages express *some* aspect. I suspect, however, that there is little value in this notion of a universal set of concepts, a different subset of which is expressed in each language. Consider that such a claim becomes empirically irrefutable once every concept appearing in any one of the languages of the world is admitted to this universal set; cf. also Schlesinger, 1971, pp. 117–118.

context to make the meaning clear. That such a system works is shown by ISL, which functions as a language in a great variety of situations.

It appears therefore that the belief in a universal semantic core is not supported by the data. For all the peoples of the world, it is probably true that the structures of the mind are similar; the ways of perceiving the world *may* be similar (though this has been questioned), but this does not entail that their languages express similar things. For, as Cassirer (1953) has insisted, language, far from reproducing reality for us, forms reality and represents it on its own terms. And these terms differ from language to language.

Returning to linguistic change, I propose that languages may change not only in respect to their surface structures, but also in respect to the underlying semantic structures expressed by them. Slobin's paper not only amply illustrates the former kind of change, but also takes account of the latter. Much more material regarding change in the contents expressed by language is to be found in the work of Cassirer (1953) and of Weisgerber (1962), both of whom follow Wilhelm von Humboldt. Evidently these changes are less easily observed than those of surface structures, and moreover they are less easily explained. Consider for instance one type of change in the underlying relations which one might call *assimilation*. The change discussed by Slobin from end state of an event to the past tense would be an instance of assimilation occurring in child language. A similar example is the extension of the patient category by Gvozdev's son, who first included in it only objects that were moved in space (quoted in Bowerman, 1973, p. 201). Recently, a number of writers on child language have reported that such expansion of underlying semantic relations occurs regularly (Braine, 1976; Brown, 1973; Bloom, Miller, & Hood, 1975; Edwards, unpublished paper; cf. also Clark, 1974; McNeill, 1975; Schlesinger, 1974). A lack of differentiation between categories appears in ISL, which has as a rule the same sign for an action and its habitual actor (e.g., *tailor* and *sew*), a phenomenon akin to functional shift in spoken language. Elsewhere (Schlesinger, 1974, 1977) I have shown how the instrumental in English—and in many other languages as well—is assimilated into the agentive relation in constructions like *the axe cut the logs*. It seems reasonable to hypothesize that such assimilations are a very general phenomenon in language.

What are the determinants of such assimilatory changes? Slobin's four charges evidently do not provide an answer to this question. It is reasonable to suppose that there is a limit to the number of distinctions a language can make in its surface structure, and that therefore underlying notions have to merge so as to gain access to linguistic expression. But this does not explain why it is precisely some particular relation which is assimilated to another in a given language, whereas a different pattern holds in a different language. Here we are faced with the puzzling question of the interaction of language and cognition in creating what Weisgerber (1962) has called the linguistic "intermediary world" ("Zwischenwelt") which represents the way language perceives reality in describing it. In my present role as a maker of comments, not a presenter of a paper, it does not behove me to delve into this problem, which is just as well because I am rather mystified by it. But I would like to stress that this is an eminently worthwhile problem which is central to the concern of Slobin's paper: language change. Judging from the rate of his progress in recent years, I would not be surprised if Dan Slobin comes up with part of the answer very soon.

REFERENCES

Bloom, L., Miller, P., & Hood, L. Variation and reduction as aspects of competence in language development. In A. Pick (Ed.), *Minnesota Symposia on Child Psychology*. Vol. 9. Minneapolis: University of Minnesota Press, 1975.

Bowerman, M. Structural relationships in children's utterances: Syntactic or semantic? In T. E. Moore (Ed.), *Cognitive development and the acquisition of Language*. New York: Academic Press, 1973. Pp. 197–214.

Braine, M. D. S. *Children's first word combinations. Monographs of the Society for Research in Child Development*, 1976, *41* (1, Serial No. 164).

Brown, R. *A first language: The early stages*. Cambridge, Mass.: Harvard University Press, 1973.

Cassirer, E. *The philosophy of symbolic forms*. Vol. 1. *Language*. New Haven, Conn.: Yale University Press, 1953.

Clark, R. Aspects of psycholinguistics in the context of the symposium. Paper presented at the UNESCO Symposium on Interactions between Linguistics and Mathematical Education, Nairobi, Kenya, 1974.

Cohen, E., Namir, L., & Schlesinger, I. M. *A new dictionary of sign language*. The Hague: Mouton, 1977.

Edwards, D. Constraints on actions: A source of early meanings in child language. Unpublished paper.

Fischer, S. Two processes of reduplication in the American Sign Language. *Foundations of language*, 1973, *9*, 469–480.

Havers, W. *Handbuch der erklärenden Syntax*. Heidelberg: Car Winters, 1931.

McNeill, D. Semiotic extension. In R. L. Solso (Ed.), *Information processing and cognition: The Loyola Symposium*. Hillsdale, N.J.: Lawrence Erlbaum, 1975. Pp. 351–380.

Namir, L., & Schlesinger, I. M. The grammar of Sign Language. In I. M. Schlesinger and L. Namir (Eds.), *Sign Language of the deaf: Psychological linguistic and sociological perspectives*. New York: Academic Press, in press.

Schlesinger, I. M. The grammar of sign language and the problem of language universals. In J. Morton (Ed.), *Biological and social factors in psycholinguistics*. London: Logos Press, 1971. Pp. 98–121.

Schlesinger, I. M. Relational concepts underlying language. In R. L. Schiefelbusch and L. L. Lloyd (Eds.), *Language perspectives—Acquisition, retardation and intervention*. Baltimore, Md.: University Park Press, 1974. Pp. 129–151.

Schlesinger, I. M. Acquisition of grammar—What and how should we investigate. In W. von Raffler-Engle (Ed.), *Child language—1975 (Word,* 1971, *27,* 187–194).

Schlesinger, I. M. *Production and comprehension of utterances.* Hillsdale, N.J.: Lawrence Erlbaum, 1977.

Slobin, D. I. Cognitive prerequisites for the development of grammar. In C. A. Ferguson and D. I. Slobin (Eds.), *Studies of child language development.* New York: Holt, 1973. Pp. 175–208.

Weisgerber, L. *Von den Kräften der deutschen Sprache.* Düsseldorf: Schwann, 1962.

16

Some Notes and Queries on Language Change

GILLIAN SANKOFF

Université de Montréal

I think it should first be said that Dan Slobin's opening remark that "most of what I have to say has been lying on library shelves for a long time" is a far too modest characterization of the paper, whose great merit is its creative bringing together of a vast array of facts and findings in a strong demonstration of their bearing on language universals. His four "charges" are well reasoned, highly thought-provoking and, to my mind, go a long way toward accounting for the striking parallels he points out in the various change situations. Showing the complex interaction of these four "charges" in influencing and constraining language change, he escapes any allegation of simplistic functionalism. Nevertheless, there are problems in any kind of functionalist approach to the structure of language, and I think a word of caution is in order, directed not only to Slobin but, given the increasing popularity of such approaches in recent years, to all of those (including myself) who have proposed analyses along these lines. We do not, for example, know what it really means for a language to be "fully" expressive or what are the "necessary semantic and pragmatic distinctions" that a language must make. Nor can we say with any assurance how far is "too far" in the discussion of a tendency for Language to segmentalize when it "has gone too far from the principle of one-to-one mapping or semantic transparency in some area of its structure" (p. 192). What we can do, however, following Slobin's innovative lead, is to pay attention to the kinds of parallels that exist in various areas of grammar and over various kinds of language change in order to try to find answers to such questions. In other words, I thoroughly concur with the approach of the paper, and my cautionary note is simply intended to stress (a) the state of our ignorance of what "fully expressive," "necessary distinctions," and "too far" might mean, and (b) the consequent necessity of tackling such problems from the other end, that is, by investigating how various languages handle the informational, communicative, expressive, symbolic, and other demands put on them (cf. Hymes' [1964, 1970] discussion of linguistic "means" and "resources").

I am also in agreement with Slobin's argument that situations of change, and especially rapid change, provide an excellent opportunity to observe the competitive interaction of the various tendencies he discusses. In terms of the four "charges," I wish he had discussed redundancy, that one of Hockett's (1963, p. 19) proposed universals which seems to underlie some of the argumentation, particularly the charge to "be quick and easy." This charge obviously reduces redundancy, but to which of the charges do we ascribe the importance of *maintaining* a fairly high level of redundancy in language? It certainly bears on processibility as well as on expressivity.

The survey of literature in the four empirical areas Slobin discusses is impressive, and those sections that are somewhat thin probably attest to a thinness of empirical work rather than to an oversight on Slobin's part. I refer here mainly to the "historical" section of "be clear" (p. 192), to a reliance on assertion rather than on particular case studies in the "pidgin–creole" section of "be clear" (p. 194) (and this despite the fact that the assertion in question is my own!), and to the complete omission of a "contact" section for "be quick and easy." Directing our attention to those areas in which more work needs to be done might be one important outgrowth of this paper.

If a few sections were thin, the majority were surprisingly rich. I particularly enjoyed the discussion of the two basic ways in which languages can become unclear (the "historical" section of "be processible"), the comparisons of child acquisition of inflectional systems and relative clauses in Turkish and Serbo-Croatian (the "child language" section of "be clear"), and the section on rhetorical expressivity. One minor quibble here: I am not at all sure that speakers of creoles and adult speakers of all natural languages find themselves "taking the role of the listener, actively programming [their] speech to be effective and intelligible in a given discourse situation" (p. 189) to a greater extent than do pidgin speakers (though this may well apply to child speech). In a limited contact vernacular as much as in any other language, speakers must be concerned with intelligibility at least, and probably also with effectiveness, even though the contact vernacular is required to be "effective" only over a limited range of situations and topics.

Lastly, though I certainly appreciate the reasons for avoiding, in a paper of this length, "the question of the source of change and the complex issue of the degree to which children are responsible for linguistic change," I think these are questions to which Slobin might profitably turn his attention, building on the classic Weinreich, Labov, and Herzog (1968) essay on the subject.

REFERENCES

Hockett, C. F. The problem of universals in language. In J. Greenberg (Ed.), *Universals of language*. Cambridge, Mass.: M.I.T. Press, 1963. Pp. 1–29.

Hymes, D. Introduction: Toward ethnographies of communication. In J. J. Gumperz and D. Hymes (Eds.), *The ethnography of communication. American Anthropologist*, 1964, *66* (6, pt. II), 1–34.

Hymes, D. Linguistic theory and the functions of speech. *Proceedings of International Days of Sociolinguistics*. Rome: Istituto Luigi Sturzo, 1970. Pp. 111–144.

Weinreich, U., W. Labov, & Herzog, M. I. Empirical foundations for a theory of language change. In W. Lehmann (Ed.), *Proceedings of the Texas Conference on Historical Linguistics*. Austin: University of Texas Press, 1968. Pp. 97–195.

17

Semantics and Miniature Artificial Languages

SHANNON DAWN MOESER

Memorial University of Newfoundland

The natural language system involves a complex set of interacting variables. Any investigation into its nature, whether it be by observing regularities in the system or by experimental manipulation of specific variables, carries the danger of interpretations being confounded by the co-occurrence of variables. That is, effects that appear due to one variable may in actuality arise from some co-occurring, unspecified variable which the researcher has not considered in his analysis.

One way to control for this problem is to simplify the materials being used in the research. Miniature artificial languages offer an experimental tool with which to investigate the psychological processes involved in the acquisition and processing of language structure. Because these systems contain only a few variables, the danger of confounding is greatly reduced. Because they are specifically designed by the experimenter, they allow for the independent manipulation of variables which in natural language are not independent.

Preparation of this paper was supported by Canada Council Grant No. S74-0177.

THE EXPERIMENTAL PARADIGM

All miniature artificial languages have a linguistic component consisting of verbal symbols and a set of rules for combining these symbols into strings. Many miniature languages also have a referential system consisting of a set of visual objects designed to correspond in some way to the linguistic component. The symbolic system, rule system, and referential system correspond respectively to the phonological, syntactic, and semantic components of natural language. However, in the artificial language, each of these components has a much less complex structure than its natural language counterpart. There are seldom more than 20 elements in the symbolic system, and sometimes as few as 5 or 6. The syntactic system may include class membership, order, and co-occurrence rules, but it can always be described by a very small number of rewrite symbols. The referential field contains nothing resembling the richness of the real world; it is entirely visual, there is no action, and each individual word refers to an individual element rather than to a set of elements as is more common with natural languages. This simplification serves two purposes: one, to make it possible for a subject to learn and use the language within a single experimental session; and two, to study variables in isolation from the interactions found in complex systems.

A number of different learning paradigms are used in artificial language research, but most studies follow a general discovery pattern. Subjects are presented with a set of symbol strings or "sentences" which have been formed from the language symbols and rule system. The strings are presented one at a time and the corpus which is presented does not include all permissible combinations generated by the grammatical rules but only a subset of these. Later the subjects are tested on whether or not they have acquired knowledge of the rule system. The test may be presented as a memory exam, in which subjects are asked to recall or identify the strings they have seen. In this case, it will be their errors that are of interest. If most of the errors are consistent with the structural system, it would indicate that the subjects were able to induce the rule inherent in the presented material and used this rule to construct their productions or make recognition judgments. Often subjects given this type of test cannot verbalize the rule that they were using, although their actions indicate that they were making use of it (e.g., Braine, 1971; Reber, 1967).

In a variation of the discovery paradigm, subjects may be initially instructed about the nature of the experimental task. They will be tested on their ability to distinguish between grammatical and nongrammatical strings, none of which were part of the original corpus.

Although the type of test can differ among experiments, they are all designed to determine whether the subjects were able to abstract a rule structure from the corpus of linguistic patterns which were presented, and if so, what type of rule structure was abstracted. The answer is provided by analyzing the subjects' production of, or response to, novel combinations of elements that were not part of the original corpus.

There are two additional paradigms which do not follow the discovery learning pattern outlined above. In one, the subject is asked to make up possible strings and is informed after each production whether or not it is acceptable (Hunt, 1965; Miller, 1967). Thus he must form verbal hypotheses as to what the system might embody and test these hypotheses by forming strings. This procedure tends to elicit complex cognitive strategies from the college students who are generally used as subjects and does not appear to be applicable to most language acquisition situations. The other paradigm, which I have recently employed, is not concerned with rule discovery but with rule use. Subjects learn to associate identical symbolic systems with different referential fields and are tested on their ability to process the rule or remember specific verbal information. These studies are designed to gain an understanding of the semantic variables underlying language organization.

Validity of the Paradigm

Investigators working with miniature languages assume that their findings can provide data relevant to questions of language acquisition and use. These are investigations of rule-governed systems, and as such, their results should be interpretable in terms of other rule-governed systems. By the simplification of structure, it is hoped to observe the operation of a number of linguistic variables under an experimental control that could never be achieved with natural language. However, although there is general agreement that miniature language research provides important data to the study of human cognitive processes, the linguistic interpretation of the results has been challenged by some linguists and psycholinguists.

Generally, the validity of using an artificial language to investigate psycholinguistic questions is questioned on two grounds: First, it is suggested that rule systems in natural languages have specific formal properties corresponding to language processing abilities possessed by humans and that these properties are altered or lost by the arbitrary selection and simplification of rules in the artificial system. Second, it is suggested that young children possess language learning abilities which are lost by puberty. Both these criticisms assume that humans possess a special language processing ability, in addition to and different from their more general cognitive abilities, a position that is neither supported by recent research in comparative psychology (Gardner, & Gardner, 1975), nor in accord with many theories of cognition (e.g., Sinclair-deZwart, 1973).

When we strip away the claim of a special language ability, we are left with the argument that artificial language studies are not suitable because they have adopted an analytic approach to the study of language. Yet doesn't a simplification process occur in any research? Even the observer in a natural setting must arbitrarily decide what to record and what to ignore. Given that any investigative technique arbitrarily narrows our scope, the use of many different research procedures is probably our best check against drawing unwarranted conclusions. Results obtained from experimental studies should be compared with those obtained using more naturalistic procedures; insights derived from linguistic analyses should be tested in a more controlled setting.

Much of the criticism directed at miniature language research comes from a misunderstanding of what is being attempted. The purpose of this research is not to investigate linguistic rules in detail but to attempt to understand the psychological processes involved in verbal rule acquisition and use. Thus miniature languages are designed to reflect only certain characteristics of natural language. If language word order is being investigated, the miniature language will contain only a simple word order rule; if selection restriction rules are being investigated, the language syntax will be more complex. To make the artificial language more complex simply because natural languages are more complex would be to defeat the purpose of using this experimental paradigm. Complexity is introduced only when it is shown to be necessary. If, for instance, even a very simple rule system is processed differently when semantic referents are present as compared to when they are not present, it suggests that a referential system should be incorporated into all artificial language designs. However, the facts can be ascertained only if the two conditions are compared. With an artificial language one can compare a "meaningful" system with a "meaningless" one, and thus evaluate the contribution of meaning to the acquisition and use of a linguistic rule system.

Many artificial language studies have been designed to investigate how the syntactic code is acquired, and their findings used to explain the processes underlying infant language learning. This research has been criticized on the grounds that infants bring to language acquisition special psychological skills that adults no longer possess (e.g., Bever, Fodor, & Weksel, 1965). Yet there is no strong empirical evidence to support this belief. Asher and Price (1967) compared language learning at various ages using an experimental situation which closely resembled a natural learning environment. The subjects heard Russian commands at the same time as they saw a model acting out these commands. Some, in addition, were required to copy the model. Thus learning took place by observing—and sometimes joining in—an activity which was related to a linguistic message. The test required that subjects respond appropriately to a new set of commands, some of which contained combinations different from any presented in the training sessions. Results showed a learning improvement with age under both training conditions: Children below puberty level were much *poorer* than college students in learning the language. If children possess a special learning ability, why was it not evident here?

Most of the evidence favoring a special linguistic aptitude in children is anecdotal. A child and his parents go to live in a foreign country. The child picks up the new language with almost magical speed while his parents show little aptitude for the language even after one or two years. Smith and Braine (1971) offer perhaps the best answer to these stories:

> All that these anecdotes demonstrate is that an adult who lives in a subculture where his native language is known need not be motivated to learn, and that a child who is sent to the local school or nursery in a foreign country is subject to what are surely very effective conditions for learning: massive exposure to the language together with overwhelming pressure to learn.
>
> Another fact relevant to these anecdotes is that the natural measure of linguistic achievement—ability to communicate with peers—contains a strong bias in favor of the child . . . the younger the learner, the less there is to learn. [p. 21–22]

In other words, the children are placed in situations were there is more motivation to learn, and are subjected to an easier test of language proficiency. Also, the children are more often exposed to a language that contains relatively simple syntactic and cognitive structure. Adults are given less opportunity to build up their knowledge from a simple base. In the Asher and Price study, children and adults were exposed to the same language corpus and given the same comprehension test, and the results suggest that it is adults who possess the superior language acquisition skills.

The problem with using miniature language studies to explain first language acquisition in infants lies not with the possibility that infants possess skills unavailable to adults, but with the probability that adults possess skills unavailable to the infant. The subjects in these experiments will bring to the language learning task special strategies which have been acquired through their experience as a language user. Thus these studies cannot give us information regarding the specific language learning strategies used by infants but can only investigate the general psychological processes that must underlie such specific strategies.

THE RESEARCH

Research on Class Order Learning

In many languages, the order of words in the sentence provides information regarding basic grammatical relations. Some of the earliest miniature language studies investigated acquisition of word order rules. One common paradigm involved using a semantically empty language, that is, a system which did not include a nonverbal reference field. Subjects were presented with strings in which symbols or groups of symbols were always shown in the same position. An example would be the following sequence: *ly, my, ga, mr, gr, la*. The letters *l, m,* and *g* always occupy the first position in the sequence, *y, a,* and *r* always occupy the final position. Thus the language structure could be described by three phrase structure rules:

$$S \rightarrow A + B$$
$$A \rightarrow l, m, g$$
$$B \rightarrow y, a, r$$

With these systems, tests of learning involve measuring the subjects' tendencies to place the symbols in the correct positions in new combinations which were not part of the original corpus. (In our example, *lr* would be a grammatical sequence, although it was not presented during training. Its production during the testing session would suggest that the word order rule had been acquired.) A number of experiments have shown that subjects learn these order contingencies (Braine, 1963; Smith, 1966b) and that such learning is best characterized by a position rule (Smith, 1966a; Smith & Gough, 1969).

Children are capable of acquiring such position rules. Braine (1963, 1966) and Smith (1966b) used 8- to 10-year-old children as subjects. Braine (1963) also reported that 4-year-olds could learn position rules, although in his experiment animal sounds were used instead of words, and pictures of the animals were presented along with the verbal stimuli. Thus these young subjects could have been learning to place pictures in certain positions rather than to place sounds in certain positions. However, in a recently completed experiment, I have found that 4-year-olds can rapidly acquire auditory order regularities of nonsense word combinations presented without any visual referents for the words.

This class order structure has also been incorporated into artificial languages that have a semantic reference system. In the most common paradigm (e.g., Esper, 1925), subjects are presented with two-syllable nonsense words in conjunction with a set of stimuli which vary along two easily discriminable dimensions (such as shape and color). The first syllable of the nonsense words is always paired with one dimension of the stimuli (e.g., color) and the second syllable is always paired with the other dimension (e.g., shape). For example, see the set of combinations illustrated in Figure 17.1.

Subjects are asked to learn to associate each two-syllable name with its two-dimensional referent; then they are tested on their acquisition of the language rule by being shown color–shape combinations which were not part of the training corpus. Subjects show systematic response tendencies which Foss (1968) suggests can best be described as a result of learning to

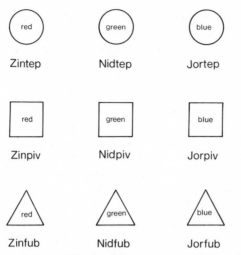

| Zintep | Nidtep | Jortep |

| Zinpiv | Nidpiv | Jorpiv |

| Zinfub | Nidfub | Jorfub |

Figure 17.1 An example of the words and referents used in the Esper artificial language paradigm. Words and stimuli are from Foss (1968).

pair single-syllable responses with stimulus values, and, in addition, a simple semantic position rule (e.g., "color syllables precede shape syllables").

Thus, class order rules are acquired in systems containing semantic referents and in systems without them. How do the two types of learning compare? I have carried out two studies comparing position learning in a language with only syntactic rules versus one with both syntactic and semantic position rules. Moeser (1969) presented subjects with a miniature language in which the same word classes did not always appear in an identical sentence position. Here we have a case more analogous with natural language. Sometimes a word class occurred at the end of a string, other times in the middle. However, the order of word classes was always invariant: A preceded B, and B preceded C. Three class combinations were used (AB, ABC, and ABCC), and there was a fourth class consisting of two words which could arbitrarily occupy nearly any position in the string. Some subjects received the string of nonsense words without a reference field; others were required to associate each word in the string with a stimulus in a visual reference system. In the nonsemantic condition, word class was definable only from sentence position; in the semantic condition, word class was definable both from sentence position and from stimulus attributes (e.g., all A-class words were associated with round objects, all C-class words with angular objects, etc.). To test the learning of word order, subjects were given a multiple-choice exam that required them to choose the correct alternative from a group of sentences that differed only in their order permutations. There were no significant differences between conditions on this test, although we know from other types of measures that subjects in the semantic condition paid little or no attention to learning the order of words in the sentences (they spent all their time learning to associate words with their referents) whereas subjects in the nonsemantic condition consciously concentrated on learning the sentence positions of various words. Word order appeared to be acquired almost automatically, whether or not attention was paid to it.

The second study comparing semantic and syntactic position learning was a developmental study. Three groups of children were used, of ages 4:0 to 4:3, 5:3 to 5:6, and 6:6 to 6:9. They heard four sequences of nonsense words and were asked to recall them. The block of sequences, and the recall tests were repeated several times, using the procedure developed by Moeser and Olson (1974). Some of the subjects had previously learned to associate the nonsense words with blocks of various designs, others had played word games which encouraged them to attend to the sounds of the words. The 4- and 5-year-olds who had a semantic system with which to associate the nonsense words were slightly superior on a test of rule learning, but there were no differences at the 6-year-old level. By the age of 6, the results of children using a syntactic classification rule and those using a semantic classification rule were indistinguishable except on a special test designed to see whether children in the semantic condition had acquired a semantic rule. Again the evidence suggests that semantic referents make little difference in the acquisition of a simple order rule.

Research on Selection Restriction Learning

Assume that we wish to account for the following four sequences: AX, AXC, AYC, AYCC. They can be generated by a set of rewrite rules as follows:

$$S \rightarrow A + B$$

$$B \rightarrow \begin{Bmatrix} X + (C) \\ Y + C + (C) \end{Bmatrix}$$

The B rule provides a co-occurrence restriction. If the X is chosen, it may or may not be followed by one C; if the Y is chosen, it must be followed by one or two Cs. It is easy to demonstrate that natural languages contain many such selection restrictions.

The data regarding acquisition of such selection restrictions in meaningless artificial languages have been somewhat ambiguous. Smith (1965, 1966a, 1969) used a system with four classes of letters (M, N, P, and Q) such that a sequence consisted of either MN or PQ structure; although his subjects learned that M and P letters came first and N and Q letters occurred last, they did not learn that N letters depended on the occurrence of M letters, and Q letters depended on the occurrence of P letters. Segal and Halwes (1965, 1966) found that subjects presented with two rules (S → A + B, and S → B + C) learned only the simple rule S → X + Y, where the X class consisted of words belonging to the A class plus some B-class words and the Y class consisted of words belonging to the C class plus some B-class words. Thus they generated not only AB and BC sequences but also AC and BB sequences. Smith (1968) did show some learning of the co-occurrence restrictions if positional regularities were eliminated; his subjects learned that two symbols from one class occurred together and two symbols from another class occurred together, but that members of both classes could not occur together. In other words, the subjects formed classes on the basis of co-occurrence instead of position in the sequences. As in the other studies, however, Smith (1968) failed to find acquisition of the position rule and selection rule concurrently.

On the other hand, there are a number of studies in which concurrent acquisition of both rules has been shown. Braine (1965) reported that subjects given sequences aXb and pXq not only learned that a and p went first, X went second, and b and q went last, but also that b was contingent on a and q and p. Braine (1966) found that subjects could learn that certain sequences followed one marker item (g) while other sequences followed another marker item (f). They acquired concurrently four sequence forms: fA, gPQ, fAgPQ, and gPQ fA. Even more complex rule systems have been acquired in studies using finite-state languages (Miller, 1958, 1967; Reber, 1967, 1969; Saporta, Blumenthal, Lackowski, & Reiff, 1965). Here a great number of permissible sequences were generated, and subjects are required to use these combinations as a basis for abstracting information about the rule structure generating them.

All of the studies that showed acquisition of the more complex rule structure have in common the fact that each restriction class contained only one symbol. In both of Braine's (1965, 1966) studies, the marker items, that is the classes which denoted the selection restriction rule, contained only one word. All of the finite-class languages had only one word per class, and a maximum of five difference symbols were presented in any one language. The subjects had to acquire only the rule for combining these symbols; they did not have to form classes concurrently with acquisition of the combination rules.

Consider what occurs when there are more items in the co-occurrence classes. Moeser and Bregman (1973) used the following syntactic rule system:

$$S \rightarrow A + B$$
$$A \rightarrow (D) + M$$
$$B \rightarrow \begin{Bmatrix} X + (C) \\ Y + C + (C) \end{Bmatrix}$$
$$C \rightarrow (D) + N$$

Such a system will generate 18 acceptable sequence combinations, less than the number generated by the finite-state languages. There were, however, eight symbols in each of the classes M and N, four each in classes X and Y, and five in class D. After 3200 exposures to sequential combinations, the subjects showed no learning of the rule structure. Yet Moeser and Bregman (1972) had found that with an almost identical system, subjects exposed to word combinations showed some rule learning after 240 exposures. In the earlier experiment, there were four words in classes M and N, and two in classes X, Y, and D. Although the subjects did not acquire the selection restriction rule (B rule), they did learn some positional rules. When the class size is increased, even positional learning seems to be eliminated.

Children do not restrict themselves to a vocabulary of five words while acquiring the grammatical restrictions of their native language. Nor do they initially produce articles and prepositions, the words which would correspond to the "frame" provided in the Braine studies. Therefore it is unlikely that the studies using "meaningless" artificial languages serve as a prototype for children's first language acquisition.

Thus we must turn to studies in which a semantic system was provided along with the symbolic system. Subjects given this task seem to approach the learning situation differently from those presented with a nonsemantic language. Moeser (1969) asked subjects to "think out loud" as they worked at acquiring the language. Here is a sample from a subject in the nonsemantic condition:

> -*Riz* seems to come at the beginning and so does *bef*, and *voy* seems to come at the end.
> -*Cag* seems to come at the end.
> -*Cim* is always in the middle, it's never at the beginning or the end.
> -*San* is in the middle.
> -*Mul* is practically always at the end.
> -*Pum* is always at the beginning and *tob* is always at the end when present.
> -Only *nep*, *riz*, *bef*, and *pum* come at the beginning.
> -I can't even tell one from the next any more.
> -All the words are three letters long, with a vowel in the middle and they are easy to mix up.

This subject concentrated on learning the positions of words in the strings and he found it quite a difficult task. In this particular experiment there were only 14 different words; if the subject had been presented with a set of 29, as in the Moeser and Bregman (1973) experiment, it is likely that he would have found this strategy impossible to employ.

The following sample was also from the Moeser (1969) experiment but taken from a subject in the semantic condition:

-*Nep* has something to do with roundness, I think.

-*Nep* is the round figure.

-*Kas*, I think, is blackness.

-*Voy* is associated with no colour.

-*Voy* is associated with orientation upwards.

-*Mul* is the association of the rectangle and the semi-circle.

-*Nep* is the semicircle.

-*San* is two mirror sort of in each other.

-*Mul* is the association of two figures.

-*Nep* is *that* figure.

-*San* is two figures, within each other.

-*Voy* is blackness, *san* is each thing associated with each other, *mul* is association.

-*Voy* is right side up.

-*Dex* is triangularity.

-*Tob* is a dark line.

-*Kas* is blackness.

-*Riz* is triangle.

-*Bef* is semicircle; *pum* is double-triangle.

-*Cag* is one on top of the other; *riz* is an object; *voy* is a direction.

-*Wup* is triangle; *jow* is rectangle.

-*Jow* is rectangle.

-*Cag* is one on top of the other.

This subject ignored the positions of words in the linguistic strings and con-centrated on learning to associate the words with their referential attributes. Sometimes he made incorrect hypotheses, and later changed them. For example, he first said that *voy* was associated with no color, then with an upward orientation, then with blackness, then with right side up. He seemed to be working on two hypotheses with this word, one that it was associated somehow with the shading of figures and the other that it was associated with the orientation of figures. Sometimes the subject was too specific in his criteria, as, for example, when he first said the *mul* was the association of the rectangle and the semicircle and later had to amend this to the association of any two figures; but generally he appeared to make more overgeneralization errors. For example, *nep* was first described as having to do with roundness (there were four round figures), then as being a semicircle (there were two semicircular figures), and finally narrowed down to a specific figure. This prototype accords closely with accounts of children's vocabulary acquisition.

Subjects shown a reference field learn to associate the words in the language with specific attributes of the field, but this cannot help them acquire the selection restriction rules unless a further specification is added. The referential field must reflect these restrictions. In other words, I am arguing that syntax is an elaboration of the lawful events and relations found in the semantic system.

Consider the experiment by Moeser and Bregman (1972). Subjects were exposed to the lawful strings of the language in one of four conditions: A *words only* condition in which only the symbol system was presented; an *arbitrary figures* condition in which figures were presented along with the symbol system but the correspondence between the word classes and figures was arbitrary; a *class correspondence* condition, in which the figures presented with the symbol system were grouped so that the words of a given class referred to visual forms of a given type; and a *syntax correlation* condition, in which the visual forms were not only correlated with verbal classes but the selection restrictions were incorporated into their design. The systems are illustrated in Figure 17.2 and examples of stimuli are shown in Figure 17.3.

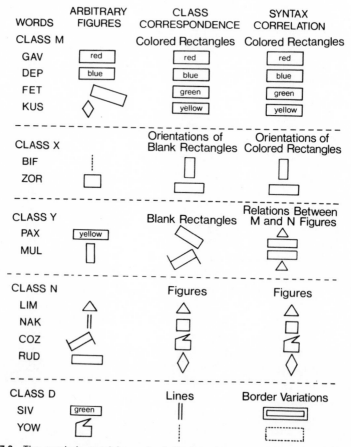

Figure 17.2 The symbols used in each of the learning conditions of the Moeser and Bregman (1972) experiment.

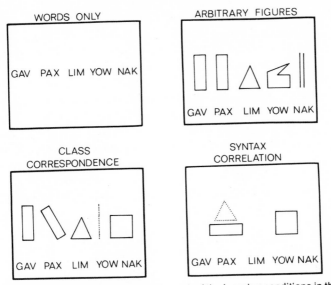

Figure 17.3   An example of a stimulus card in each of the learning conditions in the Moeser and Bregman (1972) experiment.

The language syntax used in the experiment could be described by the following rewrite rules:

$$S \rightarrow A + B$$
$$A \rightarrow M + (D)$$
$$B \rightarrow \begin{Bmatrix} X + (C) \\ Y + C + (C) \end{Bmatrix}$$
$$C \rightarrow N + (D)$$

Now refer to Figure 17.2. In both the class correspondence and syntax correlation conditions, M words referred to colored rectangles and N words to geometrical figures. However, in the syntax correlation condition, the X, Y and D referents were incorporated into the M and N referents, and the selection restriction rule was made necessary by the visual design. (A Y-word referred to an association of an M and N figure; thus if a Y word is present, there must also be an N word. An X word referred to an orientation of an M referent and thus did not necessitate the presence of an N word). In the class correspondence condition, the X, Y, and D referents were illustrated as independent units. In the arbitrary figures condition, the figures simply acted as a restatement of the information carried in the verbal system.

Subjects were tested by having to choose between pairs of grammatical and ungrammatical strings presented without reference fields. Only subjects in the syntax correlation condition were able to acquire all the rules, including the selection restriction rule; subjects in the class correspondence condition were quite good at acquiring the class order rules; those in the arbitrary figures condition were no better at acquiring the syntax rules than those not shown any reference field.

Moeser and Bregman (1972) suggested that the acquisition of the language structure consisted of (1) learning to associate each word with its referent, (2) learning the semantic rules (how the referents were organized), and (3) learning to map words onto specific sentence positions. For the three reference conditions, (1) and (3) were approximately equal, only the semantic rules differed, yet the differences in semantic structure had a major effect on the acquisition of language syntax. The subjects did not acquire an abstract syntactic structure; they acquired a set of semantic rules which they used to make judgments about the grammaticality of sentences.

When the subjects received a meaningless artificial language, they concentrated on learning position regularities, yet they were no better at acquiring position rules than subjects who concentrated on matching single words to perceptual concepts. Thus, it is proposed that the language learner expends his major efforts in trying to correlate his perceptual–cognitive structures to the linguistic expressions he hears. He does not form hypotheses about "grammar." His syntactic expressions are elaborations of the conceptual groupings he has formed, and the order regularities are acquired with little or no conscious effort.

Infant Language Learning

Moeser (1971) suggested that the results of these studies had a direct implication for theories of infant language learning. At approximately the same time, Macnamara (1972) proposed that "infants learn their language by first determining independent of language, the meaning which a speaker intends to convey to them, and by working out the relationship between the meaning and the language" (p.1). Here we have two different approaches to the investigation of language acquisition, both arguing that language abilities are mapped onto already-present cognitive structures. The subjects learning the miniature language were adults, and exposed to a learning situation much simpler than the complexities of the infant's world, yet the conclusions reached as a result of the experimental study were very similar to those reached by Macnamara from his analysis of research in infant language learning.

To further support the proposal that infants acquire their language using a semantic strategy, we tested young children, using the artificial language procedure. Moeser and Olson (1974) trained 4-year-olds to associate non-sense words with blocks of various designs, then tested their ability to recall two-word verbal sequences with the blocks absent. An illustration of the blocks is shown in Figure 17.4. The experimental group received a referential system containing an inherent semantic rule (pair → round block and square block) which corresponded to the language syntactic rule (S → A + B); the referential systems used with the control groups did not have this correspondence. Subjects in the experimental group were significantly superior in recall of verbal sequence. Again, when there was a correspondence between semantic rule and syntactic rule, language processing appeared to be easier.

In a follow-up study, we tested the ability of 4-year-olds to recall verbal pairs after being trained with the referential systems shown in Figure 17.5.

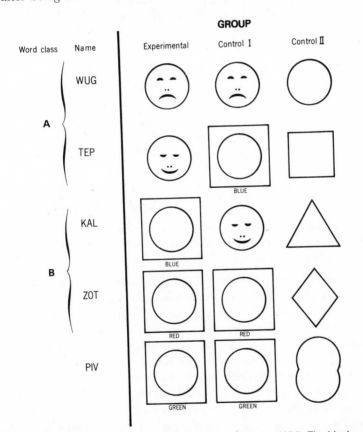

Figure 17.4 The words and stimuli used by Moeser and Olson (1974). The blocks used by the experimental and Control I subjects were designed so that the round blocks fit into the holes in the center of the square blocks.

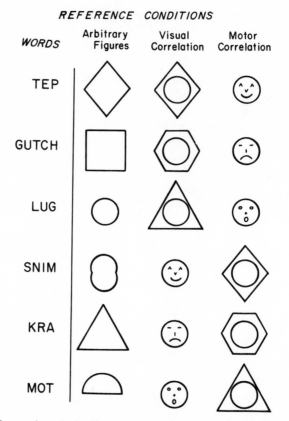

Figure 17.5 The words and stimuli used in the experiment. In the visual correlation and motor correlation conditions, the round blocks fit into the holes in the center of the larger blocks.

Here, in the visual correlation condition, the semantic rule corresponded to the syntactic rule, but the order of words in the sequence did not correspond to the order in which the children normally manipulated the blocks. (The first word in the sequence always referred to a large geometrical block, the second word to a small round block. Observation of the subjects in the experiment revealed that they all put the round blocks in the geometrical ones; they did not place the geometrical blocks around the round ones, even when the experimenter referred to a geometrical block first.) In the motor correlation condition, the semantic rule corresponded to the syntactic rule, and the order of words in the sequences was correlated to the child's actions towards the blocks. Two control groups were used, one which was trained to associate the nonsense words with arbitrary referents (the arbitrary figures condition in Figure 17.5) and one which heard only the nonsense word sequences.

Only the subjects in the motor correlation group were significantly superior to the control groups in remembering the verbal pairs; subjects in the visual correlation group were not significantly better than the control groups. Thus, in order to facilitate processing, not only did the syntax rule have to correspond to the visual properties of the objects but also to the order in which the child manipulated the objects. It appears that in very young children at least, the representation system may be organized more in terms of the child's actions toward the referential field than in terms of his visual images of it. In an earlier paper (Moeser & Bregman, 1973), we expressed the belief that early language acquisition was built upon a foundation of visual imagery, because our adult subjects had based their verbal organizations on visual relationships. Here is a case of a particular strategy available to older subjects which may not be so accessible to infants. Instead of perceptually based semantic rules, the infant's semantic system may be organized more in terms of action patterns, much as Sinclair-deZwart (1973) has suggested. However, such a modification would not alter our basic hypothesis that syntactic rules are an elaboration of cognitive organizations.

Most artificial language studies use a fairly restricted semantic system, consisting of a few visual symbols arranged into various designs. In this study, some movement was introduced into the system. It seems likely that the incorporation of motion into other artificial language studies might provide additional data on the language acquisition process. For example, Nelson (1975) has found individual differences in infant's initial language learning strategies, with some children concentrating on the acquisition of a referential vocabulary and others paying more attention to words that denote relational expressions (i.e., words referring to activity). These differences may arise from different cognitive styles which continue beyond this early developmental stage. They may arise from particular linguistic experiences which occur early in the language acquisition phase. Using a miniature language incorporating motion, we could test some of these possibilities.

Research on Semantic Organization

Movement in the reference system is only one way in which variables of the semantic rule structure can be manipulated. My most recent experiments have been designed to investigate how the cognitive system underlying language comprehension and memory is affected by the type of organization present in the reference field. In these experiments, both reference fields are correlated with the language syntax, but they differ with respect to the way in which the visual attributes are arranged. For example, see Figure 17.6. In semantic system "b" the referential field is designed in terms of discrete elements arranged as a linear association, much the same way as words in a

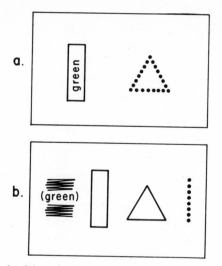

Figure 17.6   An example of the reference fields used by Moeser (1975a, b): (a) the holistic reference field; (b) the linear reference field.

language; in semantic system "a," these same elements have been combined into two perceptual organizations.

Moeser and Bregman (1972) used two groups which differed mainly with regard to how the same symbolic elements were organized, as can be seen in Figure 17.3. In the syntax correlation condition, the elements were combined into relatively holistic units; in the class correspondence condition, they were presented in a linear array. Only the selection restriction rules were not incorporated into the design of the class correspondence reference system. If we ignore the scores on the selection restriction questions, subjects in the syntax correlation condition were still superior at rule learning to those in the class correspondence condition. Furthermore, only in the syntax correlation condition did differences in complexity of rule structure not affect the acquisition process. In the class correspondence condition (and in all other conditions), the greater the number of possible combinations, the more difficult it was for subjects to learn the syntax rules. In other words, the addition of combination variations to a holistic arrangement did not affect learning, whereas the addition of combination variations to a linear display resulted in a poorer learning performance.

In some recent experiments, I have first trained subjects to associate individual nonsense words with individual perceptual attributes (for example, they might learn that *bif* refers to the color red, *dak* to a horizontal rectangle, *hib* to a vertical rectangle, *rud* to a square, *tep* to a dashed line, etc.) In this way, word-referent learning is speeded up, and can be eliminated as a factor in the experiment. Attention can then be directed solely at the learning and processing of combinations, that is, at variables which affect the formation of an underlying organization or structure.

After subjects had learned the word-referent associations, Moeser (1975b) presented four-word verbal sequences in conjunction with the elements organized into either semantic system "a" or semantic system "b" in Figure 17.6. Half the subjects in each reference condition heard a language in which the word order referred to the elements in a left-to-right sequence (color–orientation–shape–line); the others heard a language in which the elements were described in a left–right–left–right sequence (color–shape–orientation–line). Thus there were four experimental groups: (1) those shown system "a" while they heard a left-to-right verbal sequence; (2) those shown system "a" while they heard an alternating verbal sequence; (3) those shown system "b" while they heard a left-to-right verbal sequence; and (4) those shown system "b" while they heard an alternating verbal sequence.

After they had been exposed to the combinations, subjects were tested on their ability to discriminate between lawful and unlawful verbal sequences presented without visual referents. Both groups who had been shown system "b," and the group shown system "a" with the left-to-right verbal sequence were equally good at judging lawful sequences. The group given system "a" and a language order that necessitated breaking up the perceptual units was significantly poorer than the other three groups. Thus differences between word class orders were found only with respect to semantic system "a," that is, only when the holistic reference system was used. When the referential stimuli were presented as a linear array of independent elements, whether or not they were presented in a sequence that corresponded to their perceptual order had no effect on rule processing. However, when they were presented as part of an organizational system, the subjects found the rule processing task more difficult with a word order that required that the elements be processed independently of this organization, even though they had initially learned to associate individual words with these individual elements. Perceptual organization appeared to be encoded into the semantic rule system so that it affected judgments of lawfulness even when the visual array was not present.

This same type of effect was found when the task involved memory for verbal combinations rather than judgments of lawfulness (Moeser, 1976). Also, using the two reference fields shown in Figure 17.7, Moeser (1976) reported that subjects exposed to verbal combinations in conjunction with the integrated field (Figure 17.7a) were superior at remembering verbal sequences to those presented with the linear field (Figure 17.7b).

To summarize, subjects exposed to a reference field in which the elements were organized into configurations were superior to those exposed to a

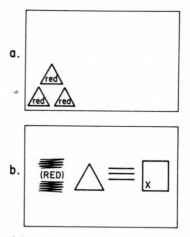

Figure 17.7 An example of the reference fields used by Moeser (1976): (a) the holistic reference field; (b) the linear reference field.

reference field containing a linear sequence of elements at acquiring language rules (Moeser & Bregman, 1972) and at remembering specific verbal sequences (Moeser, 1976), when the order of words in the sequences was congruent with the organization of the perceptual field. However, subjects exposed to the holistic field were poorer at rule processing (Moeser, 1975a, b) and at remembering sequences (Moeser, 1976) when the order of words in the sequences violated the selection restriction rules inherent in the perceptual field. Thus, the unitization information contained in the reference field affected performance both when it was helpful and when it was detrimental to the task at hand.

These results suggest that information regarding the organization of a reference system is incorporated into the underlying conceptual system. Furthermore, it does not appear that this incorporation simply involves the addition of "tags" or "markers" to the representation. For example, let us consider the argument that language acquisition consists of adding more and more features to the core concept originally associated with the word. All subjects in these experiments first learned to associate single words with single visual elements. These must be regarded as the core concepts. Then, subjects in the integrated condition had to learn additional information about these concepts, such as the fact that a color concept always coexisted with a shape concept. This additional information could be represented as a set of selection restriction markers incorporated into the core concepts. In the linear condition there were similar co-occurrence restrictions, but these were not "built-in" to the visual field and would not necessarily have to be encoded as selection restrictions. The presence of selection restrictions can thus be used to explain why subjects in the integrated condition performed so poorly when exposed to a word order which violated the order inherent in the reference field. The absence of selection restrictions in the linear condition can be used to explain why word class order had no effect on performance in this condition. However, with this line of reasoning, it must follow that subjects in the linear condition should be superior on memory tasks—they will have less information to remember. Yet they were significantly poorer on a number of memory tasks (Moeser, 1976). Therefore, these results are difficult to explain within a framework which regards language acquisition as a simple addition of primitive features.

A more fruitful approach may be to view language acquisition as a process of acquiring organized units of knowledge, and changes to that knowledge brought about both by synthesis of the original units into more complex units and by analysis of the units into their component parts. This view is similar to the description of concept acquisition offered by Nelson (1974). Within this framework we can explain the miniature language results. For example, we would predict that subjects in the integrated condition would first acquire the simple concepts as independent units in the word/referent training session. Later, the exposure of the integrated perceptual structures would encourage a modification of the original conceptual units into synthesized larger units. When both verbal and perceptual units were correlated, subjects in the integrated condition should show a superior performance because they had fewer conceptual units to process than subjects in the linear condition. When verbal and perceptual units were not correlated, subjects in the integrated condition should show an inferior performance because they would have to analyze the incoming conceptual information into its component parts. These are the results that were obtained. Thus, the artificial language experiments suggest that the underlying conceptual structure of language is best represented as a system of configurations and that the combination of these configurations into larger units or their analysis into smaller units is an important variable in the processing of linguistic information.

SUMMARY

With the miniature artificial language, we find that the design of a referential system has a strong effect on the processing of the linguistic system presented in conjunction with it. Moeser and Bregman (1972, 1973) showed that subjects could not learn even a relatively simple linguistic rule system unless this was accompanied by a referential system reflecting the linguistic restrictions. In later studies (Moeser, 1975a, b, 1976), it was found that organizational factors inherent in the referential system affected the ease with which a linguistic sequence was processed. These results suggest that to comprehend or to remember a verbal sequence, an individual must translate this sequence into a semantic representation incorporating the characteristics of the referents that the sequence describes. In other words, the underlying or base structure of language contains characteristics of the nonverbal environment. The linguistic communication is mapped onto this underlying structure in terms of a set of cognitive–linguistic rules.

These cognitive–linguistic rules are only now beginning to be investigated. Moeser (1975a) suggested that one such rule might be that attributes of a conceptual unit are best described by a sequential series of words. This would explain why double-embedded sentences are not part of our language system, even though acceptable in terms of the linguistic rule system. Moeser (1976) argues for another cognitive–linguistic rule: A series of words describing elements in a single conceptual unit are better retained as linguistic units than if they refer to a set of independent conceptual units. This would explain why verbal sequences that describe events that can be easily integrated into perceptual units are better remembered. Moeser (1975c) shows how this rule can be applied to a natural language situation. Both of these rules assume that the underlying conceptual structure reflects holistic characteristics of the reference events, an assumption supported both by the results of individual studies and by the complete program of research. The argument for an elemental representation of the conceptual structure is not supported when all of the experimental results are considered together.

Artificial language research offers an excellent opportunity for investigating the language semantic system in detail. Up to now, the total corpus of research has been fairly limited in scope because most of the studies have concentrated on linguistic variability rather than referential variability. The reference fields used in my experiments are only an extremely small subsample of the possible variations that could be made, yet even this incomplete sample shows the powerful effect that reference has on language processing.

REFERENCES

Asher, J. J., & Price, B. S. The learning strategy of the total physical response: Some age differences. *Child Development*, 1967, *38*, 1219–1227.
Bever, T. G., Fodor, J. A., & Weksel, W. On the acquisition of syntax: A critique of "contextual generalization." *Psychological Review*, 1965, *72*, 467–482.
Braine, M. D. S. On learning the grammatical order of words. *Psychological Review*, 1963, *70*, 323–348.
Braine, M. D. S. The insufficiency of a finite state model for verbal reconstructive memory. *Psychonomic Science*, 1965, *2*, 291–292.

Braine, M. D. S. Learning the positions of words relative to a marker element. *Journal of Experimental Psychology*, 1966, *72*, 532–540.

Braine, M. D. S. On two types of models of the internalization of grammars. In D. I. Slobin (Ed.), *The ontogenesis of grammar*. New York: Academic Press, 1971.

Esper, E. A. A technique for the experimental investigation of associative interference in artificial linguistic material. *Language Monographs*, 1925, No. 1.

Foss, D. J. An analysis of learning in a miniature linguistic system. *Journal of Experimental Psychology*, 1968, *76*, 450–459.

Gardner, B. T., & Gardner, R. A. Evidence for sentence constituents in the early utterances of child and chimpanzee. *Journal of Experimental Psychology: General*, 1975, *104*, 244–267.

Hunt, E. Selection and reception conditions in grammar and concept learning. *Journal of Verbal Learning and Verbal Behavior*, 1965, *4*, 211–215.

Macnamara, J. Cognitive basis of language learning in infants. *Psychological Review*, 1972, *79*, 1–13.

Miller, G. A. Free recall of redundant strings of letters. *Journal of Experimental Psychology*, 1958, *56*, 485–491.

Miller, G. A. Project Grammarama. In *The psychology of communication: Seven essays*. New York: Basic Books, 1967.

Moeser, S. D. Learning of a miniature linguistic system: Effects of external referents and order of word classes. Unpublished master's thesis, McGill University, 1969.

Moeser, S. D. The effects of semantic referents on the learning of syntax. Unpublished doctoral thesis, McGill University, 1971.

Moeser, S. D. Iconic factors and language word order. *Journal of Verbal Learning and Verbal Behavior*, 1975, *14*, 43–55. (a)

Moeser, S. D. The effect of reference field organization on language processing. *Memory and Cognition*, 1975, *3*, 370–374. (b)

Moeser, S. D. Memory for language organization in concrete and abstract sentences. *Memory and Cognition*, 1975, *3*, 560–568. (c)

Moeser, S. D. The effect of reference field organization on verbal memory. *Journal of Experimental Psychology: Human Learning and Memory*, 1976, *2*, 391–403.

Moeser, S. D., & Bregman, A. S. The role of reference in the acquisition of a miniature artificial language. *Journal of Verbal Learning and Verbal Behavior*, 1972, *11*, 759–769.

Moeser, S. D., & Bregman, A. S. Imagery and language acquisition. *Journal of Verbal Learning and Verbal Behavior*, 1973, *12*, 91–98.

Moeser, S. D., & Olson, A. J. The role of reference in children's acquisition of a miniature artificial language. *Journal of Experimental Child Psychology*, 1974, *17*, 204–218.

Nelson, K. Concept, word and sentence: Interrelations in acquisition and development. *Psychological Review*, 1974, *81*, 267–285.

Nelson, K. The nominal shift in semantic–syntactic development. *Cognitive Psychology*, 1975, *7*, 461–479.

Reber, A. S. Implicit learning of artificial grammars. *Journal of Verbal Learning and Verbal Behavior*, 1967, *6*, 855–863.

Reber, A. S. Transfer of syntactic structure in synthetic languages. *Journal of Experimental Psychology*, 1969, *81*, 115–119.

Saporta, S., Blumenthal, A. L., Lackowski, P., & Reiff, D. G. Grammatical models and language learning. In S. Rosenberg (Ed.), *Directions in psycholinguistics*. New York: Macmillan, 1965.

Segal, E. M., & Halwes, T. G. Learning of letter pairs as a prototype of first language learning. *Psychonomic Science*, 1965, *3*, 451–452.

Segal, E. M., & Halwes, T. G. The influence of frequency of exposure on the learning of a phrase structural grammar. *Psychonomic Science*, 1966, *4*, 157–158.

Sinclair-deZwart, H. Language acquisition and cognitive development. In T. E. Moore (Ed.), *Cognitive development and the acquisition of language*. New York: Academic Press, 1973.

Smith, K. H. Mediation and position learning in the recall of structured letter pairs. *Psychonomic Science*, 1965, *2*, 293–294.

Smith, K. H. Grammatical instrusions in the recall of structured letter pairs: Mediated transfer or position learning. *Journal of Experimental Psychology*, 1966, *72*, 580–588. (a)

Smith, K. H. Grammatical instrusions in the free recall of structured letter pairs. *Journal of Verbal Learning and Verbal Behavior*, 1966, *5*, 447–454. (b)

Smith, K. H. Conditional and unconditional co-occurrence restrictions in the recall of bigrams. *Psychonomic Science*, 1968, *12*, 379–380.

Smith, K. H. Learning co-occurrence restrictions: Rule induction or rote learning? *Journal of Verbal Learning and Verbal Behavior*, 1969, *8*, 319–321.

Smith, K. H., & Braine, M. D. S. Miniature languages and the problem of language acquisition. Unpublished paper (obtained from K. H. Smith), Psychology Department, Bowling Green State University, 1971.

Smith, K. H., & Gough, P. B. Transformation rules in the learning of miniature linguistic systems. *Journal of Experimental Psychology*, 1969, *79*, 276–282.

18

Miniature Artificial Languages as Research Tools

I. M. SCHLESINGER

Hebrew University of Jerusalem and
Israel Institute of Applied Social Research

In her paper Shannon Moeser discusses two criticisms of research with miniature artificial languages (MALs). One of these pertains to the artificiality of such research; regarding this, she correctly observes that abstraction and simplification are the essence of laboratory experiments and, far from invalidating them, should be considered an advantage. Moeser also refutes the claim that adult subjects are no longer able to learn language with the same capabilities the young child brings to bear on the learning task, and that we are therefore studying something radically different in the lab. I quite agree with Moeser's defence of MALs, in which she follows Smith and Braine (in press): MALs are a valid technique, in principle. We seem to differ, however, in our evaluation of the prospects for this research methodology. Moeser is apparently optimistic, whereas I tend to be somewhat more skeptical. This skepticism stems from reviewing results of studies done so far with MALs. Many of these may have revealed something about the learning of rules or about the organization of memory (Braine, 1968), and it is not this aspect I am concerned with here. The only issue I intend to discuss is the contribution of MAL research to our understanding of language acquisition. In the following, I shall try to explain the reasons for my circumspection.

The major cause of my dissatisfaction is the objectives of MAL studies so far. Many of these set out to simulate in the laboratory what was assumed to occur in the child learning language. Experiments followed in the footsteps of knowledge rather than breaking new ground. Let me give a few examples.

Following Katz's (1966, pp. 274–275) suggestion of hypothesis testing as a mechanism of language acquisition, Hunt (1965) showed that hypothesis testing is indeed an efficient procedure of learning a MAL. On the other hand, starting from a different theoretical basis, Reber (1967, 1969) showed that a MAL can be learned by "implicit learning" (i.e., Gibson's "perceptual learning") and Braine (1971) demonstrated that a grammar can be attained by passive learning. What each of these experiments goes to show is that the suggested mechanisms can *possibly* account for language learning. What has not been shown is that these are actually the mechanisms responsible for it. Researchers working with MAL are accordingly usually very modest in the claims they make regarding their achievements. Thus, Palermo and Eberhart (1971) defend themselves against Slobin's (1971) criticism by claiming that their experiment (Palermo & Eberhart, 1968) at least proves that a certain phenomenon that had been claimed to be difficult for traditional learning theories "is nothing unique to language." This, it seems to me, is not a very ambitious goal for an experiment.

When Braine (1963b) showed how the child learns by position learning he was demonstrating in the lab a process which his observations of children (Braine, 1963a) led him to believe was responsible for the acquisition process. But does the child learn a language in a way similar to that of Braine's experimental subjects? It is now generally recognized that Braine's theorizing in that early period suffers from a neglect of semantics. In the 1970s, theorists began to insist that the child learns rules of grammar in association with extralinguistic referents. Independently, Moeser and Bregman (1972, 1973), conducted experiments that showed that learning of syntactic rules is facilitated when its structure correlates with that of its referential field. If, as seems safe to assume, MAL research from now on will take semantics into account, this should be viewed as Moeser's lasting methodological contribution. It is interesting to note in passing, however, that early work with MALs starting with Esper (1925), in fact did include semantic reference, and that only for a short period in the 1960s MAL research proceeded as if language learning took place in a semantic vacuum. This, of course, was due to the influence of the then prevalent theoretical orientation. Moeser went against this trend and this is one of the few cases in which MAL researchers did not simply follow the lead of others, but set out to explore new hypotheses.

In general, however, much of MAL research rested content with demonstrating in the lab the existence of processes assumed to occur in nature. At the time the experiments were performed, this may have had some useful function in allaying doubts concerning a learning account of language and in showing the existence of certain learning mechanisms. Here, the researchers stood ground against the then fashionable disavowal of empiricism. From our present-day vantage point, however, the importance of these experiments seems to have been rather shortlived. We may admire the ingenuity expended in designing the experiment, and it is perhaps just because of this ingenuity that the results sound so disappointing. It is almost embarrassing to read the authors' summation of what they have achieved. Thus, Foss (1968a): ". . . the present hypothesis is that Ss discover systematicity, and utilize it in further behavior." But, he admits,

> what needs to be clarified is the nature of the mechanism that discovers such systematicity as may be represented in the stimuli, and how and under what conditions the device extends the systematicity to new inputs.

This is precisely what we have wanted to know all along. Or take the conclusion arrived at by Smith and Gough (1969): "that in the learning of at least one miniature language, as in the acquisition of natural languages, transformations are in evidence." On reading such summaries, one can hardly be blamed if one's enthusiasm for MALs flags.

Let us consider now a different kind of experimental hypothesis. Unlike the studies discussed above, which are concerned with the question of what *kinds* of rules are learned or what general mechanism is responsible for such learning, there are those which investigate the *conditions* of learning those rules. It seems that here MALs might contribute to our knowledge in more significant ways. Foss (1968b) studied the effect of number of instances of a given rule and of sequencing of instances. Palermo and Parrish (1971) investigated the effect of two variables on rule acquisition: (a) the number of different instances exemplifying the rule which were presented to the learner, and (b) the number of repetitions of an instance exemplifying the rule. They found that what matters is the amount of presentation, regardless of whether this consisted of a small number of instances presented several times or a larger number presented fewer times. They point out that it would seem to follow that children growing up in a lexically restricted environment can still acquire the rules of language, provided the small variety of exemplars is repeated a sufficient number of times. While it may be premature to extrapolate from these results to the learning of natural languages in view of the vast differences in complexity of the systems involved, in the sophistication of learners, and so on, studies like these at least concentrate on hitherto unexplored regularities. The latter can be more readily studied by MALs than by investigating language learning in a natural setting, because of the greater freedom of experimental manipulation possible with the former. Smith and Braine (in press) discuss further studies of this type.

As a case study of what might or might not be gained from experimenting with MALs, I propose to discuss in somewhat more detail two of Moeser's recent experiments, which have been presented at length in her present paper. Moeser (1975a, b) manipulated the organization of the referential field and assessed the effect of this on rule learning. These studies and that of Moeser (1976) may have implications for the problem of information storage, but my concern is only with the importance of these experiments for the acquisition of language; and it is to this aspect I shall address my remarks.

Moeser shows that when the referential field is integrated, a MAL with object coding is easier to learn than one with dimension coding, because of the discrepancy between the language structure and the structure of the referential field in the latter case. It seems that subjects find it difficult to fragment a holistic representation (object and attribute) for the purpose of linguistic expression (object$_1$ + object$_2$ + attribute$_1$ + attribute$_2$). Consider now what this may show about language learning. What would be a case of structures of natural language fragmenting holistic representations? The only one that comes to my mind is (1), which is obviously more difficult both in production and in comprehension than (2);

(1)   *Jane, Jill and Joan are blond, black and brunette, respectively.*
(2)   *Jane is blond, Jill is black and Joan is brunette.*

The reason is that (1), but not (2), requires storing the order of names and assigning the hair colors in the right sequence, and such "order information" is difficult to retain, as has been amply demonstrated by experiments with that psycholinguist's hobby horse—the self-embedded sentence (see Schlesinger, 1968, pp. 98–118, 129–140, and 1975, for a discussion). It might seem that this difficulty can account for structures like (1) being acquired later than those like (2). This in itself would be a rather meagre conclusion. Moreover, one might question the justification for extrapolating from this experiment on the grounds that subjects were not required to judge the appropriateness of the linguistic description to its referent, but only the acceptability of linguistic structure, which is something the child learning language is not required to do.

In all fairness, one should add, however, that this is not what Moeser claims the experiment proves. Instead, she suggests a possible parallel to her finding in the "iconic" aspects which have been proposed as possible explanations of the predominant word order in natural languages (Jakobson, 1963) and in language acquisition. But the relation between the iconic factors studied in her experiments and those observed in natural language is tenuous, at best. It seems that the operation of iconic factors in language learning can be studied more directly; cf. Jakobson's (1963, p. 269) observation that in Russian, in which word order is free, children acquire the subject–verb–object order first, and see also Slobin (1973) and Park (1970). Here, too, it seems rather futile to replicate in the laboratory what we know to happen outside it.

In working with MALs, there is a temptation for the investigator to be carried away by the possibility of doing tidy experiments with a very pliable tool. MALs may play the role of the sorcerer's apprentice; instead of serving the needs of investigation, they may dictate what is to be investigated. If this technique is to be relevant to studying language acquisition, far more attention should be paid to formulating new significant hypotheses for the testing of which MALs seem to offer some special advantage. One of the directions to pursue would be an investigation of the effect of linguistic and semantic complexity on rate of learning. In natural languages these variables are confounded to a large extent. I think Moeser's work has shown how linguistic and semantic complexity can be manipulated independently in the laboratory. Instead of resigning ourselves to waiting for rare occurrences like that of the Hungarian- and Serbo-Croatian-speaking child (Slobin, 1973), we might resort to MALs for tackling this problem.

Another possibility has been discussed by Smith and Braine (in press). They suggest that MALs may be a tool for testing linguistic theories and provide information relevant to the construction of such theories. If a rule hypothesized to occur in grammar cannot be learned by subjects in a simplified artificial language, then the grammar may be in need of revision. Further, Smith and Braine propose that the subjects' performance "be examined to determine what rule system best characterizes what they did learn" and that the latter be then considered for incorporation into the linguistic theory. They even hope that MAL research may discover "hitherto unnoticed classes of rules which are relatively salient for human beings and which might form the basis for fresh analyses of recalcitrant problems of grammatical descriptions." Since no one seems so far to have tried to put these suggestions into practice, it is difficult to venture an opinion on the feasibility of the approach.

In short, there are hypotheses to be found which deserve study by MALs. One should be aware, however, that there are also certain problems and inherent limitations in this type of research; to prevent future disappointments, these should be taken into consideration. I propose to discuss them in the following under two headings: limitations due to the nature of experimental material, and those due to the nature of experimental subjects.

The problem with experimental materials has been mentioned in passing by Moeser: "The referential field contains nothing resembling the richness of the real world; it is entirely visual; there is no action, and each individual word refers to an individual element rather than to a set of elements as is more common with natural languages." So far, then, MALs have been more like a roster of proper names than like a dictionary. For some experiments such simplification may be all for the good. After all, it is precisely the possibility of simplification that constitutes one of the main advantages of a laboratory experiment, as Moeser correctly points out. For certain kinds of hypotheses, however, we may be abstracting from just those properties which account for the processes occurring in learning outside the laboratory. If Braine's (1963b) early experiments are not a likely paradigm for natural language learning, this is because he excluded from them what we today regard as essential in the learning process: the referential field. We should ask ourselves in the case of each experiment whether we are not structuring the referential field in a way which vitiates our objectives.

As for the limiting characteristics of the referential field mentioned by Moeser, it seems that some of these are remediable. MALs can be invented that are far richer than those presently used, although this brings with it the complication that learning sessions would have to be far longer, in some cases perhaps longer than is practical. It would be easy also to introduce into a MAL words that refer to classes of elements, as is the case in natural language. The introduction of action would be more difficult, but one might think of ways to achieve this by using manipulable objects rather than drawings (cf. Moeser & Olson, 1974). This would presumably be necessary in any case if the purpose of the experiment is to study the acquisition of rules determining how semantic relations are expressed in language; note that previous MAL experiments limited themselves to one semantic relation which one might perhaps call "attribute of."

A more vexing problem not mentioned by Moeser is the following. The concepts referred to by words in natural language very often contain instances of a great variety, and it is one of the more arduous tasks of the child to learn which objects or events count as instances of the concept and which do not. It is not always safe to abstract from this process of moving from overextension to the correct use of the word. Hence a similar variety will often need to be introduced into the set of elements referred to by a single MAL word. On the other hand, these elements should have sufficient similarity to each other to justify their being called by the same name: An arbitrarily compounded class is also not a suitable analogue of the natural language learning situation. In sum, MALs will have to be adapted, and such adaptations seem feasible. The only constraint on the malleability of MAL which may be insurmountable in principle is the one discussed by Premack and Premack (1974): Certain logical concepts—such as "if—then," or "or," and so on—do not seem to have perceptual counterparts.

In view of these difficulties, one might ask: Why should research with MALs limit itself to an artificial referential field? After all, an artificial language could be employed which refers to actual objects and events, or to pictures of these. This is in fact the way Braine (1968) has employed an artificial language in studying the acquisition of the gender distinction. Likewise, drawings of actual events have been used in a comparison of the learning of two different syntactic transformations (Schlesinger, 1977). The only reason I can see for preferring abstract drawings like those used by Moeser is the fact that they are less conducive to natural language mediation by the learner. When faced with familiar objects or everyday situations, or drawings thereof, the learner presumably tends to formulate these internally in his native language and translate from there into "artificialese." As a consequence, the experiment becomes quite unlike first language learning, which involves no such translation. Such translations may be curtailed, though not entirely disposed of, by a referential field constituted of more abstract materials.

But, if this is so, then the following recommendation seems to be in order. Instead of the rectangles and circles and other rather familiar geometrical designs used by Moeser, which after all have natural language names, nonsense figures with low association value should be used. Such figures have often been employed in perception experiments, and their construction presents no special difficulty. However, the problem that would have to be dealt with is how to define perceptually distinct classes of figures that would go under the same MAL "name."

The last problem I want to discuss here has to do with the subjects we necessarily must work with in MAL experiments. Ideally, these should be children at the age when they acquire their first language, and, moreover, they should be shielded from bilingual interference from the vernacular. But this seems somehow to be impracticable. Now, Moeser is right in refuting the criticism that the mechanism by which children acquire language is unavailable to the adult subject, and disconfirming evidence for the critical period hypothesis has also been presented by Braine (1968, 1971). The real problem, however, lies elsewhere, and this is acknowledged only in passing by Moeser. The task of the more mature subject in learning a MAL is radically different from that of the child learning his native language, because the former is in effect learning a second language. Intrusions from the learner's first language are impossible to control and may often distort the results considerably. Moeser and Bregman (1973) in fact report a case of a subject translating into categories of English grammar, and who knows how many more did so without being fully aware of it? For some recent experimental evidence for the effect of a subject's native language on his dealing with a MAL, see Miller and McCrimmon (1970).

There is nothing I know that can be done about this inherent limitation of work with MAL. But one should notice that this is a more serious problem for some kinds of hypotheses than for others. If rules are investigated which have no parallel with the subject's native language (or any language he knows), the danger of such contamination is minimized. Braine (1968) has employed MALs to investigate the acquisition of the arbitrary assignment of gender to inanimate objects (as in French). In one MAL the male and female classes correlated with the sex of the persons referred to, and in the control condition this constraint was waived. Subjects in the control condition were obviously not influenced by their native language, but neither were those in the experimental condition, because they were speakers of English, and English has practically only natural gender.

It may be argued, however, that for an English speaker there would be negative transfer in this experimental condition, because his experience with English would lead him not to expect the assignment of gender to inanimates. Note, however, that Braine intended to assess the facilitating effect of semantic correspondences. Hence, if in spite of the detrimental influence of the native language such an effect showed up, it could be viewed as a genuine one.

In other words, often the direction of the influence of the native language can be surmised and therefore taken into account. In the experiment mentioned above, I compared a transformation involving the addition of a suffix with that involving the reduplication of an element. Since affixation, but not reduplication, is frequent in Hebrew, one might expect that the effect of Hebrew, which was the subject's native language, would be to facilitate the acquisition of the suffix transformation. From the opposite finding one might then validly infer that reduplication is easier than affixation. Actually I found no difference in ease of acquisition, and this was sufficient to disconfirm the hypothesis that reduplication is a less easily learned transformation.

To summarize, MALs should not be employed to confirm in a roundabout way the feasibility of learning language in a way we know children to learn it; instead they should be put to the service of exploring hypotheses that can be less easily studied in a natural learning situation. The necessity to use subjects for whom the MAL is a second language imposes constraints on the applicability of the technique, but if suitable caution is exercised it does not abolish its usefulness. These remarks concern only work on MALs which is pertinent to language learning. Moeser's paper contains other interesting material, much of it a discussion of her own imaginative work, to which I cannot do justice here.

REFERENCES

Braine, M. D. S. The ontogeny of English phrase structure: The first phase. *Language*, 1963, *39*, 1–13. (a)

Braine, M. D. S. On learning the grammatical order of words. *Psychological Review*, 1963, *70*, 323–348. (b)

Braine, M. D. S. Miniature linguistic system experiments and grammar acquisition. Paper presented at the American Psychological Association Symposium, Fall 1968.

Braine, M. D. S. On two types of models of the internalization of grammars. In D. I. Slobin (Ed.), *The ontogenesis of grammar*. New York: Academic Press, 1971. Pp. 153–186. (a)

Braine, M. D. S. The acquisition of language in infant and child. In C. Reed (Ed.), *The learning of language*. New York: Appleton, 1971. Pp. 153–186. (b)

Esper, E. A. A technique for the experimental investigation of associative interference in artificial linguistic material. *Language Monographs*, 1925, No. 1.

Foss, D. J. An analysis of learning in a miniature linguistic system. *Journal of Experimental Psychology*, 1968, *76*, 450–459. (a)

Foss, D. J. Learning and discovery in the acquisition of structured material: The effect on number of items and their sequence. *Journal of Experimental Psychology*, 1968, *27*, 337–344. (b)

Hunt, E. Selection and reception conditions in grammar and concept learning. *Journal of Verbal Learning and Verbal Behavior*, 1965, *4*, 211–215.

Jakobson, R. Implications of language universals for linguistics. In J. H. Greenberg (Ed.), *Universals of language*. 2nd ed. Cambridge, Mass.: M.I.T. Press, 1963. Pp. 263–278.

Katz, J. J. *The philosophy of language*. New York: Harper & Row, 1966.

Miller, A., & McCrimmon, N. Stimulus and response variations in learning artificial linguistic systems. *Psychological Reports*, 1970, *27*, 215–222.

Moeser, S. D. The effect of reference field organization on language processing. *Memory and Cognition*, 1975, *3*, 370–374. (a)

Moeser, S. D. Iconic factors and language word order. *Journal of Verbal Learning and Verbal Behavior*, 1975, *14*, 43–55. (b)

Moeser, S. D. The effect of Reference field organization on verbal memory. *Journal of Experimental Psychology: Human Learning and Memory*, 1976, *2*, 391–403.

Moeser, S. D., & Bregman, A. S. The role of reference in the acquisition of a miniature artificial language. *Journal of Verbal Learning and Verbal Behavior*, 1972, *11*, 759–769.

Moeser, S. D., & Bregman, A. S. Imagery and language acquisition. *Journal of Verbal Learning and Verbal Behavior*, 1973, *12*, 91–98.

Moeser, S. D., & Olson, A. J. The role of reference in children's acquisition of a miniature artificial language. *Journal of Experimental Child Psychology*, 1974, *17*, 204–218.

Palermo, D., & Eberhart, V. L. On the learning of morphological rules: An experimental analogy. *Journal of Verbal Learning and Verbal Behavior*, 1968, *9*, 410–416.

Palermo, D., & Eberhart, V. L. On the learning of morphological rules: A reply to Slobin. In D. I. Slobin (Ed.), *The ontogenesis of grammar*. New York: Academic Press, 1971. Pp. 225–230.

Palermo, D. S., & Parrish, M. Rule acquisition as a function of number and frequency of exemplar presentation. *Journal of Verbal Learning and Verbal Behavior*, 1971, *10*, 44–51.

Park, T. The acquisition of German syntax. Unpublished paper, University of Munster, Germany, 1970.

Premack, D., & Premack, A. J. Teaching visual language to apes and language deficient persons. In R. L. Schiefelbusch and L. L. Lloyd (Eds.), *Language perspectives—Acquisition, retardation and intervention*. Baltimore, Md.: University Park Press, 1974. Pp. 347–376.

Reber, A. S. Implicit learning of artificial grammars. *Journal of Verbal Learning and Verbal Behavior*, 1967, *6*, 855–863.

Reber, A. S. Transfer of syntactic structure in synthetic languages. *Journal of Experimental Psychology*, 1969, *81*, 115–119.

Schlesinger, I. M. *Sentence structure and the reading process*. The Hague: Mouton, 1968.

Schlesinger, I. M. Why a sentence in which a sentence in which a sentence is embedded is embedded is difficult. *International Journal of Psycholinguistics*, 1975, *4*, 53–66.

Schlesinger, I. M. *Production and comprehension of utterances*, Hillsdale, N.J.: Lawrence Erlbaum, 1977.

Slobin, D. I. On the learning of morphological rules: A reply to Palermo and Eberhart. In D. I. Slobin (Ed.), *The ontogenesis of grammar*. New York: Academic Press, 1971. Pp. 215–224.

Slobin, D. I. Cognitive prerequisites for the development of grammar. In C. A. Ferguson and D. I. Slobin (Eds.), *Studies of child language development*. New York: Holt, 1973. Pp. 175–208.

Smith, K. H. Conditional and unconditional co-occurrence restrictions in the recall of bigrams. *Psychonomic Science*, 1968, *12*, 379–380.

Smith, K. H., & Braine, M. D. S. Miniature languages and the problem of language acquisition. In T. G. Bever and W. Weksel (Eds.), *The structure and psychology of language*. New York: Holt, in press.

Smith, K. H., & Gough, P. B. Transformation rules in the learning of miniature linguistic systems. *Journal of Experimental Psychology*, 1969, *79*, 276–282.

19

Children's Command of the Logic of Conversation

JOHN MACNAMARA

McGill University

The understanding of sentences usually involves the generation of certain related propositions, and it is with the capacity of children to perform such operations that this paper is concerned. In particular I will explore children's ability to generate sentential implicatives and presuppositions and to draw from them certain indirect implications (these terms will be explained below). Such operations constitute part of linguistic competence, though they are closely connected with more general cognition and with the logic of ordinary thought. I also believe that they are involved in the learning of language in a crucial manner. The learning of language is basically, though by no means solely, the assigning of sentences to meanings. A child would never learn a language if he were not able to guess successfully what an utterance meant, and to guess successfully is to have access to meaning independent of speech (see Macnamara, 1972).

The sort of expressions we shall study can be interpreted correctly only if one is able to appreciate their effect on the truth values of propositions they govern, and sometimes such propositions are unstated. For example, the

The research was funded by a Canada Council grant to John Macnamara. The substance of Experiment 2 was reported in an article: Macnamara, J., Baker, E., & Olson, C. E. Four-year-olds' understanding of *pretend, forget* and *know*: Evidence for propositional operations. *Child Development*, 1976, *47*, 62–70.

sentences *John avoided (didn't avoid) visiting his aunt* both presuppose that John did not want to visit his aunt. The sentences *John managed (didn't manage) to visit his aunt* presuppose that he did want to visit her. Terms like *avoid* and *manage*, then, can be learned meaningfully only by someone who knows something of the psychology of action; sometimes we like what we do, and sometimes we do not. One must also be able to interpret an implicit negative in *avoid* whose force applies to the sentential complement of *avoid* as well as to the presupposition which expresses motivation. In other words, learning the meaning of such terms depends on the prior ability to interpret the force of a propositional operator in proposition A on the truth value of proposition B, and proposition B may, not being explicit in the utterance, have to be generated. In addition to the interest of all this for students of language learning, I hope to show that the study of ordinary language affords a particularly promising approach to the study of mind, and to the description of cognitive development.

First, a clarification of terms, and in this I follow rather closely the lead of Van Fraassen (1968) and Karttunen (1971, 1973). Certain English verbs, when used in a sentence, normally commit the speaker to a belief in the truth of the sentential complement. Take for example the verb *force*.

(1).   A   *John forced Tom to admit guilt.*
                        B   *Tom admitted guilt.*

Normally the utterance of (1A) commits one to a belief in the truth of (1B). In other words (1A) semantically implies (1B).

It is necessary to adopt a new term, *semantically implies*, rather than *implies*, because the relationship to which I wish to draw attention is not that which logic normally calls implication or material implication. The difference between the two operators will become clear as we go along, but first we must continue with illustrations of implicative verbs. To signal the new operator, I will use a special symbol ($\Vdash$). To show that (1A) semantically implies (1B), I will write (1A) $\Vdash$ (1B), or more simply A $\Vdash$ B.

Karttunen (1971) distinguishes six types of implicative verbs. The first is like *force*, A $\Vdash$ B. Note that we cannot conclude the negative of (1B), $-$ B, from the negative of (1A), $-$ A. We cannot conclude that *Tom did not admit guilt* from the statement that *John did not force him to admit guilt*.

The second type of verb is illustrated by *be able*. For example:

(2).   A   *Harry was not able to jump the gate.*
                        B   *Harry did not jump the gate.*

In this case A $\Vdash - $ B (we take A and B for the corresponding affirmatives). Note that we do not get A $\Vdash$ B; a person does not necessarily do all that he is able to do. Karttunen's third type is like *manage*.

(3).   A   *Jim managed to finish the assignment.*
                      B   *Jim finished the assignment.*

Here we have A ⊩ B; and we also have − A ⊩ − B; if Jim did not manage to finish the assignment, he did not finish it. This marks a difference from the implication operator of standard logic. If we replaced semantically implies with the implies of logic, we would lose the negative implicative of *manage*. Granted A → B we could not from − A conclude − B, that is, we could not conclude − A → − B. To attempt to do so would be to commit the error of denying the antecedent. This is the first reason for adopting a special operator for ordinary language.

The other three types of verb contain an implicit negative.

Prevent:
(4).   A   *Mary prevented Jane from registering.*
                      B   *Jane registered.*

This gives us A ⊩ − B, but not − A ⊩ B.

Hesitate:
(5).   A   *Harriet did not hesitate to complain.*
                      B   *Harriet complained.*

This time we have − A ⊩ B, but not A ⊩ − B.

Avoid:
(6).   A   *Joyce avoided going to the party.*
                      B   *Joyce went to the party.*

This yields both A ⊩ − B and − A ⊩ B. In the latter case, normal intonation is particularly important.

We can define presuppositions with sufficient accuracy for our purpose by means of the same operator. Sentences that contain one of the six types of verb frequently have obvious presuppositions (P). For example, *let* is a verb of type three: A ⊩ B and − A ⊩ − B.

(7).   A   *Dad let Wendy go to school.*
                      B   *Wendy went to school.*
                      P   *Wendy wanted to go to school.*

The point about presuppositions is that they stand whether the parent sentence is affirmed or denied. This is not true of implicatives. So (7P) stands whether (7A) is affirmed or denied. That is, A ⊩ P and − A ⊩ P. Or more simply, AV − A ⊩ P. This can be taken as a formal definition of presupposition.

We can now appreciate a second reason for rejecting material implication as the logical operator involved in implicatives. Let us illustrate with *avoid*:

(8).

    A   *John avoided going to see his aunt.*

  − A   *John didn't avoid going to see his aunt.*

    P   *John does not like going to see his aunt.*

    B   *John went to see his aunt.*

  − B   *John didn't go to see his aunt.*

In this set, P is a presupposition of both A and − A, while A $\Vdash$ − B and − A $\Vdash$ B. This is all we wish to be able to conclude from A and from − A. Katz (1973) has pointed out that AV − A, → P is not the relationship of presupposition, since it would have the inconvenience, among others, of admitting only necessary truths to the status of presuppositions. Other inconveniences arise in connection with the implicative relationship. If we tried to represent it with the implication sign, A → B, we would be forced to admit two results of which we want only one. Granted A → B, if A is true, we can conclude that B is too (*modus ponens*); in addition, if − B is true, we can conclude that − A is too (*modus tollens*). The operator *semantically implies* admits only *modus ponens*, not *modus tollens*. The reason is that is would be bizarre, on learning that John went to see his aunt (8B), to conclude that he did not avoid going to see her (8 − A). The trouble is that (8 − A) involves (8P), but (8B) does not. Similarly if from (8 − B) we conclude (8A), the same presupposition would be involved. In ordinary English the statement that someone went to see his aunt or did not go to see her does not necessarily imply that he does not like going to see her. Even if we learned that someone avoided going to see his aunt yesterday, we cannot, on hearing that he went to see her today, conclude that he did not *avoid* doing so today, because he may, for one thing, have had a change of heart toward her. Hence the reason for a special operator, *semantically implies*.

    In the experiments that follow, we will be concerned with implicatives and presuppositions and also with what we call indirect implications. The sentences of (9) illustrate the third type of relationship.

(9).

    A   *Harry forgot to bring the car.*

    B   *Harry did not bring the car.*

    P   *Harry was expected (possibly by himself)*
           to bring the car.

    C   *Somebody was disappointed.*

Forget is a Type 6 verb, so A $\Vdash$ − B; P is a presupposition, so A $\Vdash$ P. But we can also conclude (9C) on the basis of (9A), or more clearly on the basis of (9B) and (9P) combined. To expect something which does not happen is to be disappointed. This relationship is a *meaning postulate* in Carnap's (1956) terms, that is, a relationship of equivalence among lexical items which is specified in the lexicon.

EXPERIMENT 1

The first experiment concentrates on implicatives. Our intention was to select expressions of each of the six types and study 4-year-olds' understanding of them. After some exploratory work with children we hit upon the following list which serves quite well, provided we are prepared to make one or two adjustments:

1.	*X* **made** *Y do something*	$A \Vdash B$
2.	a. *X* **wasn't able** *to do something*	
	b. *X* **wasn't big enough** *to do something*	$-A \Vdash -B$
3.	*X* **let** *Y do something*	
	X **didn't let** *Y do something*	$A \Vdash B \ \& \ -A \Vdash -B$
4.	—	
5.	*X* **wasn't afraid** *to do something*	$-A \Vdash B$
6.	*X* **turned off** *the apparatus*	
	X **didn't turn off** *the apparatus*	$A \Vdash -B \ \& \ -A \Vdash B$

We could not find a suitable expression of Type 4, but the positive form of Type 6 serves instead. Strictly speaking, we cannot exclude the possibility that someone did not do what he was not afraid to do. However, to the child we felt that it probably did. The expression *turn off* does not give rise to a sentential complement. It does, however, give rise to an understanding about the state of an apparatus, and that understanding can be taken as a proposition. Strictly speaking, the expression *didn't turn off* does not give rise to a semantic implicative of the sort that *turn off* does. Nevertheless, there is at least a powerful suggestion that if somebody did not turn off an apparatus, it is still on. In the context of a story in which the apparatus was on, the implicative does go through.

We composed stories that incorporated the key expressions, and questions that would test understanding of the various related propositions. We were well aware that the contents of the story might set up response biases in favor of *yes* or *no* and these we attempted to circumvent in various ways. In composing the stories, we adopted two strategies. Where possible, we composed negative as well as positive versions so that the correct response sometimes varied. In this way a bias to say *yes*, for example, would sometimes lead to a wrong response and sometimes to a right one for the same story. The second strategy was to compose a single story frame and vary the persons and objects mentioned in it. As far as possible, the persons and objects were counter-balanced across the key expressions in the hope of reducing the effect of response bias connected with particular objects. Take, for example, the objects, a chocolate cake on a high shelf and a kite in a tree. It might be that young children would have a strong tendency to say *yes* to a question *Did Mary want the chocolate cake?* and not nearly so strong a bias to say *yes* to *Did Jane want the kite?* Suppose further that the first question was posed in connection with a story in which someone *let* Mary get the cake, and the second with one in which someone *made* her get the kite. To the first question, *yes* is the correct answer, and to the second it is *no*. A response bias would yield a difference between the two responses, and it would be impossible to disentangle it from the understanding of *let* as opposed to *made*. The difficulty disappears, however, if both objects are used in connection with both verbs. In the appendix, we set out the story frames, the sets of names and objects we employed, and the key expressions which were used with them. We also employed a form of statistical analysis which is independent of response bias, signal detection.

Subjects and Procedure

All of the children who took part belonged to English-speaking middle-class homes in the west end of Montreal Island. In order not to put too many questions to an individual child, we divided the stories and their associated questions into two sets. We selected 20 children from each of two nursery schools, one group for each set of stories and questions. Group 1 was told the stories in which the key sentences contained the words *made, wasn't able, turn off, didn't turn off*, and *wasn't afraid*. Group 2 was told the stories that contained *let, didn't let*, and *wasn't big enough*. Each group was told some other stories and asked some other questions which are mostly not relevant to the present study. However, the second group was told a story which had *glad* in its key sentence. There were positive and negative versions of this story with each of which was associated a pair of questions, one aimed at a presupposition and one at an indirect implication. The basic idea is that if one is, or is not, glad of something, there is a presupposition that the thing is true. In one of our stories a child is, or is not, glad that dinner is ready. The indirect implication is that the child is correspondingly hungry or not hungry.

In each group the number of boys and girls was roughly equal. In Group 1, the average age was 4 years, 6 months; in Group 2, it was 4 years, 9 months. Within each group, the stories were told in a different random order to each child, but the order of questions was constant.

The children who were all native speakers of English were seen individually in school. After hearing each story, a child was asked to repeat it to make sure he had heard and remembered the important details. If he made any mistakes, he was corrected or reminded.

Statistical Analysis

Statistical analysis of the data is complicated by three considerations: The "measures" are repeated and are not, therefore, independent; there are logical dependencies among the answers; and apart from factors largely controlled for in the composition of the stories, there is a possibility of response bias, in favor of *yes* or *no*. For our primary statistical analysis, we adopted a model based on signal detection theory (e.g., Pastore & Scheirer, 1974). The model handles two responses at a time and applies only when we expect one of them to be *yes* and the other *no*. It enables us to evaluate whether the group of children reliably discriminated truth ("signal") from falsehood ("noise"). For our purpose we identify an expression that demanded *yes* as correct response with the presentation of signal, and one that demanded *no* with the presentation of noise.

The model may be thought of as making the following assumptions. Children differ in their inclination to respond affirmatively, and the inclination is increased or reduced by their grasp of the truth or falsehood of the proposition to which the question is addressed. When the inclination to respond affirmatively exceeds a certain criterion point, the child says *yes*, otherwise he says *no*. There are thus two hypothetical distributions of "inclination-to-affirm" values, one for the true proposition and one for the false one. For convenience, we assume that these distributions are normal with unit variance, but our test of significance is appropriate for any continuous distributions.

The children's ability to detect the truth value of the unstated propositions is quantified as d', the sensitivity parameter of signal detection theory. It is independent of response bias. To determine the reliability of children's discrimination, it is necessary to establish whether d' differs significantly from zero. For this purpose we assume only that the hit rate and the correct rejection rate are estimates of binomial probabilities. The usual standard error of a binomial proportion may then be employed before applying a z-transformation to obtain a confidence interval for d'. We report a p value with each d' to indicate whether it is significantly different from zero. A significant and positive d' indicates that the children, as a group at least, detected the truth values of the unstated propositions to which the questions were addressed.

Our method of evaluating the reliability of the children's discrimination is apt to underestimate their abilities in two respects. First, if children set different criterion points on their "inclination-to-affirm" scale, the estimate of d' tends to be too small (Pastore & Scheirer, 1974). Secondly, if children differ from each other in their probabilities of detecting truth or rejecting falsehood, the binomial standard error attributes too much error to our estimates (Feller, 1968, pp. 230–231) and makes it more difficult to demonstrate the significance of d'. However, the effects under investigation here are sufficiently strong to outweigh the conservative nature of our tests.

Where appropriate, we used more familiar statistical techniques, and we also examined the extent to which children conformed to the logical structure of a whole set of responses. Our style of exploration forced us to combine the data in various ways which may be confusing to the reader. After setting out our findings in detail, then, we will synopsize them in the order of the six implicative verbs.

Results

IMPLICATIVE: *MADE* AND *WASN'T ABLE*.

Table 19.1 contains the numbers of correct responses to the specified question types (see the appendix). The responses to the implicatives yield $d' = 2.56, p < .01$. This means that most children correctly assigned truth values to the unstated implicatives. In order to do so, they must somehow have known that the complement of *made* in a positive sentence is true and the complement of *wasn't able* is false. May we remind the reader that the same set of stories were employed with both expressions, so the analysis is appropriate.

TABLE 19.1

Number of Correct Responses for *Made* **and** *Wasn't Able*

Type of question	Made	Wasn't able	Both
Implicative	18 (Y)	18 (N)	16
Presupposition	10 (N)		
Both of the above	8		

Note: The same 20 children answered all three questions: Y = correct answer, *yes*; N = correct answer, *no*.

IMPLICATIVE: *WASN'T ABLE* AND *WASN'T AFRAID*.

Eighteen children correctly responded *yes* to the question which asked about the complement of *wasn't afraid* and as we have seen, 18 correctly responded *no* to the corresponding question connected with *wasn't able*. These were the same children. The figures yield a significant $d' = 2.56, p < .01$. Once again, most children correctly varied their response from affirmative to negative, though this time both of the key expressions were negative.

IMPLICATIVE: *LET* AND *DIDN'T LET*.

The data obtained with the positive and negative stories containing *let* are given in Table 19.2. Responses to the implicative questions yielded $d' = 2.12, p < .01$, a highly significant result. Note, however, that only 14 children correctly responded *no* to the implicative question following upon *didn't let*.

Perhaps the children who responded *yes* were more sophisticated than we imagined and realized that people sometimes do what they are not let do, in the sense of refused permission. That is, the overall performance may be more impressive than it appears to be in Table 19.2.

TABLE 19.2

Number of Correct Responses for *Let* **and** *Didn't Let*

Type of question	Let	Didn't let	Both
Implicative	18 (Y)	14 (N)	13
Presupposition	18 (Y)	18 (Y)	16
Both of the above	17	12	10

Note: The same 20 children answered all three questions: Y = correct answer, *yes*; N = correct answer, *no*.

IMPLICATIVE: *WASN'T BIG ENOUGH* AND *LET.*

The same children answered the questions that dealt with the implicatives of these two expressions, and since the one requires the answer *no*, the other *yes*, we can apply the signal detection model. All 20 children answered *no* correctly in the *wasn't big enough* stories, and 18 answered *yes* to the implicative question connected with *let*. Since all children answered one question correctly, there is, strictly, no statistical test possible, since the criterion point is an infinite distance from the mean of the distribution for correct rejection. However, we adopt a conservative position and replace the 20 with $19\frac{1}{2}$. When we do this, we obtain $d' = 3.24, p < .01$. Just as some children correctly attributed truth values to the implicative complements of *let* and *didn't let*, so they did to the corresponding complements of *let* and *wasn't big enough*.

PRESUPPOSITION: *MADE* AND *LET.*

These two verbs give rise to contrary presuppositions which were tested with a single question of the form *Did X want to do Y?* (see the appendix). The two questions were, however, put to different children and we tested the reliability of their response patterns with a simple test of the difference between two proportions. In effect, we asked whether 18 affirmative responses out of 20 for *let* significantly differed from 10 affirmative (incorrect) responses for *made*. The test yielded $z = 2.86, p < .01$; so there are grounds for believing that some children grasped the relevant presuppositions and varied their responses in accordance with the propositional logic that assigns truth values to them.

IMPLICATIVE AND INDIRECT IMPLICATION: *TURNED OFF* AND *DIDN'T TURN OFF.*

The response pattern for the *turn off* stories is given in Table 19.3. Responses to the question that was addressed to the implicative yielded $d' = 2.68$, $p < .01$. Those to the question that was addressed to the indirect implication implication yielded $d' = 2.32$, $p < .01$. Indeed the level of responding to this set of questions showed a good grasp of the unstated implicatives and indirect implications, and of their truth values.

TABLE 19.3

Number of Correct Responses for *Turned Off* **and** *Didn't Turn Off*

Type of question	*Turned off*	*Didn't turn off*	Both
Implicative	17 (N)	19 (Y)	17
Indirect implication	17 (N)	18 (Y)	17
Both of the above	16	18	16

Note: All question were answered by the same 20 children: Y = correct response, *yes*; N = correct response, *no*.

INDIRECT IMPLICATION AND PRESUPPOSITION: *GLAD* AND *NOT GLAD.*

As in Tables 19.1 and 19.2, so here, in Table 19.4, the negative response seemed more difficult than the positive one. In applying the signal detection test, we replaced the number 20 with $19\frac{1}{2}$. For questions addressed to the indirect implicative, we obtain $d' = 2.80$, $p < .01$. So, though there may have been a bias in favor of responding *yes*, there are good grounds for believing that at least some children were able to overcome it and distinguish truth from falsehood in this connection.

There does not seem to be an appropriate statistical test to evaluate responses to the presuppositional questions. Nevertheless, the level of responding was

TABLE 19.4

Number of Correct Responses for *Glad* **and** *Not Glad*

Type of question	*Glad*	*Not glad*	Both
Indirect implication	20 (Y)	14 (N)	16
Presupposition	20 (Y)	19 (Y)	19
Both of the above	20	13	13

Note: All questions answered by the same 20 children: Y = correct response, *yes*; N = correct response, *no*.

so good (as the key sentence changed from positive to negative) that a statistical test is hardly necessary to rule out the fear that response bias alone explains it.

SUMMARY

Our statistical analyses yield significant evidence that most children responded in accord with the schema of propositional implicatives from which we took our departure. They seemed just as at home with verbs that follow the $A \Vdash B$ and $-A \Vdash -B$ rules as with ones that follow the $-A \Vdash B$ and $A \Vdash -B$ rules. And most children varied their responses appropriately when the same verb permitted two implicative relations. That is, most children varied from *yes* to *no* appropriately in response to implicative questions as *let* changed to *didn't let* and as *turned off* changed to *didn't turn off*.

Moreover, there was convincing evidence that the children as a whole grasped the indirect implications to which the stories gave rise and correctly assigned them truth values. Likewise, they grasped and correctly assigned truth values to the presuppositions.

Our statistical analysis depended on different responses being correct, but we can also inquire whether children who correctly followed the propositional relationships on one occasion also followed the same relationship on another occasion. The possibilities are restricted by the fact that the stories were divided between two groups of children, and we cannot find repetitions of all operations. There are two types of implicative relationships we can examine. The same children were asked about the expressions that contained *didn't let* and *wasn't big enough* $(-A \Vdash -B)$. In fact, 14 children answered both questions correctly. That is, all the children who grasped the negative implicative associated with *didn't let* grasped the same relationship with *wasn't big enough*. The other implicative relationship we can examine is that related to *didn't turn off* and *wasn't afraid* $(-A \Vdash B)$. Fifteen children grasped this relationship on both occasions and coped with the implicit negatives in *turn off* and *afraid*.

The same children were tested on the *let* and *glad* stories, so we can see how they handled the presuppositions on the two occasions. Eighteen answered the relevant question correctly in connection with the positive versions of each; 17 answered it correctly in connection with the negative ones; and 15 answered both questions correctly on both occasions. These figures speak for themselves. There is no reason to expect that a child who performs a propositional operation in relation to one expression should perform the same operation in connection with another. He might simply not know part of the meaning of the second expression. However, if he does give the right answer on both occasions, the case that he is indeed following such a propositional operation is strengthened. And so it is with our children.

The implicatives and indirect implications associated with the *turned off* and *didn't turn off* stories form a single set of logical interdependencies. As we have seen, from whether mother did or did not *turn off* the apparatus, one concludes whether or not it was on (implicative); from whether or not it was on, one concludes whether or not the child could listen to the program (indirect implication). That is, the truth value of the indirect implication (itself (unstated) depended on the truth value of the unstated implicative. From Table 19.3, we learn that 16 of the 20 children answered all four questions correctly, which is convincing evidence that a great many of them followed the interdependencies. But what of the 4 children who did not answer all questions correctly; did they assign the incorrect values to the implicatives and satisfy the interdependencies nonetheless? In fact 2 did and 2 did not, not a very satisfactory result. Yet if we count the 2 who did, in all, 18 of the 20 children responded in a manner that conformed to the interdependencies of the implicatives and indirect implications. This is an impressive result, as readers of Wason and Johnson-Laird's (1972) studies of adult logic will appreciate.

Discussion

The above set of results shows that small children aged about $4\frac{1}{2}$ understood very well the complicated set of semantic implications that we investigated. Clearly their correct responses are not the result of a simple response strategy such as always saying *no* or always saying *yes*. Each of those responses was wrong as often as it was right. Moreover, the odds against random responding are truly astronomical

Some to whom we have shown these results have "objected" that all we have done is shown that 4-year-olds know the meaning of certain words. In a sense, this is true. However, the meaning of sentences in which our set of words occurs is complicated in a most interesting manner. These words give rise to sentential components (or propositional components) whose truth value is given implicitly together with the parent sentence. The focal point of our study is that children so young were able to grasp sentential components and determine their truth value under such conditions. Moreover, we saw evidence of such children's ability to grasp unstated presuppositions and indirect implications, and we shall see more of this in the next experiment.

We hope in all this to have contributed to the description of children's intellectual powers at that stage which Piaget calls "preoperational." For Piaget, this stage, which extends from age 2 to 7, is prelogical. Piaget does not, to our knowledge, consider such logical operations as we have investigated. In general, 4-year-olds failed the logical tests to which Piaget put them, and hence his description of children's minds between 2 and 7 is largely negative. It is pleasant to be able to report some logical operations that they can perform. More of all this in the general discussion.

EXPERIMENT 2

The second experiment is basically similar to the first, but it concentrates on presuppositions and indirect implications. We selected three expressions that give rise to presuppositions and indirect implications, told stories that incorporated the key expressions to 4-year-olds, and questioned them about the relevant propositions. The three key verbs are, *pretend*, *know*, and *forget*.

Method

Our main body of subjects consisted of two groups of 4-year-olds very similar to those of Experiment 1. In each group, the numbers of boys and girls were roughly equal. The mean age of each group was about 4 years, 6 months. All attended nursery school where they were tested individually, and all were native speakers of English. One group was tested with problems related to *pretend* and *forget*, the other on problems related to *know*. Each child was asked all the questions related to the material with which he was to be tested.

The children were told the stories individually. In order to be sure they had listened, they were asked to repeat the stories, and when they faltered they were prompted. After retelling a story, they were asked questions that revealed whether they had picked up the implications, presuppositions, and indirect implications of the key sentence.

There were two slightly different versions of each story, one in which the key sentence was positive and one in which it was negative. Otherwise the versions differed only in the name of participants and in the objects they manipulated. These variations were counterbalanced across positive and negative versions. Each child was tested on two different occasions, separated by several days, once on the positive version and once on the negative one. Half the children in each group were tested first on the positive version and half on the negative; for the others the reverse order was followed. The order in which the questions were asked, that in which they are set out below, was constant across children. The group that was tested on stories incorporating *pretend* and *forget* were tested first on the *forget* story.

Our plan is to present the main data under three major headings, one for each of the three words. Each set of data will be followed by a brief discussion, and we will round off the paper with a general discussion.

Pretend

The following is the positive version of the story:

> Robert was a little boy who lived in a big house beside his school. He went to school every day except when he was sick. When he was sick he would stay at home until he was better. One day Robert was late coming down to the kitchen. He was late for breakfast. His mother looked at him very carefully. She felt his forehead with her hand. She said, "Robert, you're pretending you're sick."

The negative version ended, "Harry, you're not pretending you're sick." Each child was asked to repeat the story, and if he made any important errors, he was corrected. Then he was asked the following questions, the same ones for each version.

Questions:
1. Was Robert really sick? (Implicative)
2. Should Robert go to school? (Indirect implication)

RESULTS

The data are set out in Table 19.5. The children's responses indicate that they were able reliably to discriminate the truth of the indirect implication tested in Question 2: $d' = 2.17\ p < .01$. The reliability of their grasp of the unstated logical implicative which was tested in Question 1 is less clear, $d' = 1.03\ p > .05$

The simple logic of the story is that if Robert is sick (determined by whether he is pretending or not pretending to be sick), he must stay at home; if he is not sick, he must go to school. We can now ask how many children responded to each version in a manner that is compatible with this logic. The answer is that 19 so responded to the positive version and 14 to the negative one. There may be more randomness than these figures suggest, and some of the children

TABLE 19.5

Numbers of Correct Responses for *Pretend*

Type of question	Story version		
	Positive	Negative	Both
Indirect implication	19 (Y)	14 (N)	13
Implicative	18 (N)	8 (Y)	8
Both of the above	18	8	8

Note: The questions were posed to 20 children. The parenthetical letters indicate whether the correct response was *yes* or *no*.

who seemed to follow the logic may have been successful by chance. In fact, in response to the negative version, 12 children erroneously, to our way of thinking, said that Robert was not sick; 6 of the 12 said he should go to school (and conformed to our logical model), and 6 said he should not go to school.

One should not conclude from this, however, that the correct responses were also random. In one pilot study[1] we told the positive version twice to 20 different 4-year-olds and on each occasion asked them if Robert should go to school. Ten children gave the correct response both times. In another pilot study we told the negative version twice to yet another 20 4-year-olds and asked the same question. On the first occasion 9 gave the right answer and on the second 12 did. The only change was that 3 who answered wrongly the first time answered correctly the second time.

Forget

The following is the positive version:

> There once were two friends called Mary-Jane and Dick. They used to play together in Dick's backyard. Sometimes Mary-Jane would bring a big coloured ball that she had, and sometimes she would bring a truck, and she and Dick would play with her ball or her truck. One day, Mary-Jane and Dick were playing together and they decided that they would play after dinner that night. They decided that Mary-Jane would bring *one* of her toys. They chose which toy she would bring and they were looking forward to playing with it. After dinner Dick came outside to wait for Mary-Jane. When Mary-Jane came outside, *she forgot to bring the ball.*

The negative version was similar, but ended, "she didn't forget to bring the dolly."

Questions (the same for both versions):
1. Was Dick disappointed? (Indirect implication)
2. Did Mary-Jane have the ball with her? (Implicative)
3. Was Mary-Jane supposed to bring the ball? (Presupposition)
4. Was Mary-Jane supposed to bring the truck? (Control question)

RESULTS

The data for *forget* are set out in Table 19.6, where it will be seen that, for each version, *yes* was right twice and so was *no*, but to different questions. The data provide compelling evidence that the children grasped both the indirect

---

[1] Throughout the paper, there are numerous references to pilot studies which were carried out while we were perfecting our technique. These were done in the same manner as the final studies on exactly the same sorts of children, but the children were not made to repeat the stories before questioning and the form of the question often varied slightly from its final form.

TABLE 19.6

Numbers of Correct Responses for *Forget*

Type of question	Story version		
	Positive	Negative	Both
Indirect implication	17 (Y)	19 (N)	16
Implicative	20 (N)	18 (Y)	18
Presupposition	19 (Y)	18 (Y)	17
Control	13 (N)	12 (N)	10
All of the above	12	12	10

Note: The questions were posed to 20 children. The parenthetical letters indicate whether the correct response was *yes* or *no*.

implication tested in Question 1, $d' = 2.68$, $p < .01$, and the logical implicative tested in Question 2, $d' = 3.24$, $p < .01$.

Question 4 was the most difficult. It was included as a control for evaluating responses concerning the presupposition, to see if there was a tendency for children to agree that children are supposed to bring things. The signal detection analysis, this time contrasting responses to Questions 3 and 4, revealed that there was indeed such a bias, but the children also demonstrated statistically reliable comprehension of the presupposition in both the positive version, $d' = 2.03$, $p < .01$, and the negative version, $d' = 1.53$, $p < .01$, of the story. With only one exception, all the children who correctly answered Question 4 also answered correctly the other three questions for that particular version of the story. And the 10 children who answered correctly this question both times are the 10 who answered correctly all other questions. They seem to have been the ones who grasped that Mary-Jane was supposed to bring only *one* of the two toys, that the one she forgot or did not forget to bring was the one she was supposed to bring, and that Dick's disappointment depended on whether or not she brought what she was supposed to bring.

Once again we can ask how many children conformed to the logical model. In their responses to the positive version, 18 did; and in their responses to the negative ones, 18 did too. However, we have seen from responses to the control question (number 4) that grasp of the logic was weaker than these figures suggest. Of the 18 who seemed to be quite logical in their responses to the positive version, 5 responded incorrectly to Question 4, thus raising doubts about their grasp of the logic. Five of the 18 whose responses to the negative version seemed logical also responded incorrectly to Question 4. Nevertheless, the overall performance is impressive.

Once again, pilot studies bear out the main result. In one, we obtained a very similar pattern of responses for the positive version with 20 different

4-year-olds. In another, the positive version was told twice to 40 other 4-year-olds, and 29 said on both occasions that Dick was disappointed. In a third pilot study, the negative version was told twice to yet another 29 4-year-olds. On the first occasion, 11 said Dick was not disappointed; on the the second, 13 did, the only change being that 2 who first gave the wrong answer gave the right one the second time.

A logician, inclined to make such translations, might represent our findings as follows:

Positive: p if and only if q and not r
Negative: not p if and only if q and r

where p = Dick was disappointed; q = Dick expected something; and r = that thing happened. In order to apply the correct meaning postulate, the child had to know the contents of the propositional components—to expect something which does not happen is to be disappointed; to expect something which does happen is not to be disappointed. Notice, however, that the appropriate logic for assigning truth values to the indirect implications is propositional (or formal or sentential) logic. The propositions once constituted, truth values can be assigned on the basis of the propositional connectives without further reference to the proposition's contents. But more about this in the conclusion.

Since the same children were examined on both *pretend* and *forget*, we can look at how they fared on similar operations on the two occasions. Associated with each story was one implicative and one indirect implication. The numbers of correct responses are set out in Table 19.7. Of the 8 children who grasped the implicative connected with the two versions of the pretend story, 7 grasped it also in connection with the two versions of the *forget* story. And 10 children grasped the indirect implication connected with both versions of the two stories. Of the 7 children just mentioned, 6 grasped the implicative and indirect implications related to both versions of both stories.

TABLE 19.7

Numbers of Children Who Responded Correctly for Both
Pretend **and** *Forget*

Type of question	Story version		
	Positive	Negative	Both
Indirect implication	16	13	10
Implicative	18	7	7
Both of the above	15	6	6

Note: The questions were posed to 20 children.

As a test of the consistency of the children's discrimination across the two types of question and the two key words, an analysis of variance was performed on the data for implicatives and indirect implications from the two stories. For indirect implications, responses were coded as 1 for *yes* and 0 for *no*, while for implicatives the coding was 1 for *no* and 0 for *yes*. With this coding, correct responses, based on the appropriate propositional operation, result in a high score for the positive version and a low score for the negative version, so that a difference between the versions reflects the children's grasp of the propositional components. The coding also implies that any difference observed between responses concerning implicatives and concerning indirect implications is confounded with any bias that favors either *yes* or *no* responses.

The dichotomous data from the 20 subjects were systematically pooled to form 5 macrosubjects, each comprising the data from 4 subjects, after the manner described by Murdock and Ogilvie (1968). The data for each macrosubject were converted to proportions and subjected to the usual arcsine transformation (e.g., Winer, 1971, p. 872). If the observations were sampled from a binomial distribution, the highest-order interaction mean square may be expected to be approximately .25 for macrosubjects of size four (see Murdock & Ogilvie, 1968, for details).

The design of the analysis of variance was a completely crossed four-way factorial: 2 stories (*pretend* and *forget*) × 2 versions (positive and negative) × 2 types of question (implicatives and indirect implications) × 5 macrosubjects. The only significant effect that emerged was the main effect of versions: $F (1, 4) = 28.90$, $p < .01$. As expected, scores were higher on the positive versions. This finding corroborates the results of the signal detection analyses, indicating that the children detected and responded to the unstated propositional components.

None of the four interaction terms came close to significance. This result is compatible with the view that the children did not vary in their ability to apprehend the truth value from one type of question to the next or from one story to the next.

Know

The following is the positive version of the story:

> There once were a brother and sister called Christopher and Susan. They were playing a game in the living-room one day. Christopher was hiding things and Susan was trying to find them. Christopher hid a comb, an elastic band, a penny and a pencil. Before Susan had started to look for the things, Christopher and Susan came into the kitchen holding each other's hands. Christopher said to his

mother: "Mummy, Susan knows that I hid the penny under the cushion of the green chair." Their mother came into the living room and looked underneath the cushion, but the penny was not there.

The negative version had the boy say: "Mummy, Susan doesn't know that I hid the penny under the cushion of the green chair."

Questions (same for both versions):

1. Was Christopher telling a lie? (Indirect implication)
2. Did Christopher say Susan knew where the penny was? (Explicit in story)
3. Did mother find the penny under the cushion? (Explicit in story)
4. Did Christopher put the penny there? (Indirect implication)
5. Did Christopher say the penny was there? (Presupposition)
6. Did Christopher know the penny was not there? (Indirect implication)

RESULTS

Because the correct answer to each question, except Question 2, was the same for both versions, it was not possible to apply the signal detection test to responses to Questions 1, 3, 4, 5, or 6. Accordingly, we discuss the results descriptively before considering statistical inferences that may be drawn involving Question 2. The data are presented in Table 19.8.

It is well known (e.g., Piaget, 1932) that many 4-year-olds consider the utterance of a falsehood to be a lie, whether or not the speaker knew that what he said was false. In a pilot study with 20 other 4-year-olds, we found 16 were of this opinion. Thus, most of the 20 children in our experiment could be expected to say Christopher was telling a lie, even if he did not realize that what he said was false. In fact, we found that 16 children answered Question 1 correctly on both occasions, affirming that Christopher was telling a lie.

TABLE 19.8

Numbers of Correct Responses for *Know*

Type of question	Story version		
	Positive	Negative	Both
1. Indirect implication	17 (Y)	18 (Y)	16
2. Explicit in story	11 (Y)	14 (N)	8
3. Explicit in story	18 (N)	18 (N)	16
4. Indirect implication	15 (N)	17 (N)	15
5. Presupposition	13 (Y)	10 (Y)	9
6. Indirect implication	8 (Y)	5 (Y)	3
Types 1, 2, 4, 5, and 6	4	2	2

Note: The questions were posed to 20 children. The parenthetical letters indicate whether the correct response was *yes* or *no*.

There seems to have been a special difficulty related to Question 6: "Did Christopher know the penny was not there?" Perhaps it was that, to answer that question correctly, one had to handle several superficially conflicting strands of information: Christopher "said" the penny was under the cushion; he had hidden the objects and ought to know; no one had interfered with the objects; mother looked and saw the penny was not there. This appears to have been too much for most of these 20 young children.

Question 2 was an important one for this discussion, as it indicates whether the children were indeed demonstrating their understanding of the word *know*. A signal detection analysis provided no evidence that the children, as a group, took account of the word *know* in the story, $d = .65, p > .10$. The reason may have been the unavoidable syntactic complexity of both the parent sentence and Question 2.

It is conceivable that a few of the children may have both taken account of the word *know* as indicated by their response to Question 2 and grasped the indirect implications and presuppositions tested in Questions 1, 4, 5, and 6. Although only two children in fact responded correctly to all five of these questions in both versions, this number is significantly more ($p < .05$) than expected under the hypothesis of independent responding to the five questions as estimated from the marginal correct-response rates. This finding is consistent with, but does not prove, the notion that at least these two children were sensitive to the word *know* and to the presuppositions it engenders. Nevertheless, the number of children is so much smaller than the corresponding numbers for the *pretend* and *forget* stories that we can safely conclude that the *know* story was far more difficult and in fact exceeded the information processing powers of all but two.

While most children seem to have ignored *know* and the difficult presuppositions associated with it, we must remember that 16 children said on both occasions that Christopher told a lie. The response was probably logical, on their terms, so long as it was guided by the recognition that Christopher had said the penny was under the cushion (Question 5) and it was not there, as evidenced by the fact that mother did not find it there (Question 3). How many children responded in a manner that is compatible with such logic? In fact, 16 did in response to the positive version, 9 did in response to the negative one; these same 9 responded in this manner on both occasions. Thus while certain aspects of the story may have escaped most children, many of them seem to have grasped enough to make impressive logical deductions.

The results receive support from a pilot study in which 20 4-year-olds were told the positive version twice and 15 said on both occasions that Christopher told a lie. In another pilot study, 20 different 4-year-olds were told the negative version twice and 12 responded correctly both times.

CONCLUSION

What have we succeeded in showing? I believe that I have adduced evidence as compelling as the area readily permits that many children aged 4 are able to grasp presuppositions and implicatives of all six types, and to assign them truth values correctly. In other words, these children showed in certain cases understanding of the semantic system which generates presuppositions and assigns truth values to sentential complements.

Can we conclude from all this that the children had a rule associated with each of the key expressions to assign a truth value to any sentential complement? For example, did the children know that if X *made* Y do something, then Y did that something, whoever Y was and whatever the something? The answer must be an affirmative, though a guarded one, because the results we obtained for the implicative of *made* were obtained over four different Ys and four different actions. The only reason for being guarded about the rule is that one could no doubt suggest sentential complements so far outside the child's experience that the child would simply give up the attempt to grasp them and never reach the point of assigning them a truth value. But, no doubt, one could manipulate adults in the same way.

While we allow the child a rule that assigns truth values to the sentential complements of the key expressions, can we conclude that for the child each key expression was a member of a class of such expressions? In other words, are there any grounds for believing that the child's linguistic competence, as distinct from the knowledge he can formulate, marks *made* as an A $\Vdash$ B type of verb, of which there may be many others? Here we are on less firm ground. Nevertheless, we did study two expressions in which the A $\Vdash$ B implication was involved (*made* and *let*) and the children handled both equally well. We studied three expressions which involved the $-$A $\Vdash$ $-$B relationship (*not big enough, not able*, and *did not let*) and again the children handled all three almost equally well. Three key expressions involved the A $\quad$ $-$B relationship (*turned off, pretend*, and *forget*); none caused any problem to the children. Four key expressions involved the $-$A $\Vdash$ B relationship (*didn't turn off, wasn't afraid. was not pretending*, and *didn't forget*). Of these only the negative of *pretend* caused any real problem for the children, and we saw that this may have been due to ambiguity of the implicative relationship. Unfortunately we studied only one expression, *let*, of the A $\Vdash$B and $-$A $\Vdash$$-$B type, but both relationships were well handled by the children. We had three verbs of the A $\Vdash$ $-$B and $-$A $\Vdash$B-type (*turned off, pretend*, and *forget*) and with the exception of *pretend* the children handled both relationships with ease. The conclusion is that we have some grounds in our findings for stating that the children effectively treat the A of the implicative rule as a variable as well as the B. But in fact we can be a little bolder, because to understand one of these expressions is to know its implicative force. For example, one could not understand *forget* without knowing that it was implicitly negative, that it meant something like *did not remember*, and in consequence that its sentential complement is false. The question of whether the child interprets *forget* as belonging to a class of expressions reduces to whether he understands more than one such expression, and the answer is that many children do.

Presuppositions about which we questioned the children were involved in five of our stories: *let, made, glad, forget*, and *know*. Of these, the presupposition associated with *know* proved the most difficult; still 9 children answered the relevant question correctly in connection with the negative as well as the positive version of the story. The presupposition of *made*, too, caused some difficulty, but those of the other three expressions seemed readily accessible to the children. Indeed it seems reasonable to conclude that our children found certain presuppositions as easy to handle as implicatives. This is interesting because implicatives are sentential complements and, as such, largely explicit in the parent utterance; the implicative logic merely assigns a truth value to the complement. For example, *John forgot to bring the car* has as complement *John brought the car* (syntactic problems aside); the implicative force of *forget* is to make the complement false. The presupposition is further from the parent utterance: *John was expected to bring the car*. It is derived by replacing in the parent utterance *forget* with a verb that conveys part of its meaning. The truth value of the presupposition is then assigned by the presuppositional logic. For example, *made* in our study gave rise to a negative presupposition: *X wanted to do Y*. Whereas *forget* gave rise to an affirmative one: *X was expected to do Y*. However, we should not be surprised that such presuppositions should be handled as easily as implicatives by our children, since they could not understand the key expression without being able to apply the presuppositional logic. We should, then, be no more surprised at their ability to handle implicative and presuppositional logic than that they understood such terms as *let* and *forget*.

In four of our tests, the indirect implication depended upon a correct assessment of either an implicative or a presupposition or both. One could only say whether one could watch the TV program if one knew whether the TV was on or off, and that depended on whether mother had or had not *turned it off*. One could properly say whether the little boy ought to go to school only if one knew whether or not he was sick, and that in turn depended on whether or not he was *pretending* to be sick. One could say whether or not the little girl was disappointed only if one knew whether or not the little boy had brought out a particular toy *and* whether or not the little girl expected him to bring out that one. One could say that the little boy was telling lies only if one knew that he had said something *and* it was untrue. The truth value of the unstated indirect implication depended on the truth value of one or more other unstated propositions.

The signal detection test showed that the children appropriately varied their answer to the indirect implication questions associated with the *turned off*, *pretend*, and *forget* stories; because the corresponding response associated with the *know* story was affirmative for the negative and positive versions, the test was not appropriate. There can be little doubt that some children evaluated the indirect implications by means of the propositional schema we have just outlined.

From this it follows that children of 4 establish semantic relations among lexical items of the sort that we have called meaning postulates. For example, to *lie* (for the child) is to "say something which is not true." To be *disappointed* is to "expect something which does not happen." Note that I am not proposing such postulates as definitions; they merely represent some common meaning. The point I wish to emphasize is the not too startling one, that vocabulary items are not learned in isolation from one another but that their meanings form interrelated networks.

Though, in general, one might wish to express meaning postulates by means of some such operator as $\Vdash$, in the context of our stories we can use the biconditional, if and only if. Ordinarily when it occurs between propositions, we have to do with propositional or sentential logic (formal logic, in Piaget's terms). We may now ask whether or not our children gave evidence of propositional logic. Before answering, we must point out that the relation between logic, as formalized in a textbook, and psychology is unknown and probably quite complicated (see, for example, Beth, 1961, & Parsons, 1960). The only sense in which formal logic is clearly psychological is that it is the product of a human psyche. Nevertheless, it is not clear that the psychological processes that developed logic are themselves formal logic. Of these processes we know almost nothing. So there is very little hope of finding a satisfactory answer to even so circumscribed a question as, Do the reasoning processes of a professional logician reveal formal logic?

The question then becomes, Did our children show evidence of an abstract propositional logic which is as powerful as propositional logic? Before replying to this, a word about "abstract" is necessary. Many adults who show an unshakable logic of some sort in their interpretation of propositions have never studied logic and so could not formulate their logic in terms of abstract symbols. Moreover, many adults in logic class are unable to make much sense of an abstract system. A more appropriate form of our question, then, would be, Did our children reveal logical powers of a type that can be represented in abstract form only by a logic as powerful as propositional logic?

Before answering, we are obliged to confront the popular belief that Inhelder and Piaget (1958) have established, that children under the age of

12 cannot normally reason at the level of "formal operations." Indeed the belief is that Piaget has established that, under the age of 7, children cannot reason at the level of the logic of classes or the logic of relations. Our children were much younger than 7.

There is some difficulty in interpreting what Inhelder and Piaget mean by the logic of formal operations, but in some contexts it seems to be equivalent to propositional logic. And in logic, propositional logic means the system that assigns truth values to combinations of propositions as a function of the truth value of the individual propositions and the logical connectives among them. Now, clearly, very young children speak and act as if the truth of S involves the falsehood of *not S*. That is a postulate of propositional logic. So, clearly, Inhelder and Piaget cannot have proved that children are devoid of logic powers as powerful as any part of propositional logic.

Moreover, Inhelder and Piaget asked children to solve problems in physics, such as which of a set of possible variables influence the rate of oscillation of a pendulum? They represented states of variables as propositions and outcomes as propositions which were implied by combinations of the "variable propositions." They explained the younger children's failures mainly as failures in logic. Leave aside such formidable problems as how to explain to a young child the difference between rate of oscillation and the speed of the pendulum; Inhelder and Piaget are claiming a negative, and to establish their case they have to prove that in no context or in no problem could a young child show reasoning powers that are to be attributed to some general reasoning system of power equal to the basic axiomatic system we call propositional logic. Negatives are proverbially difficult to establish, and it is hardly surprising that they did not succeed in establishing this one.

But what of the children in this study? I believe that some of them showed themselves capable of establishing the truth values of implicatives, presuppositions, and indirect implications on hearing the key sentences in suitable contexts. Does it follow that they employed a logical system to do so, and one which is as powerful as propositional logic? We cannot be sure of either. If they did employ a logical system, it was as powerful as propositional logic, but we cannot be sure that they employed a logical system. But the reason we cannot be sure is the interesting one that we can never be sure that anyone is ever employing a logical system. In other words, our doubts apply to adults as much as to children; and the evidence that the children used a logical system equivalent to propositional logic is exactly the same as the evidence that adults do.

Let us review the relevant findings. We counterbalanced the objects in the stories, so correct answers were not tied to particular objects. We tested for the same propositional relation several times. Where possible, we examined the effect of negativing the key sentence. We employed a statistical technique that was independent in all relevant ways of response bias, even if such bias varied from child to child or from one set of objects in the stories to another. Through all these screening tests, some children emerged as giving the right answers to questions that explored the truth relations between key sentences on the one hand and implicatives and presuppositions on the other; and to questions which explored the truth relations between implicatives and presuppositions on the one hand and indirect implications on the other. I might add that whereas Inhelder and Piaget had their children work with visible, tangible materials; ours worked with unstated propositions.

Our children's responses are not to be explained by saying that they might have imagined the scene and read off the outcomes without recourse to any propositions or any propositional connectives. The ability to represent in imagination those events that were relevant postulates the prior ability to interpret the key propositions (see Pylyshyn, 1973). Nor can the findings be explained by simply saying that the children relied on associations between words. Just as they undoubtedly used their imaginations, they undoubtedly used associations between words. But again they could use the correct associations only if they had the ability to retrieve them (since they were not explicit in the stories). That ability presupposes the ability it hopes to explain. The correct associations depended on whether the key sentence was affirmed or denied, and on the connectives among the propositions.

When some people speak of applying a logical system, they mean that there is a necessary connection between the truth of the conclusion and the truth of the premises. If the premises are true and the correct logical steps have been taken, the conclusion is necessarily true. Did our children experience such a necessary connection? Here we have no evidence beyond what has already been cited. Indeed, there are no operational tests of such an experience. Further, Wason and Johnson-Laird (1972) show how easy it is to create a false experience of certainty and to dissipate a correct one. One has to rely on the word of the experiencer, then. We do not have even that, and it is difficult to see how it could be usefully obtained. Nevertheless, some children showed just the sort of robust adherence to the correct interpretation across various stories and from positive to negative versions that would in an adult normally be accepted as an indication that they were applying a logical system. We see no additional reason to doubt that the children were.

Learning a language involves establishing meaning postulates and applying a system of rules to propositions so as to generate related propositions and assign their truth values. It is such a system that we have been studying. We cannot at this point explain its origin in the child. We have confined ourselves to showing its existence. However, we can be quite sure that it plays a major part in language learning, as it does in language interpretation.

One may be surprised at what we now see to be the mastery of reasoning in ordinary language displayed by young children, particularly if one has experience of how much adults fumble in logic class. There are several reasons for the difference, but one must be the extreme parsimony with which ordinary language encodes information, leaving the interpretative system to work out whatever implicatives, presuppositions, and indirect implications are appropriate. The convenience to that restricted workspace which we call short-term memory must be considerable.

ACKNOWLEDGMENT

I am particularly grateful to Nancy Katz, who discussed the ideas upon which the research is based, and to Chet Olson, who helped with the statistical problems.

APPENDIX

A. Story frame and variables employed with *made wasn't able, wasn't big enough, let, wouldn't let,* and *wasn't afraid.*

Once there were two little children called
1. Kenneth and Sandra
2. William and Janet
3. David and Carolyn
4. Colin and Jennifer

(The boy) was the oldest, but he and (the girl) were about the same size. One day they were playing together in the
5. playroom
6. kitchen
7. backyard
8. hallway

They were
1. looking for something to play with
2. looking for something to eat
3. trying to reach their kite which was caught in a tree
4. getting ready to go outside

9. They saw their toy train, but to reach it one of them had to stand on a table.
10. They saw a chocolate cake, but to reach it one of them had to stand on a chair.
11. To get the kite, one of them would have to climb up on the branch of a tree
12. To reach their coats in the closet, one of them had to stand on a stool.

Made: (The boy) made (the girl) (do act specified in 9–12).
   Question 1. Did she. . . .?   (Implicative)
          2. Did she want to. . . .?   (Presupposition)

Wasn't able: (The girl) wasn't able to (do act specified in 9–12).
Question 1. Did she. . . .?   (Implicative)

Wasn't big enough: (The girl) wasn't big enough to (do act specified in 9–12).
Question 1. Did she. . . .?   (Implicative)

Let and wouldn't let: (The boy) (let) (the girl) (do act specified in 9–12).
Question 1. Did she. . . .?   (Implicative)
         2. Did she want to. . . .?   (Presupposition)

B. Stories employed with *turned off* and *didn't turn off.*

$\left\{\begin{array}{c}\text{Kim}\\\text{Sara}\end{array}\right\}$ was a little girl who was sitting by herself in the living room one day.

   Her mother then came into the room. She $\left\{\begin{array}{c}\text{turned off}\\\text{didn't turn off}\end{array}\right\}\left\{\begin{array}{c}\text{the TV.}\\\text{the radio.}\end{array}\right\}$

   Question 1. After her mother came in, was the $\left\{\begin{array}{c}\text{TV}\\\text{radio}\end{array}\right\}$ still on?

            (Implicative)
          2. Could $\left\{\begin{array}{c}\text{Kim}\\\text{Sara}\end{array}\right\}\left\{\begin{array}{c}\text{see the picture on the TV}\\\text{hear the music on the radio}\end{array}\right\}$ after her mother

             came in?   (Indirect implication)

C. Stories employed with *glad* and *wasn't glad.*

$\left\{\begin{array}{c}\text{Cathy}\\\text{Mary}\end{array}\right\}$ was a little girl who was playing by herself one day.
$\left\{\begin{array}{l}\text{She was looking forward to reading her favorite book.}\\\text{Then Tommy, the boy next door, rang the bell.}\end{array}\right\}$
Her mother came to the door and called her.
She $\left\{\begin{array}{c}\text{was}\\\text{wasn't}\end{array}\right\}$ glad that $\left\{\begin{array}{l}\text{dinner was ready.}\\\text{Tommy came over to play with her.}\end{array}\right\}$
   Question 1. $\left\{\begin{array}{l}\text{Was dinner ready?}\\\text{Did Tommy come over to play with her?}\end{array}\right\}$ (Presupposition)
          2. $\left\{\begin{array}{l}\text{Was she hungry?}\\\text{Did she like Tommy?}\end{array}\right\}$ (Indirect implication)

REFERENCES

Beth, E. W. Première partie. In E. W. Beth and J. Piaget, *Epistémologie mathématique et psychologie.* Paris: Presses Universitaires de France, 1961.

Carnap, R. *Meaning and necessity.* (2nd ed.) Chicago: University of Chicago Press, 1956.

Feller, W. *An introduction to probability theory and its applications.* Vol. 1. (3rd ed.) New York: Wiley, 1968.

Inhelder, B., & Piaget, J. *The growth of logical thinking from childhood to adolescence.* New York: Basic Books, 1958.

Karttunen, L. Implicative verbs. *Language*, 1971, *47*, 340–358.

Karttunen, L. *Presuppositions of compound sentences. Linguistic Inquiry*, 1973, *4*, 169–193.

Katz, J. J. On defining "Presupposition." *Linguistic Inquiry*, 1973, *4*, 256–260.

Macnamara, J. The cognitive basis of language learning in children. *Psychological Review*, 1972, *79*, 1–13.

Murdock, B. B., & Ogilvie, J. C. Binomial variability in short-term memory. *Psychological Bulletin*, 1968, *70*, 256–260.

Parsons, C. Review of Inhelder and Piaget (1958). *British Journal of Psychology*, 1960, *51*, 75–84.

Pastore, R. E., & Scheirer, C. J. Signal detection theory: Considerations for general application. *Psychological Bulletin*, 1974, *81*, 945–958.

Piaget, J. *The moral judgment of the child.* London: Kegan Paul, 1932.

Pylyshyn, Z. W. What the mind's eye tells the mind's brain. *Psychological Bulletin*, 1973, *80*, 1–24.

Van Fraassen, B. Presupposition, implication and self reference. *Journal of Philosophy*, 1968, *65*, 132–152.

Wason, P. C., & Johnson-Laird, P.N. *Psychology of reasoning: Structure and content.* Cambridge, Mass.: Harvard University Press, 1972.

Winer, B. J. *Statistical principles in experimental design.* (2nd ed.) New York: McGraw-Hill, 1971.

20

Testing for Propositional Logic

SEYMOUR PAPERT

Massachusetts Institute of Technology

I would like to begin with some methodological comments, and I can best make my point by telling you about a little experiment I did very casually and without any statistical precautions. It is about the first story, *made*. Macnamara said *John made Jill stand on the table*, and then the question was, "Did Jill stand on the table?" My story was different in one respect. I set up a model in which there was something out of reach, and there was a table. There was also a ladder next to the thing that was out of reach. I told the story exactly as Macnamara did and had the children repeat it. I told it to four children and asked, "Did Jill stand on the table?" One child said, "no," and, when asked how Jill got the thing, replied, "She climbed the ladder."

The point of my little experiment is that it set up a conflict in the child's mind. There was the ladder and there was the table, and the child answered without taking into account the key sentence which Macnamara is counting on. Notice that I am not saying that the child failed to hear that sentence, just that he may not have attended to it. The children whom Macnamara tested might have taken account of the fact that the thing wanted was high up and that there was a table present. He could, without performing any propositional operation on the sentence which contained *made*, have said that Jill stood on the table.

The point about conflict is a crucial one. When Piaget tested children's ability to conserve quantity of liquid when the liquid was poured from one vessel into another, he established conflict. On the one hand, the child knew the liquid had come from vessel A; on the other, there seemed to be more in vessel B because it was taller. The problem with the child is not that he does not have rules to handle the different information, but that the rules can be upset by a conflict. The adult, on the other hand, holds firm to a rule in spite of the conflict. Conservation means holding to the rule that yields invariance of quantity across conditions that tend to make you think the equality was not there.

Macnamara spoke about logicians setting up adults to give the wrong answer. I rather fear that he was setting up children to give the right one. The adults are different, though. You might set them up to make a slip, but if you give them time to think about it, they are quite firm, and however much you try to upset them, they hold firm. Piaget is explicit on this point. One claims that children have mental structures to handle certain sorts of logical operations only when the children reveal a sense of necessity about the conclusion.

Perhaps I should clear up one point. It is naive to suppose that there is such a thing as "doing propositional logic." There are a whole lot of different kinds of mental operations that fall under the general label of propositional logic. The claim is that certain of these are not available to the child until adolescence. Clearly, there are senses of doing propositional logic that children can manage as soon as they have propositions. There are other senses of it that nobody but a professional logician can do; and maybe he will not do it in his intuitive thinking.

There is a more subtle point which is closely related to what is meant by saying that a child is using formal logic of the sort, p implies q. There are occasions when what seems like an implication is built into the child's model of action. Take, for example, the sentence *If it rains, wear your raincoat.* Now put the question: *It's raining; does Mary wear her raincoat?* It is not necessary to attribute a correct response to a grasp of the conditional sentence plus the logical operation, *modus ponens.* Rather, our whole history has made putting on one's raincoat a part of the operational meaning of rain. Now despite my methodological questions, I really think that a lot of Macnamara's results would stand up even when properly controlled; but if they did, I would say that they were showing something different. They would be showing that part of the meaning that has been built into words like *make to* is that the thing happened.

Contrast this with what children will say if we avoid this by taking arbitrary p and q; for example, *Whenever Mary wears a hat, she wears a coat,* or *If Mary wears a hat, she wears a coat.* It is amazing how late in life, not before 11 or 12, children manage to deal with this. It might be that the failure is not properly described by saying the younger children do not have propositional logic. But there is a body of facts about the minds of children which show that the use of implication does not seem natural, intuitive, or easy for children.

I would like to distinguish between an implicative relation of the type $A \Vdash B$ being in the child's understanding of *made to* and the child's correctly interpreting *made to*. Perhaps the way to test it would be to introduce a new term of the same type to the child, one for which he has not had a chance to develop a whole scheme of operations, and I will engage that it will be very difficult to get the child to interpret it as you wish him to. In other words, for Macnamara's theory to be right, there should be a certain decoupling of the scheme $A \Vdash B$ from the actual terms which already instantiate it, so that the child could use it with new terms of the appropriate sort. The point is not so much which are right, his findings or Piaget's, but how they are related. I believe that if you could tidy up both sets of experiments, you would find that there really is a difference between the reasoning powers of an adult and those of a child, and the difference is not all due to language problems. If you set up the conservation of weight problem with two balls of clay, and you secretly remove some from one ball, on seeing the evidence of the weighing scales, young children say they must have been mistaken, whereas older children say you have tricked them.

One of Piaget's best insights into the actual processes of mental development is that before mental schemata appear in full form at the intellectual level, there is a preparation for them at some other level. One can, as it were, see their shadows before one can see them. Often the preparation is an action schema; the form of the schema is built into a plan of action in something that we might call a concrete form. What I suggest is that the findings presented to us are evidence of such a preparation of complicated schemata. The findings are prefigurings of schemata that have come to be called propositional, and do not emerge until the child is very much older.

Index